TURMOIL IN
AMERICAN PUBLIC POLICY

TURMOIL IN AMERICAN PUBLIC POLICY

SCIENCE, DEMOCRACY, AND THE ENVIRONMENT

Leslie R. Alm, Ross E. Burkhart,
and Marc V. Simon

 PRAEGER

AN IMPRINT OF ABC-CLIO, LLC
Santa Barbara, California • Denver, Colorado • Oxford, England

Library of Congress Cataloging-in-Publication Data

Alm, Leslie R., 1950–
    Turmoil in American public policy : science, democracy, and the environment / Leslie R. Alm,
Ross E. Burkhart, and Marc V. Simon.
        p. cm.
    Includes bibliographical references and index.
    ISBN 978-0-313-38536-0 (alk. paper) — ISBN 978-0-313-38537-7 (ebook)
    1. Environmental policy—United States. 2. Environmental policy—United States—Citizen
participation. 3. Science and state—United States. 4. Environmental policy—Canada. 5.
Environmental policy—Canada—Citizen participation. 6. Science and state—Canada. I. Burkhart,
Ross Earl. II. Simon, Marc V. III. Title.
    GE180.A525 2010
    333.720973—dc22   2010001307

ISBN: 978-0-313-38536-0
EISBN: 978-0-313-38537-7

14 13 12 11 10   1 2 3 4 5

This book is also available on the World Wide Web as an eBook.
Visit www.abc-clio.com for details.

Praeger
An Imprint of ABC-CLIO, LLC

ABC-CLIO, LLC
130 Cremona Drive, P.O. Box 1911
Santa Barbara, California 93116-1911

This book is printed on acid-free paper ∞

Manufactured in the United States of America

Contents

Preface

How do natural scientists fit into the U.S. environmental policymaking process? That is the key question this book addresses and attempts to answer. It is a complicated question, and it has a complicated answer.

To deal with these complications, we offer a textbook format that is grounded in empirical evidence. The format is that of a standard textbook that delineates major topics and themes, followed by reflection questions and suggested readings for students. The findings from hundreds of personal interviews with natural scientists and social scientists, completed over the past twenty years (including this year), provide the empirical evidence. The result is a book that explores the intricacies of the science–policy linkage that pervades environmental policymaking in the United States. We create a framework that students at both undergraduate and graduate levels can appreciate; one where they can delve into the murky world of politics that marks American public policymaking. At the same time, it is a framework that allows policymakers, scientists, and other interested parties to consider the philosophical and practical question of why linking science to environmental policymaking in a meaningful way is such a difficult task.

Our book is built on a foundation set forth by the many studies of environmental policymaking that have been conducted over the past several decades. Many of these studies and what their authors say about the interface of science and policy are highlighted throughout the chapters. As much as possible, we put the names of those we are citing right in the text so readers can identify whose works we are outlining. If readers want to get the full gist of the arguments being presented, they can then explore far beyond what we have highlighted by going directly to the primary sources. We hope that by putting the names of these scholars in the middle of the conversation (as well as in a reading list at the end of each chapter), we will provide readers with a head start to find out more about what these scholars have to say.

We feel that it is important to promote the work of these experts because doing so exposes students to the names of scholars (and others) who are at the forefront of research about how science and scientists affect environmental policymaking in the United States. Although it is always problematic to include every individual who has something valuable to say about a substantive field of study, in this instance we do want to point out a few of the scholars who have guided our research. Prominent in our review of what scholars have said about the relationship of science to policy are the works of Robert Bartlett, Lynton Caldwell, Ellis Cowling, David Guston, Helen Ingram, Sheila Jasanoff, Michael Kraft, Judith Layzer, Kai N. Lee, William Leiss, Karen Litfin, Dorothy Nelkin, Roger Peilke, Jr., Walter Rosenbaum, Dan Sarewitz, Brian Silver, Zachary Smith, Aaron Wildavsky, and Edward O. Wilson. As readers will see, the works of these experts, as well as works by many other scholars, are conspicuous throughout this text. We hope readers will enjoy the propositions and ideas put forth by those who have spent a good deal of their lives exploring the science–policy linkage to environmental policymaking in the United States.

This book is designed to give readers the ability to explore the complexities of linking science to policy in today's world. As you read this book, it is important to keep in mind that it is our intention to give special weight to the views of both social scientists and natural scientists regarding the science–policy linkage. We do this because we think that one of the keys to improving how science gets meaningfully used in the environmental policymaking process is how well distinct and different disciplines interact.

Scientists live and work in a society defined by complexity, and they are influenced by both political and scientific interactions. Most of the time these interactions are explained by social scientists, who comment on the way the political world conducts its business. It is our purpose to give natural scientists a chance to tell their side of the story. We do this by letting natural scientists explain to readers (in their own words) what they think about the science–policy linkage. We then compare natural scientists' perceptions with the views of social scientists. And the results are telling. Again, we hope that readers enjoy seeing how scientists perceive the world, as told in their own words.

In completing this book, we have benefited from the advice and counsel of many people. We would especially like to thank the many scientists who accepted our invitation to talk about the science–policy linkage and who graciously shared their thoughts and ideas with us. We thank the College of Social Sciences and Public Affairs at Boise State University and the Department of Political Science at Bowling Green State University for their encouragement and support, as well as Dan Abele and the Canadian Embassy for their financial support over the years.

Above all, we thank our significant others: Barbara, Maria, and Christy.

CHAPTER 1

Science, Democracy, and
the Environment

We will restore science to its rightful place, and wield technology's wonders. . . . We will harness the sun and the winds and the soil to fuel our cars and run our factories.

President Barack Obama, *Inaugural Address*, January 20, 2009.

INTRODUCTION

Several decades ago Lynton Caldwell wrote that making the linkage of science to environmental policymaking in the United States democratic system was not easy because individually each of these systems—science, democracy, and the natural environment—in and of itself is complex, paradoxical, and poorly understood.[1] There should not be any doubt in readers' minds that this assessment remains true today. If there is doubt, the following chapters should go a long way to dispel that doubt.

But before we get to the intricacies and entanglements that lie at the heart of linking science to environmental policymaking, take a brief look, as intimated by Caldwell, at the state of each of these systems today. Pick up a daily newspaper, watch the local or national news on television, or go online to explore what is happening in the areas of science, democracy, and the environment. When you do, it will not take you long to see that we are facing what appears to be challenging (some might say catastrophic) problems in most every geographical location on earth. Attempts to spread democracy throughout the world, at least to date, have left much to be desired. Environmental issues rack every nation, with the shadow of global warming settling across every continent and falling on every human being. Science is left in the wake, asking more questions than it provides answers. This is not to say there is no hope. It is only to say, as lamented by Caldwell some time ago, that when one looks at mixing science, democracy, and the environment, things get messy. And maybe it is all right that it is messy. We will look anyway.

While reflecting on the central role of science and technology in contemporary economic and social development, Sheila Jasanoff makes the case that democratic

1

governments are presumed to be capable of discerning their citizens' needs and wants, and deploying science and technology effectively to meet these needs and wants.[2] Jasanoff further posits that

> democratic theory cannot be articulated in satisfactory terms today without looking in detail at the politics of science and technology [because] contemporary societies are constituted *as knowledge* societies [and] it is no longer possible to deal with such staple concepts of democratic theory as citizenship or deliberation or accountability without delving into their interaction with the dynamics of knowledge creation and use.[3]

This is a profound statement about the linkage of science to democracy. According to Jasanoff, one cannot adequately contemplate democracy without having a deep, detailed understanding of the *politics* of science. Walter Rosenbaum makes an even stronger case regarding the importance of science to democracy when he pronounces that two of the enduring issues in American environmental policymaking are which government institutions and leaders should shape the nation's environmental policies, and what role science, and the scientific community, should assume in the process.[4] Think about that for a moment. Of all the possible issues surrounding environmental policymaking in the United States, one of our foremost environmental scholars chooses two that together represent the quest to successfully link science to policy.

Rosenbaum is not alone in this characterization of American democracy. Alexander Keynan argues that the rapid growth of science and its importance to the modern state have increased the necessity of exploring the relationship among science, scientists, and governments, and the role of scientists in the formulation of national policy.[5] It is now clear that policymakers and the public are increasingly turning to scientists for advice in dealing with environmental issues.[6] In fact, it is claimed that most environmental issues would not even exist as policy problems except for the input of scientists,[7] and that there is only one way to adequately protect our natural environment and that is by "bringing both science and democracy to the fight for environmental protection."[8]

Yet, some argue that the notion of democracy—ultimate rule by votes of the people—is irrelevant to science because science is concerned with the discovery of truths that are not affected by what scientists think or by issues that can be decided by votes.[9] Along these lines, others argue that science and scientists are ineffective in attempting to inform the democratic process.[10] Look carefully at the words of Bruce Smith.

> Policy can never be solely the simple reflection of scientific expertise, no matter how broad gauged and well informed that expertise may be. . . . The policy process seems clearly bound to wrestle with the issue of how to blend the findings and the methods of science with the power struggles and value conflicts of democracy. The challenge of the nation is to reconcile the integrity and the disciplined search for truth of science with the openness and procedural fairness of democracy.[11]

What Smith proclaims is that science cannot provide all the answers to our public policy needs (something we will discuss in detail later in this book). But Smith does provide the full measure of the problem: how do we assure that science is properly integrated into the American public policymaking process? As we proceed to discuss and search for the answer to this question, keep in mind that the answer may lie in the way science is connected to human purpose, in the way we gauge directions from the tenets of democracy, and in the way we maintain our bearings during turbulent times.[12] Ultimately, any discussion about science being linked to policy and politics has to be grounded in visions of democracy.[13]

AMERICAN PUBLIC POLICYMAKING

This book is about how scientists (and science) fit into the American environmental policymaking process. However, before we get to that specific topic, students should have a basic understanding of how the United States public policymaking process works in general. Hence, our first substantive chapters furnish a basic overview of the American public policymaking process, followed by an explanation of how this process incorporates the concerns of environmental protection and the tenets of science.

At first glance, the study of American public policymaking does not appear to be such a daunting task, especially when one reads the comforting words of Paul Sabatier:

> In the process of public policymaking, problems are conceptualized and brought to government for solution; governmental institutions formulate alternatives and select policy solutions; and those solutions get implemented, evaluated, and revised.[14]

The policymaking process appears straightforward and easy to conceptualize. Yet, following this brief introduction, Sabatier goes on to explain that the policy process is "extremely complex," involving hundreds of actors (interest groups, governmental agencies, legislatures at different levels of government, researchers, journalists, judges), time spans of a decade or more, dozens of different programs at multiple levels of government, debates, litigation, regulatory administration, disputes of deeply held values with large amounts of money and authoritative coercion; truly a complicated process where the stakes are almost always high.[15] B. Guy Peters supports Sabatier's assessment of the complexity of public policymaking in the United States, skillfully using Mark Twain's utterances about patriotism being the last refuge of fools and scoundrels to criticize the fact that the concept of public policy has become a refuge of the same sort because in today's world of public policymaking, most everything government does is now labeled *policy*.[16]

As expressed previously, public policymaking in the United States rests within a seemingly inexhaustible set of concepts and processes that have been described as predominantly "chaotic,"[17] and as "fluid, dynamic, and malleable."[18] The chaotic nature of public policymaking and the difficulty of portraying its impact are fittingly summarized by Peters and Jon Pierre as follows:

> [T]he study of public policy could be described as shooting at a mobile target with a somewhat malfunctioning rifle. The target is changing course frequently—or does not change course when we expect it to—and our weapon is far from perfect in composition and robustness.[19]

In this regard, students of American public policymaking must deal with the fact that public policy includes all political activities and institutions, "from voting, political cultures, parties, legislatures, bureaucracies, international agencies, local governments, and back again, to the citizens who implement and evaluate public policies."[20] One must consider the fact that politics is predominant, with governments of different ideological orientations making different choices with respect to how we allocate resources.[21] One must also differentiate between federalism and separation of powers, between pluralism and elitism, and between fragmentation and incrementalism. Simply put, those interested in the study of American public policy are faced with the proposition that the sheer complexity of what is going on in the public policymaking process precludes simple, straightforward, sequential types of explanation.[22]

ENVIRONMENTAL POLICYMAKING

The subfield within political science titled "public policy" is a dynamic and complex area of study. As James Anderson notes: "Public policies in a modern, complex society are indeed ubiquitous. They confer advantages and disadvantages, cause pleasure, irritation, and pain, and collectively have important consequences for our well-being and happiness."[23] When one adds *environmental* issues to this public policy mix, things become even more entangled. Environmental politics means conflicts between value systems: natural resources development versus environmental protection, individual property rights versus the government's right of eminent domain, and command-and-control regulatory systems versus market-oriented approaches. Such a combination makes for difficult reading and difficult analysis. More than two decades ago, Dean Mann—a highly respected environmental scholar—expressed the frustrations of dealing with environmental policy, and his words are still applicable today:

> Environmental policy is not an artifact of administrations, grandly enunciated by presidents, duly enacted by responsive legislatures, and efficiently administered by the executive establishment. It is rather a jerry-built structure in which innumerable individuals, private groups, bureaucrats, politicians, agencies, courts, political parties, and circumstances have laid down the planks, hammered the nails, plastered over the cracks, made sometimes unsightly additions and deletions, and generally defied "holistic" or "ecological" principles of policy design.[24]

Of more recent vintage, Norman Miller offers a critique of environmental policymaking today.

> Because environmental issues affect us in such profound ways and involve such a multiplicity of interests, they subject the legislative process to its greatest strains. . . . [O]ver the course of the last half century or so the body of laws enacted in the environmental area have influenced almost every aspect of our daily lives, and mandated the appropriation of more public and private monies than the body of law in any other area. Perhaps more significantly, environmentalism and politics are inextricably linked because substantive values, to say nothing of behavior, are at stake. Every major policy supports some interested party's view of the world and adversely affects someone else's. That is why the collective process for solving problems related to the environment is inherently adversarial.[25]

Whether or not we use Mann's or Miller's interpretation of environmental policymaking, we see that the environment remains an extremely meaningful concern of Americans, and this concern is reflected in the pervasive nature of its importance to the American people as a whole and to the profound nature of its impact on U.S. policy today.

SCIENCE AND ENVIRONMENTAL POLICYMAKING

Within the environmental policymaking context of the United States democratic system of government, we add one final ingredient—science. In straightforward but very profound terms, science has been characterized as the most powerful of all forms of knowledge,[26] with its ability to improve human life voiced as "the quintessential hallmark of the modern era."[27] In the United States, as noted earlier, environmental policy is not viewed merely as the application of science and technology to problems of the environment.[28] Still, the American culture that defines our modern-day society is rich with scientific and technological thought,[29] and policymaking is touted as a coproduction between science and society.[30] But the fit of science into the American policymaking process, including concerns about the environment, is not one that is so easily explained.

The views of Americans about the role of scientific expertise in governance have long been a source of disagreement and tension.[31] Although scientific advice is considered to be "part of a necessary process of political accommodation among science, society, and the state,"[32] democratic societies such as the United States generally do not vest the power to govern to scientists; they vest it to nonscientists.[33] Frances Lynn, keeping with the widely perceived belief in maintaining a separation between science and politics, describes the most commonly accepted role for scientists in a democracy.

> One could argue that the most appropriate role for the scientist . . . would be to self-consciously provide decision makers and the public with as much information as possible about the uncertainties in his or her work . . . and place the very difficult decision of degrees of protection and the acceptability of a risk into the political arena, where, in a democracy, it belongs.[34]

This ideal division of labor between science and politics may be what people seek, but in the United States, especially on environmental issues, it is rarely achieved. The problem—as noted by Gwynne Dyer in his book *Climate Wars*—is that environmental politics has become a left-right political conflict in the United States. Hence, unlike in European democracies, for example, in the United States, the science of climate change was disparaged and denied for two decades because the likely policies to be derived from that science were opposed by the political right.[35] Dyer goes on to note that

> in less ideological societies, climate change could be treated as a more or less neutral fact. Given the ferocity of the culture wars in the United States during the Clinton and Bush administrations, global warming was bound to become a highly contentious "values" issue in the United States, rather than a scientific one.[36]

So there is something in U.S. political culture that heightens the potential for politicization of science, particularly in environmental policymaking; this is another reason for our choice to center our attention on this policy area.

Radford Byerly and Roger Pielke, Jr., agree with Lynn's basic premise, and they also suggest that science should meet the condition of democratic accountability, consciously guided by society's goals rather than by scientific serendipity.[37] Another take on the role of scientists in a democracy is expressed by Anne Schneider and Helen Ingram, who suggest that using scientists as experts denigrates the role of the ordinary citizen, thus damaging the role of citizenship in a democracy.[38] A persistent, populist, strain of anti-intellectualism in U.S. political culture that was visible long ago to Alexis de Tocqueville, might explain these views about the tensions between science and democracy.

> Those who cultivate the sciences amongst a democratic people . . . adhere closely to facts, and study facts with their own senses. As they do not easily defer to the mere name of any fellow man, they are never inclined to rest upon any man's authority; but on the contrary, they are unremitting in their efforts to find out the weaker points of their neighbors' doctrine. Scientific precedents have little weight with them; they are never long detained by the subtlety of the schools, nor ready to accept big words for sterling coin; they penetrate, as far as they can, into the principle parts of the subject which occupies them, and they like to expound them in the vulgar tongue.[39]

Anti-intellectualism could be one of the reasons that science is so easily politicized in the United States as compared to other advanced democracies. Consider that the current chancellor of Germany, Angela Merkel, is in fact a highly qualified scientist. Margaret Thatcher, former prime minister of Britain, was an early leader on climate change policy. Both of these leaders are on the political right, yet they did not suffer political costs from their pro-environment policies, because the policies were based on a respected scientific consensus. In contrast, Al Gore is portrayed by the right in the United States as something of a buffoon or "environmental wacko" for his support of climate change science.

It is ironic that scientists and science should face such intense scrutiny in the U.S. political process, as compared to in other industrial democracies, given that in so many ways the United States owes its economic success to scientific advances. But in its political culture, whereas other countries elect leaders with PhDs, the United States public is more likely to vote for celebrities. The temptation for United States politicians to play on the anti-intellectualism of the public may have reached its zenith in the George W. Bush years, characterized by Chris Mooney as a time of "the Republican War on Science."[40]

However, no matter how you look at it, science and scientists are viewed as critical to environmental policymaking in all democracies because scientific issues permeate all environmental problems and because scientists are often the first to discover and publicize environmental problems.[41] In fact, it is argued that environmental issues such as the reduction in stratospheric ozone would not be part of the public dialogue without the influence of scientists.[42] In short, conventional wisdom posits that environmental questions are fundamentally questions of science,[43] and that most environmental issues on the current agenda would not exist were it not for scientific research.[44] As Norman Miller puts it, "every environmental problem has, at its foundation, a scientific reality, and it therefore seems axiomatic that science must play a prominent, if not pivotal, role in formulating its solution."[45] More to the point, Karen Litfin argues that the language of environmental policy debates is scientific in nature "because science is a primary source of legitimation and because scientists help to define environmental problems."[46]

At the same time, scholars recognize that it is not easy to translate the findings of science into reasonable public policies.[47] With all the importance allocated to science and scientists, questions remain about the ability of scientists to connect to a policy world that eventually relies on politicians to make the final policy decisions, with or without scientific input.[48] Simply put, science and scientists do not have the ability to resolve policy debates on their own, no matter how good the science is determined to be and no matter how much faith we have in scientists and the scientific process.[49]

Many who have spent a good part of their professional careers studying science and its linkage to environmental policymaking have doubts about the effectiveness of science to meaningfully affect policy. For instance, Daniel Sarewitz asks some very pointed questions about the linkage of science to policy in a democracy. He asks, where is the common ground between the orderly search for scientific truth and the chaotic forums of popular governance? And, shouldn't this common ground be sought in a more scientific approach to democracy rather than in a more democratic approach to science?[50] Bruce Bimber asks a series of questions relevant to understanding the politics of science: what do scientists do, why do they do it, and what difference does it make? Bimber goes on to posit that a richer analysis might ask even more detailed questions, such as which scientists are to be believed, which scientists should be discounted because of their political interests, and how government should elicit from scientists advice that is unshaped by partisanship and ideology.[51]

As you will see in the coming chapters, one of the most commonly expressed assertions about the science–policy linkage is that scientists and policymakers are said to work in two different worlds, each deeply rooted in divergent human occupations. As one noted environmental scholar points out:

> Science and politics serve different purposes. Politics aims at the responsible use of power; in a democracy, "responsible" means accountable, eventually to voters. Science aims at finding truths—results that withstand the scrutiny of one's fellow scientists.[52]

Moreover, within the context of environmental policymaking, some argue that we should go beyond just accepting the idea that scientists and policymakers work in different worlds according to different values, and set up an environmental policymaking system where scientists and policymakers are isolated from each other's influence, with barriers maintained such that scientists can complete their research with careful adherence to the canons of the scientific process, and policymakers can be protected from scientists telling them what they should decide.[53] But, is this type of environmental policy world even a remote possibility in today's environment? Is it something we should even be striving to accomplish?

To begin answering these questions and to get a flavor of the complex and controversial aspects of linking science (and scientists) to public policymaking in the United States, we offer four descriptions of the way the science–policy linkage is viewed in the context of American democracy. The four we have chosen to highlight are a representative sample of the way scholars have come to view science and environmental policymaking in the United States. In no way are these quotes a comprehensive set of all possible descriptions of the science–policy linkage. However, they do represent mainstream views of scholarship regarding the large, philosophical questions that surround the science–policy dichotomy. Moreover, these descriptions foreshadow the major themes that will be detailed in the chapters to come.

FOUR WAYS TO DEFINE THE SCIENCE–POLICY LINKAGE IN ENVIRONMENTAL POLICYMAKING

(1) Separation of Science and Politics

Ellis B. Cowling provides us with a good starting point in delineating the role of scientists in the American environmental policymaking process.

> The responsibility of scientists . . . in a democracy is to understand and clearly communicate the scientific facts and uncertainties and to describe expected outcomes objectively. Deciding what to do involves questions of societal values where scientists, as scientists . . . have no special authority. . . . The proper role for scientists . . . is to provide advice and counsel . . . to those who are charged by our society to make policy decisions. It is not a proper role for a scientist . . . as such, to seek to make (or even to have special influence on) societal decisions.[54]

Cowling's description, while brief, is quite instructive. It provides the reader with many of the critical aspects of linking science to policy *in a democracy* and also provides a prescription for how this should be completed. Note that the focus is on the "responsibility of scientists" and the "proper role for scientists," to provide advice only to policymakers and not to make value judgments about what society needs, at least not in the public setting. Indeed, Cowling even warns scientists against seeking to make such value judgments. Scientists are also to "clearly communicate" the results of their scientific investigations, a task that we will see in the coming chapters is not only difficult, but that is nearly impossible to do well. Finally, Cowling uses some of the critical words that characterize the tenets of the scientific process to describe the role of scientists: facts, uncertainties, and objectivity. Clearly, from Cowling's perspective, scientists are seen as one small, albeit significant, part of the public policymaking process where it is up to the policymakers to make societal decisions with scientists in a completely advisory role.

(2) Scientific Consensus Requires Political Action

Kai N. Lee provides a second description of the science–policy linkage.

> Without the centralizing vision of science . . . we cannot perceive the planet we share with other living things. . . . When science yields unambiguous negative implications for significant public values, action should be taken by governments. The form and content of the action will vary, but the imperative to act does not. When science yields consensus on the importance of a problem, however ambiguous the existing knowledge may be, democratic governments should consider action, initiating or continuing the collection of relevant information and building their capacity to analyze that information over time.[55]

Lee's vision of science diverges a bit from Cowling's vision (at least as expressed by these short statements) in that Lee suggests that policymakers should take action if scientific input meets certain criteria. Policymakers are not allowed to simply disregard scientific input. But the criteria are extremely stringent. Scientists must provide "unambiguous negative implications" for "significant public values." Whoa! These are very strong words, and again, as we shall see in the coming chapters, they set a bar for scientists to meet that may be unreachable. For instance, how does one define unambiguous? Is there any room for ambiguity at all? Doesn't this concept go against the very uncertainties that are inherent in the scientific process? And who defines *which* public values are *significant*? Do scientists have any say in making those determinations? Furthermore, what does *consensus* mean? That all scientists agree? That a majority of scientists agree? And under what mechanism do we reach this consensus? Still, Lee provides us with a view of public policymaking linking science directly to environmental protection, a view where science is a major participant in decision-making (a *centralizing* force) regarding the quality of life on "the planet we share with other living things."

(3) Science as the Most Legitimate Rationale for Policy

Aaron Wildavsky provides a cogent description of the science–policy linkage, emphasizing science's uniqueness and importance.

> Scientific evidence does matter. I notice that no mention is made of witchcraft as a rationale for regulation, but rather obeisance is made to science whether or not it is

what matters. Nor does any responsible person get up and say that his ideology or her worldview requires inventing or denying dangers and to hell with the evidence. As long as science is the only publicly acceptable rationale, it matters.[56]

Wildavsky's words underscore the fact that within American public policy-making, science is not only accepted as the best way of knowing, it is viewed as the only valid and responsible way to establish a knowledge base, to provide the evidence that underlies decision-making. Wildavsky recognizes the importance of ideology in America's policy-making arena and even makes light of some ways of knowing that, at least publicly, are not acceptable ways to establish what we know. However, what Wildavsky does not want us to miss is the fact that the evidence that matters most in U.S. policymaking is scientifically driven, and that we had better be prepared to deal with all the burdens that come with linking this way of knowing to policy.

(4) The Incompatibility of Scientific and Political Judgments

For our final description of the way the science–policy linkage is viewed in the context of American democracy, we chose to highlight some of the thoughts of Walter Rosenbaum.

> Risk assessment frequently compels public officials to make scientific judgments and scientists to resolve policy issues for which neither may be trained. The almost inevitable need to resolve scientific questions through the political process and the problems that arise in making scientific and political judgments compatible are two of the most troublesome characteristics of environmental politics.[57]

In characterizing risk assessment, Rosenbaum goes right to the heart of the major theme of this book: getting good science into the U.S. environmental policymaking process is highly problematic. Of course, defining the term "good" science is problematic in and of itself. But we will save that dilemma for a later chapter. For now, let's concentrate on what Rosenbaum is trying to tell us. First, Rosenbaum emphasizes the fact that scientists and policymakers are trained in different ways, and, as a matter of course, they do not know how to operate in each other's professional world. Scientists are not proficient at doing politics (or policy), and policymakers are not proficient at doing science, and neither scientists nor policymakers have a good understanding of what the other does, or how.

Further, Rosenbaum observes that science has to be filtered through the policy (or political) process. Note that in Rosenbaum's description there is no mention of the arrow going the other way. He does not argue that policy questions must be resolved through the scientific process. In this regard, it appears that Rosenbaum has put the burden of action or change upon scientists. If science is to matter, it has to matter in the political world, a world where policymakers rule and have neither the scientific understanding nor the motivation to gain scientific understanding for resolving policy questions. Hence, if the science is to be properly used, it must be presented in a way (by the scientists) that policymakers can comprehend. Yet, as Rosenbaum points out, this is no easy task. In fact, attempting to merge the world of science and the world of politics into a workable unit may simply be an insurmountable task.

THE OUTLINE OF THE BOOK CHAPTERS

As one can surmise from the descriptions provided here, huge dilemmas exist in linking science to policy. How do policymakers resolve scientific questions through the political process, while making scientific and political judgments compatible? One's attempts to answer this question lead directly to a series of additional questions: When, where, and how should scientists enter the policy-making process? Should policymakers listen to the advice of scientists? Is it really possible for scientists to provide objective analyses of their research results? Is it possible for scientific research to be separated from policy judgments?

The chapters that follow explore possible answers to these questions. Our efforts are built on a foundation set forth by the many studies of environmental policymaking conducted over the past several decades. As you proceed through this book, you will see that many of these studies and their authors are highlighted.

The goal of this book is to provide a detailed description and analysis of how scientists fit into the U.S. environmental policymaking process. The focus is on the interactions between scientists and policymakers, and on how these interactions affect eventual environmental policy outcomes. However, to meaningfully understand the science–politics interaction, one must first have a grasp of the American public policymaking process as a whole. Hence, what follows is a sequence of chapters dedicated to a general description of the public policy process, environmental policymaking, and science, followed by a detailed analysis of the science–policy linkage, with emphasis on the concepts of scientific objectivity and political advocacy.

Chapter 2 describes the characteristics of the public policymaking system as it is carried out within the constraints of American democracy. After providing a range of definitions for the concepts of "public policy" and "democracy," there is a delineation of the core characteristics that make up the American public policy-making system. In addition, several of the most common approaches to the study of public policymaking are furnished so that readers can recognize possible models to use in analyzing the workings of policy analysis. Finally, there is a brief discussion highlighting scientists as the hidden participants of the public policymaking process.

Chapter 3 describes environmental policymaking as it plays out in the United States today, including an explanation of why environmental protection is currently recognized as an important policy issue. There is also a discussion of some of the tensions that make American environmental policymaking unique. The chapter ends with a brief overview of how the science–policy linkage relates to environmental policymaking.

Chapter 4 describes the part that science plays in the environmental policymaking process. The definition of science is discussed, as well as how science is supposed to be used by policymakers. The chapter concludes with recognition of the role of individual scientists in the environmental policymaking process, both as scientists and as citizens.

Chapter 5 delves into the science–politics relationship. Articulating this relationship makes science relevant in today's environmental policymaking world. One of the biggest concerns voiced by many environmental scholars is that scientists and policymakers work in two completely different and separate worlds. This concern is discussed in detail, with an emphasis on why it is so difficult for scientists to integrate their findings into the policy setting.

Chapter 6 critically examines the ideal of objectivity in the scientific process. The fallacy of neutral science is discussed, as are the reasons why so many scientists and policymakers alike feel that we must continue to honor the ideal of objectivity, despite the constant integration of values into the scientific process. The chapter ends with a discussion of how individual scientists attempt to cope in a way that protects the integrity of their work.

Chapter 7 lays out the difficulties scientists have in balancing the rigor of their scientific work with the political values of the policymaking process. The ideas of "neutral" science and advocacy are set against each other, as scientists move from providing scientific advice to becoming outright advocates for particular policy positions. Adversarial science is discussed, including the part that skeptics play in moving science into the policy world. In addition, the importance of communication, education, media, and consensus to the science–policy linkage are explained.

Chapter 8 offers an empirical overview of the science–policy linkage from the perspective of the scientists themselves. This chapter contains findings from interviews conducted by one of the authors. It is divided into three sections, each of which focuses on the perceptions of individual scientists as they attempt to connect science to policy. The chapter begins with a discussion of the differences (and similarities) between social scientists and natural scientists. Much has been made of the difference between the ways in which social scientists and natural scientists approach their work, and this chapter delves into those differences and the ways those differences affect how scientists perceive the science–policy linkage. The chapter then moves on to distinguish differences (and similarities) between how the United States and Canada approach environmental policymaking, and, more to the point, how U.S. and Canadian scientists differ in their approaches to the science–policy linkage. The chapter concludes with a listing of the interview results, highlighting how different disciplines and different cultures affect how science is connected to the policy world.

Chapter 9 offers an overview of the science–policy linkage as it plays out in the U.S. environmental policymaking process, highlighting what the authors believe are the major challenges facing scientists and policymakers as they continue the journey into the complex world of environmental policymaking in the United States.

This book is designed to give readers the ability to explore the complexities of linking science to policy in today's world. As you read this book, it is important to keep in mind that it is our intention to highlight the views of scientists regarding the science–policy linkage, with special attention provided to the views of natural scientists. We do this because most research about how the public policymaking process works is conducted by social scientists, with little attention given to the views of the natural scientists who are conducting environmental research. We wanted to make sure that the views of natural scientists were prominent as we explored some of the large, philosophical questions concerning how science fits into the public policymaking process: questions about whether it is possible for scientists to be truly objective in completing their research and whether scientists can be advocates for environmental action while remaining within the bounds of the scientific process. Not only are these questions concerning advocacy, objectivity, and the separation of science and policy pertinent to environmental policymaking today, but they will also remain pertinent in the long term.

Despite our emphasis on natural science, we do not ignore the work of social scientists. In fact, as you read on you will see that the heart of the philosophical arguments we make is based on the work of social scientists. Furthermore, we explore differences between how natural scientists and social scientists view the tensions between scientists and policymakers.

REFLECTIVE QUESTIONS

Question 1-1

Define the term *public policy*. In other words, what do you understand public policy to mean?

Question 1-2

Do the processes of *democracy* and *science* share any particular values? In answering this question, provide a brief description of the rules each of these processes follows.

Question 1-3

Describe three changes you would make to ensure that science is properly integrated into the American public policymaking process.

Question 1-4

Answer the question that Walter Rosenbaum posed at the beginning of this chapter: Which government institutions and leaders should shape the nation's environmental policies? Be specific: don't just provide the official titles by institution, but name the people who are in charge of those institutions today.

Question 1-5

Choose one of the four descriptions of the science–policy linkage delineated in this chapter (Cowling, Lee, Wildavsky, Rosenbaum), and provide a critique of its substance. Describe what you agree and disagree with, and how you would improve its descriptive power.

SUGGESTED READINGS

Lynton Caldwell, *Between Two Worlds: Science, the Environmental Movement, and Public Choice* (Cambridge: Cambridge University Press, 1990).

Kai N. Lee, *Compass and Gyroscope: Integrating Science and Politics for the Environment* (Washington, DC: Island Press, 1993).

Karen Litfin, *Ozone Discourses: Science and Politics in Global Environmental Cooperation* (New York: Columbia University Press, 1994).

Joel Primack and Frank Von Hippel, *Advice and Dissent: Scientists in the Political Arena* (New York: Basic Books, 1974).

CHAPTER 2

American Public Policy
and Democracy

Understanding the causes and consequences of policy decisions improves our knowledge of society.

Thomas Dye, *Understanding Public Policy,* 2002.

Despite what social science may say, politics is morality. Politics is the making of choices between good and bad, choices of priorities among competing good things.

Theodore Lowi, *The End of Liberalism,* 1979.

INTRODUCTION

The purpose of this chapter is to provide students with a description of American public policymaking as it relates to a democratic system of government. Understandably, we cannot deal comprehensively with every facet of American public policymaking or provide a definitive summary of all the characteristics that are exhibited in the policy world. However, what we can do is provide a basic introduction to the American public policymaking process, including definitions of key concepts. It is our hope that this chapter establishes a solid grounding in the American way of thinking about public policy so that readers have a good grasp of the general conditions in which both scientists and policymakers engage in policymaking.

We provide definitions of *public policy* and *democracy.* We describe what scholars believe are the core characteristics of the American public policymaking process. We also offer a categorization and explanation of some of the most common approaches to the study of American public policymaking. Our listing is by no means exhaustive, but it does highlight several different ways to view and investigate the way policymaking works. In this regard, we focus on the role of scientists as hidden participants in the policymaking process as well as the vital interaction between science and citizenship. We end the chapter with a discussion of the use of science as it relates to the world of politics.

DEFINITION OF PUBLIC POLICY

Because the study of public policy is a fairly recent phenomenon in the United States, and because the deliberative, democratic policymaking process is quite rightly deemed as contentious[1] and messy,[2] observers of the policy process struggle to grasp the essence of exactly what public policy means. In fact, it is a common technique to begin books about American public policy by simply asking the question, "What is public policy?" This question is then answered by providing straightforward definitions of public policy, such as those listed here.

- A policy is defined as a relatively stable, purposive course of action followed by an actor or set of actors dealing with a problem or matter of concern;[3]
- Policy is an intentional course of action followed by a government institution or official for resolving an issue of public concern;[4]
- Public policy is a course of action made up of a series of decisions, discrete choices (including the choice not to act), over a period of time;[5]
- Public policy is a process or series or a pattern of governmental activities or decisions that are designed to remedy some public problem, either real or imagined;[6]
- Public policy is whatever governments choose to do or not to do.[7]

While these definitions portray the policymaking process in slightly different ways, there are common themes—making public policy involves an attempt by government to address society's problems; and policy is a course of action, not just an isolated, one-time government act. As a working definition of public policymaking for this book, we offer the following description by a leading scholar, Paul Sabatier:

> In the process of public policymaking, problems are conceptualized and brought to government for solution; governmental institutions formulate alternatives and select policy solutions; and those solutions get implemented, evaluated, and revised.[8]

We recognize that in the context of an increasingly globalized world, with such great interdependence among politics, markets, culture, and society, this definition does not fully account for what Diane Stone calls a "growing global public space" that affects public policymaking.[9] In the end, it should always be remembered that "policies are not simply the random and chaotic product of a political process, [they] have underlying patterns and logic, and the ideas included in policies have real consequences."[10] It is within this context that we view the public policy process.

DEMOCRACY

More than fifty years ago, E. E. Schattschneider suggested that one of the great deficiencies of American democracy was that we lacked a good, usable definition of what it actually was.[11] We may still lack such a definition. The meaning of democracy is easily confused: the Democratic People's Republic of Korea is the official name of North Korea, and former East Germany was the Democratic Republic of Germany. Neither country can seriously claim to be a democracy. Having said this, we will make a good effort here to delineate exactly what we mean when the term *democracy* is used.

In brief, democracy can be defined simply as "a form of government in which the people rule."[12] From the Greek derivation, "demos" refers to "the people" and "kratein" refers to "rule." But direct democracy—the town hall model implied by this derivation—is not possible in large societies. The United States is normally classified as a representative democracy, in which the public elects representatives who transmit their views during the policymaking process. In this way the public still serves as a vital source of knowledge and ideas for policymakers, and public input is considered a fundamental aspect of the way policy decisions are made.

Countries have evolved many forms of democracy. As noted previously, even communist countries can consider themselves democratic. As such, these countries employ a form of representation via a political party; in most cases, the party debates decisions and can establish policies (however, under the principle of democratic centralism, there is no debate *after* the policy is made). Many countries today speak of Islamic democracy, in which, as in Iran, a formal representative government is overseen by a group of religious leaders who are determined to align all government actions with Sharia (Islamic) law.

Social scientists commonly measure the level of democracy of countries around the world using either the Freedom House or POLITY scales.[13] Freedom House annually ranks countries on a seven-point scale and then reports them as either "free," "partly free," or "not free." The focus is on the political and civil liberties that citizens possess. The POLITY index employs a twenty-one-point index to rank countries on a scale from autocratic to most democratic. It focuses on factors related to the structure of government, such as constraints on executive authority, and political competition.

The United States has always ranked among the highest scoring countries on these indices. Thus, in a comparative sense, the United States has been a promi-nent example of how democracy can work in a country.

Popular understanding in the United States of the definition of democracy usually includes the factors emphasized in the POLITY and Freedom House data: elections, political competition, and civil liberties. A simple way to conceptualize democracy, then, is "majority rule with minority rights."[14] But as we examine things more closely, American democracy may not reach this ideal. For some, as Kai N. Lee says, American democracy is simply "majority rule by the minority that cares."[15] For others, it is majority rule by the minority that is wealthy enough to have influence and access. The actual role of the public in the policy process in any democracy is not clearly defined simply by the form of government. Later in this chapter we explore conceptions of the public role in American democracy.

However, we believe that the health of a democracy depends on the free exchange of ideas between those inside of government and those outside of gov-ernment. In a sense, it would be accurate to say that democracy is founded on the ability of policymakers to respond to citizens willing to speak their minds.[16]

Responsiveness, then, is one of the key features of democracy. Interestingly, responsiveness depends not just on the attitude of elected officials and bureaucrats, but as Robert Putnam argues in *Bowling Alone,* it also depends on the degree of civic engagement in society, including such mundane things as bowling leagues.[17]

Indeed, some scholars (including Putnam) argue that involving an engaged and informed public in the policymaking process goes far beyond just legitimizing the democratic system, it actually leads to better policy outcomes. For citizens to participate in a meaningful way, however, there has to be a tolerance and openness to hear all the arguments; a place where uncertainties and disparate views are laid before the public.[18] According to David Collingridge and Colin Reeve, it is the *openness* of the American political system that ensures that all sides of an argument have the ability to be heard.[19]

Another feature related to the openness of a political system is the ability of the public to get information, or *transparency.* As defined by Transparency International, an NGO (nongovernmental organization) that monitors government corruption, transparency is the principle that allows *those affected* by governmental or administrative decisions to know not only the basic facts and figures but also the mechanisms and processes by which decisions are made. Transparency requires officials to act visibly, predictably, and understandably.[20]

One of the main ways that information gets transmitted to the public is through the *media,* which explains why a free press is considered to be a central component of democracy. According to Daniel Fiorina, especially regarding environmental policymaking, it is transparency that matters most. He believes that transparency not only brings environmental issues to public attention, it also provides the necessary means to hold both government and industry accountable.[21]

Still, beyond how responsive, open, and transparent a government is, more knowledge of the American system is needed to understand how people bring about actual policy change. Some observers of the American public policymaking process assert that change can only come about through two things: persistent participation by organized advocates for change,[22] and the ability to arouse popular concern leading toward action.[23] Yet such organized advocates need knowledge of the policy process in order to affect change; that is the focus of the next section.

AMERICAN PUBLIC POLICY AND DEMOCRACY: THE CORE CHARACTERISTICS

In order to appreciate the way American public policymaking works, including environmental policymaking, we must first recognize that public policymaking is a dynamic and fluid process. It is strongly affected by several unique features of our democratic political system, in which most (but not all) public policymakers are elected officials acting within a constitutionally based system of government,[24] and in which our political culture is defined by such core beliefs as individual liberty, limited government, private property, the Protestant work ethic, social mobility based on merit, and faith in the free market.[25]

These special characteristics are often featured in standard American government and public policymaking texts. What follows here is an overview of

SUGGESTED READINGS

Lynton Caldwell, *Between Two Worlds: Science, the Environmental Movement, and Public Choice* (Cambridge: Cambridge University Press, 1990).

Kai N. Lee, *Compass and Gyroscope: Integrating Science and Politics for the Environment* (Washington, DC: Island Press, 1993).

Karen Litfin, *Ozone Discourses: Science and Politics in Global Environmental Cooperation* (New York: Columbia University Press, 1994).

Joel Primack and Frank Von Hippel, *Advice and Dissent: Scientists in the Political Arena* (New York: Basic Books, 1974).

scientists. We do this because most research about how the public policymaking process works is conducted by social scientists, with little attention given to the views of the natural scientists who are conducting environmental research. We wanted to make sure that the views of natural scientists were prominent as we explored some of the large, philosophical questions concerning how science fits into the public policymaking process: questions about whether it is possible for scientists to be truly objective in completing their research and whether scientists can be advocates for environmental action while remaining within the bounds of the scientific process. Not only are these questions concerning advocacy, objectivity, and the separation of science and policy pertinent to environmental policymaking today, but they will also remain pertinent in the long term.

Despite our emphasis on natural science, we do not ignore the work of social scientists. In fact, as you read on you will see that the heart of the philosophical arguments we make is based on the work of social scientists. Furthermore, we explore differences between how natural scientists and social scientists view the tensions between scientists and policymakers.

REFLECTIVE QUESTIONS

Question 1-1

Define the term *public policy*. In other words, what do you understand public policy to mean?

Question 1-2

Do the processes of *democracy* and *science* share any particular values? In answering this question, provide a brief description of the rules each of these processes follows.

Question 1-3

Describe three changes you would make to ensure that science is properly integrated into the American public policymaking process.

Question 1-4

Answer the question that Walter Rosenbaum posed at the beginning of this chapter: Which government institutions and leaders should shape the nation's environmental policies? Be specific: don't just provide the official titles by institution, but name the people who are in charge of those institutions today.

Question 1-5

Choose one of the four descriptions of the science–policy linkage delineated in this chapter (Cowling, Lee, Wildavsky, Rosenbaum), and provide a critique of its substance. Describe what you agree and disagree with, and how you would improve its descriptive power.

science is supposed to be used by policymakers. The chapter concludes with recognition of the role of individual scientists in the environmental policymaking process, both as scientists and as citizens.

Chapter 5 delves into the science–politics relationship. Articulating this relationship makes science relevant in today's environmental policymaking world. One of the biggest concerns voiced by many environmental scholars is that scientists and policymakers work in two completely different and separate worlds. This concern is discussed in detail, with an emphasis on why it is so difficult for scientists to integrate their findings into the policy setting.

Chapter 6 critically examines the ideal of objectivity in the scientific process. The fallacy of neutral science is discussed, as are the reasons why so many scientists and policymakers alike feel that we must continue to honor the ideal of objectivity, despite the constant integration of values into the scientific process. The chapter ends with a discussion of how individual scientists attempt to cope in a way that protects the integrity of their work.

Chapter 7 lays out the difficulties scientists have in balancing the rigor of their scientific work with the political values of the policymaking process. The ideas of "neutral" science and advocacy are set against each other, as scientists move from providing scientific advice to becoming outright advocates for particular policy positions. Adversarial science is discussed, including the part that skeptics play in moving science into the policy world. In addition, the importance of communication, education, media, and consensus to the science–policy linkage are explained.

Chapter 8 offers an empirical overview of the science–policy linkage from the perspective of the scientists themselves. This chapter contains findings from interviews conducted by one of the authors. It is divided into three sections, each of which focuses on the perceptions of individual scientists as they attempt to connect science to policy. The chapter begins with a discussion of the differences (and similarities) between social scientists and natural scientists. Much has been made of the difference between the ways in which social scientists and natural scientists approach their work, and this chapter delves into those differences and the ways those differences affect how scientists perceive the science–policy linkage. The chapter then moves on to distinguish differences (and similarities) between how the United States and Canada approach environmental policymaking, and, more to the point, how U.S. and Canadian scientists differ in their approaches to the science–policy linkage. The chapter concludes with a listing of the interview results, highlighting how different disciplines and different cultures affect how science is connected to the policy world.

Chapter 9 offers an overview of the science–policy linkage as it plays out in the U.S. environmental policymaking process, highlighting what the authors believe are the major challenges facing scientists and policymakers as they continue the journey into the complex world of environmental policymaking in the United States.

This book is designed to give readers the ability to explore the complexities of linking science to policy in today's world. As you read this book, it is important to keep in mind that it is our intention to highlight the views of scientists regarding the science–policy linkage, with special attention provided to the views of natural merge the world of science and the world of politics into a workable unit may simply be an insurmountable task.

THE OUTLINE OF THE BOOK CHAPTERS

As one can surmise from the descriptions provided here, huge dilemmas exist in linking science to policy. How do policymakers resolve scientific questions through the political process, while making scientific and political judgments compatible? One's attempts to answer this question lead directly to a series of additional questions: When, where, and how should scientists enter the policy-making process? Should policymakers listen to the advice of scientists? Is it really possible for scientists to provide objective analyses of their research results? Is it possible for scientific research to be separated from policy judgments?

The chapters that follow explore possible answers to these questions. Our efforts are built on a foundation set forth by the many studies of environmental policymaking conducted over the past several decades. As you proceed through this book, you will see that many of these studies and their authors are high-lighted.

The goal of this book is to provide a detailed description and analysis of how scientists fit into the U.S. environmental policymaking process. The focus is on the interactions between scientists and policymakers, and on how these interactions affect eventual environmental policy outcomes. However, to meaningfully understand the science–politics interaction, one must first have a grasp of the American public policymaking process as a whole. Hence, what follows is a sequence of chapters dedicated to a general description of the public policy process, environmental policymaking, and science, followed by a detailed analysis of the science–policy linkage, with emphasis on the concepts of scientific objectivity and political advocacy.

Chapter 2 describes the characteristics of the public policymaking system as it is carried out within the constraints of American democracy. After providing a range of definitions for the concepts of "public policy" and "democracy," there is a delineation of the core characteristics that make up the American public policy-making system. In addition, several of the most common approaches to the study of public policymaking are furnished so that readers can recognize possible models to use in analyzing the workings of policy analysis. Finally, there is a brief discussion highlighting scientists as the hidden participants of the public policymaking process.

Chapter 3 describes environmental policymaking as it plays out in the United States today, including an explanation of why environmental protection is currently recognized as an important policy issue. There is also a discussion of some of the tensions that make American environmental policymaking unique. The chapter ends with a brief overview of how the science–policy linkage relates to environmental policymaking.

Chapter 4 describes the part that science plays in the environmental policymaking process. The definition of science is discussed, as well as how what matters. Nor does any responsible person get up and say that his ideology or her worldview requires inventing or denying dangers and to hell with the evidence. As long as science is the only publicly acceptable rationale, it matters.[56]

Wildavsky's words underscore the fact that within American public policy-making, science is not only accepted as the best way of knowing, it is viewed as the only valid and responsible way to establish a knowledge base, to provide the evidence that underlies decision-making. Wildavsky recognizes the importance of ideology in America's policy-making arena and even makes light of some ways of knowing that, at least publicly, are not acceptable ways to establish what we know. However, what Wildavsky does not want us to miss is the fact that the evidence that matters most in U.S. policymaking is scientifically driven, and that we had better be prepared to deal with all the burdens that come with linking this way of knowing to policy.

(4) The Incompatibility of Scientific and Political Judgments

For our final description of the way the science–policy linkage is viewed in the context of American democracy, we chose to highlight some of the thoughts of Walter Rosenbaum.

> Risk assessment frequently compels public officials to make scientific judgments and scientists to resolve policy issues for which neither may be trained. The almost inevitable need to resolve scientific questions through the political process and the problems that arise in making scientific and political judgments compatible are two of the most troublesome characteristics of environmental politics.[57]

In characterizing risk assessment, Rosenbaum goes right to the heart of the major theme of this book: getting good science into the U.S. environmental policymaking process is highly problematic. Of course, defining the term "good" science is problematic in and of itself. But we will save that dilemma for a later chapter. For now, let's concentrate on what Rosenbaum is trying to tell us. First, Rosenbaum emphasizes the fact that scientists and policymakers are trained in different ways, and, as a matter of course, they do not know how to operate in each other's professional world. Scientists are not proficient at doing politics (or policy), and policymakers are not proficient at doing science, and neither scientists nor policymakers have a good understanding of what the other does, or how.

Further, Rosenbaum observes that science has to be filtered through the policy (or political) process. Note that in Rosenbaum's description there is no mention of the arrow going the other way. He does not argue that policy questions must be resolved through the scientific process. In this regard, it appears that Rosenbaum has put the burden of action or change upon scientists. If science is to matter, it has to matter in the political world, a world where policymakers rule and have neither the scientific understanding nor the motivation to gain scientific understanding for resolving policy questions. Hence, if the science is to be properly used, it must be presented in a way (by the scientists) that policymakers can comprehend. Yet, as Rosenbaum points out, this is no easy task. In fact, attempting to society needs, at least not in the public setting. Indeed, Cowling even warns scientists against seeking to make such value judgments. Scientists are also to "clearly communicate" the results of their scientific investigations, a task that we will see in the coming chapters is not only difficult, but that is nearly impossible to do well. Finally, Cowling uses some of the critical words that characterize the tenets of the scientific process to describe the role of scientists: facts, uncertainties, and objectivity. Clearly, from Cowling's perspective, scientists are seen as one small, albeit significant, part of the public policymaking process where it is up to the policymakers to make societal decisions with scientists in a completely advisory role.

(2) Scientific Consensus Requires Political Action

Kai N. Lee provides a second description of the science–policy linkage.

> Without the centralizing vision of science . . . we cannot perceive the planet we share with other living things. . . . When science yields unambiguous negative implications for significant public values, action should be taken by governments. The form and content of the action will vary, but the imperative to act does not. When science yields consensus on the importance of a problem, however ambiguous the existing knowledge may be, democratic governments should consider action, initiating or continuing the collection of relevant information and building their capacity to analyze that information over time.[55]

Lee's vision of science diverges a bit from Cowling's vision (at least as expressed by these short statements) in that Lee suggests that policymakers should take action if scientific input meets certain criteria. Policymakers are not allowed to simply disregard scientific input. But the criteria are extremely stringent. Scientists must provide "unambiguous negative implications" for "significant public values." Whoa! These are very strong words, and again, as we shall see in the coming chapters, they set a bar for scientists to meet that may be unreachable. For instance, how does one define unambiguous? Is there any room for ambiguity at all? Doesn't this concept go against the very uncertainties that are inherent in the scientific process? And who defines *which* public values are *significant?* Do scientists have any say in making those determinations? Furthermore, what does *consensus* mean? That all scientists agree? That a majority of scientists agree? And under what mechanism do we reach this consensus? Still, Lee provides us with a view of public policymaking linking science directly to environmental protection, a view where science is a major participant in decision-making (a *centralizing* force) regarding the quality of life on "the planet we share with other living things."

(3) Science as the Most Legitimate Rationale for Policy

Aaron Wildavsky provides a cogent description of the science–policy linkage, emphasizing science's uniqueness and importance.

> Scientific evidence does matter. I notice that no mention is made of witchcraft as a rationale for regulation, but rather obeisance is made to science whether or not it is

said to work in two different worlds, each deeply rooted in divergent human occupations. As one noted environmental scholar points out:

> Science and politics serve different purposes. Politics aims at the responsible use of power; in a democracy, "responsible" means accountable, eventually to voters. Science aims at finding truths—results that withstand the scrutiny of one's fellow scientists.[52]

Moreover, within the context of environmental policymaking, some argue that we should go beyond just accepting the idea that scientists and policymakers work in different worlds according to different values, and set up an environmental policymaking system where scientists and policymakers are isolated from each other's influence, with barriers maintained such that scientists can complete their research with careful adherence to the canons of the scientific process, and policymakers can be protected from scientists telling them what they should decide.[53] But, is this type of environmental policy world even a remote possibility in today's environment? Is it something we should even be striving to accomplish?

To begin answering these questions and to get a flavor of the complex and controversial aspects of linking science (and scientists) to public policymaking in the United States, we offer four descriptions of the way the science–policy linkage is viewed in the context of American democracy. The four we have chosen to highlight are a representative sample of the way scholars have come to view science and environmental policymaking in the United States. In no way are these quotes a comprehensive set of all possible descriptions of the science–policy linkage. However, they do represent mainstream views of scholarship regarding the large, philosophical questions that surround the science–policy dichotomy. Moreover, these descriptions foreshadow the major themes that will be detailed in the chapters to come.

FOUR WAYS TO DEFINE THE SCIENCE–POLICY LINKAGE IN ENVIRONMENTAL POLICYMAKING

(1) Separation of Science and Politics

Ellis B. Cowling provides us with a good starting point in delineating the role of scientists in the American environmental policymaking process.

> The responsibility of scientists . . . in a democracy is to understand and clearly communicate the scientific facts and uncertainties and to describe expected outcomes objectively. Deciding what to do involves questions of societal values where scientists, as scientists . . . have no special authority. . . . The proper role for scientists . . . is to provide advice and counsel . . . to those who are charged by our society to make policy decisions. It is not a proper role for a scientist . . . as such, to seek to make (or even to have special influence on) societal decisions.[54]

Cowling's description, while brief, is quite instructive. It provides the reader with many of the critical aspects of linking science to policy *in a democracy* and also provides a prescription for how this should be completed. Note that the focus is on the "responsibility of scientists" and the "proper role for scientists," to provide advice only to policymakers and not to make value judgments about what in so many ways the United States owes its economic success to scientific advances. But in its political culture, whereas other countries elect leaders with PhDs, the United States public is more likely to vote for celebrities. The temptation for United States politicians to play on the anti-intellectualism of the public may have reached its zenith in the George W. Bush years, characterized by Chris Mooney as a time of "the Republican War on Science."[40]

However, no matter how you look at it, science and scientists are viewed as critical to environmental policymaking in all democracies because scientific issues permeate all environmental problems and because scientists are often the first to discover and publicize environmental problems.[41] In fact, it is argued that environmental issues such as the reduction in stratospheric ozone would not be part of the public dialogue without the influence of scientists.[42] In short, conventional wisdom posits that environmental questions are fundamentally questions of science,[43] and that most environmental issues on the current agenda would not exist were it not for scientific research.[44] As Norman Miller puts it, "every environmental problem has, at its foundation, a scientific reality, and it therefore seems axiomatic that science must play a prominent, if not pivotal, role in formulating its solution."[45] More to the point, Karen Litfin argues that the language of environmental policy debates is scientific in nature "because science is a primary source of legitimation and because scientists help to define environmental problems."[46]

At the same time, scholars recognize that it is not easy to translate the findings of science into reasonable public policies.[47] With all the importance allocated to science and scientists, questions remain about the ability of scientists to connect to a policy world that eventually relies on politicians to make the final policy decisions, with or without scientific input.[48] Simply put, science and scientists do not have the ability to resolve policy debates on their own, no matter how good the science is determined to be and no matter how much faith we have in scientists and the scientific process.[49]

Many who have spent a good part of their professional careers studying science and its linkage to environmental policymaking have doubts about the effectiveness of science to meaningfully affect policy. For instance, Daniel Sarewitz asks some very pointed questions about the linkage of science to policy in a democracy. He asks, where is the common ground between the orderly search for scientific truth and the chaotic forums of popular governance? And, shouldn't this common ground be sought in a more scientific approach to democracy rather than in a more democratic approach to science?[50] Bruce Bimber asks a series of questions relevant to understanding the politics of science: what do scientists do, why do they do it, and what difference does it make? Bimber goes on to posit that a richer analysis might ask even more detailed questions, such as which scientists are to be believed, which scientists should be discounted because of their political interests, and how government should elicit from scientists advice that is unshaped by partisanship and ideology.[51]

As you will see in the coming chapters, one of the most commonly expressed assertions about the science–policy linkage is that scientists and policymakers are

If pluralism is to yield a truly democratic outcome, several assumptions must hold:

- A representative segment of the public must join interest groups;
- Interest groups must be responsive to their membership;
- Interest groups must have adequate information and regular access to policy-makers.

The pluralist perspective is especially relevant to the science–policy linkage with respect to environmental issues. Scientists can be conceived as one of many interest groups that provide input to policymakers. Yet any claims by scientists supporting a particular policy position will be countered by the criticisms of those on opposing sides of issues.[36] Ideally, policymakers will consider input from scientists as well as a variety of other interested parties on any environmental issue. The result should be a rational policy that represents the best possible balancing of popular interests on the issue.

In the elite theory of governance (see Figure 2.2), participation in the policy process is allowed only for the few that possess special characteristics such as wealth or institutional status. Government is no longer the neutral referee but is inherently biased toward the interests of large corporations and economic interests. Access is limited to those who have political power, perhaps because they can pay in the form of campaign contributions or employment for government officials and their constituents, or, on occasion, because the group has a vast

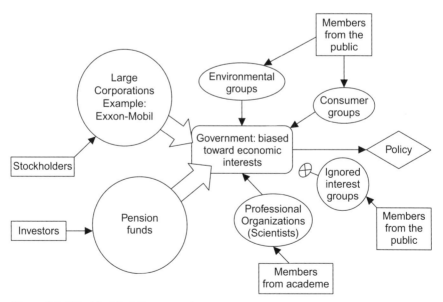

Figure 2.2 Elite Model of Democracy[1]

[1] This diagram represents the authors' depiction of the United States elitist model of democracy.

government services, regressive taxes, weak government, and limited citizen participation). Of course, the media has a powerful effect on American political culture
and on the policy process, often giving "a misleading impression about the problems
of society and how well government works."[34] As noted earlier, the media has a pivotal role in ensuring transparency. The ability to affect or control the media affects
citizens' access to information, which inevitably affects public policy.

The relationship between citizens and the policymaking process is a complex
one. The next section introduces two theoretical concepts commonly used to
describe this relationship.

Pluralism and Elitism

The theoretical frameworks of pluralism and elitism help us understand inherent
tensions in democracy in the United States. Beginning again with the observation
that direct democracy is not possible in large societies, these frameworks help us
understand how "rule by the people" can still take place.

Pluralism assumes that the people's will is transmitted to government not just
every two or four years during elections but through interest groups that lobby
government. In a sense, these are Madison's "factions" from Federalist #10. The
policymaking process is regulated by a government that acts as a neutral referee
that allows competing interest groups to have access to policymakers. Policy is the
result of this fair and open competition between interest groups, and should produce the best possible balance of conflicting demands.[35] The process is something
like that pictured in Figure 2.1.

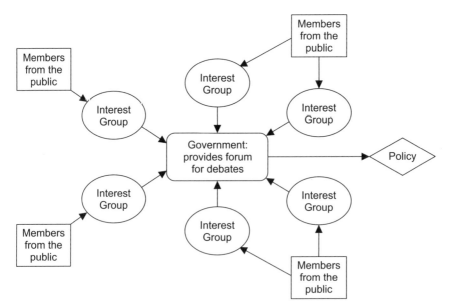

Figure 2.1 A Sample Model of Pluralist Democracy[1]

[1]This diagram represents the authors' depiction of the United States pluralistic model of democracy.

numerous points of access for interest groups to pursue their separate agendas. In the words of Roger Clark et al., the United States Constitution establishes a "deliberately fragmented and open character of decision making authority."[27] For example, today at least eighteen different departments and agencies are involved in intelligence gathering in the United States.[28] The fragmentation present today is characterized not only by institutional divisions of power but also by geographic loyalties, all of which leads to ambiguities of authority.[29] As suggested by James Smith, there "is something troubling about the relationship among experts, leaders, and citizens that tends to make American politics more polarized, short-sighted, and fragmented—and often less intelligent—than it should be."[30] Institutionally, characteristics such as federalism and fragmentation critically affect American public policy outcomes, including the outcomes of environmental policymaking.[31]

Incrementalism

Incrementalism means that policy in the United States rarely exhibits radical change; the best predictor of future policy is current policy, with small deviations. Although dynamic and innovative changes occur on rare occasions (for instance, after realigning elections such as in 1932 with the election of Franklin D. Roosevelt and 1980 with the election of Ronald Reagan), most change is painfully slow. Other democracies are not like this—in parliamentary democracies such as Great Britain, with the executive and legislative branches unified under the control of the majority party, sweeping changes are more frequent. So as Judith Layzer suggests, one of the enduring features of American policymaking is the "remarkable persistence of the status quo."[32] But one should not forget that the American political system was purposely designed to be slow and deliberate with public policymaking often "arduous, time consuming, continuous, but not impossible."[33] The founders were skeptical about human nature and expected government to evolve toward tyranny, so they designed structures that would inhibit that tendency.

Political Culture

Political culture also plays a prominent role in setting public policy in the United States. Citizens' attitudes, beliefs, and expectations about government actions create norms that affect policymaking. It matters if individuals, states, or regions view policymaking in a positive light in which those who govern strive to promote the public good in terms of honesty, unselfishness, and a commitment to the public welfare or if these entities view policymaking as a marketplace, where government should only possess a limited role. Further, it matters whether people believe that government should be controlled by a small group of policy elites or be guided by a predominance of citizen participation.

Political culture includes the concept of political ideologies, and in the United States we have a spectrum of ideologies ranging from those citizens classified as liberal (tending to favor redistributive polices, government services, progressive taxes, strong government, and maximum citizen participation) to those citizens classified as conservative (tending to favor distributive policies, minimal some of the particularly American characteristics that define policymaking in the United States, as illustrated by the recent work of Mark E. Rushefsky in his book *Public Policy in the United States: At the Dawn of the Twenty-First Century,* 4th Edition.[26] These characteristics include, among others, federalism, separation of powers, checks and balances, fragmentation, incrementalism, political culture, pluralism, and elitism.

Federalism

One of the first things students of public policymaking in the United States must realize is that American federalism—a system set up such that the national government shares power with the fifty states—has created a complex set of intergovernmental relations. Although the authority of federal, state, and local governments is set in constitutional law, the interpretation of that law has led to considerable competition among the levels to establish and retain authority. State and federal governments have different functions, and while state and local governments can act independently, they are also often tasked with carrying out policies set by the federal government. American federalism has many important consequences. First, it often makes implementation of consistent nationwide policies more difficult. Second, it allows for experimentation, in which policies can be tried at the state or local level before being adopted nationally. Third, like other features of American democracy, federalism can result in long delays in policy formation because of the need to build consensus among so many different governmental actors.

Separation of Powers and Checks and Balances

The founders of American democracy were preoccupied with preventing what they considered to be the inevitable slide of governments toward tyranny. A basic way to prevent the concentration of power in any king-like authority was to divide government into three separate branches, each with primary responsibility for carrying out certain functions (e.g., legislature makes the law, executive executes the law, judicial interprets the law). Separation of powers means the sharing of authority, and the system of checks and balances ensures that each branch has some control over the others' powers. This prevents any one branch from getting too much power, but it also slows and considerably complicates the policymaking process. In many cases, approval is needed by all three branches for a policy to be enacted and implemented. One key consequence of the American system is a bias toward the status quo; it is much easier to delay or prevent policy change than it is to implement it. Two concepts that help us understand this problem are fragmentation and incrementalism.

Fragmentation

Fragmentation means that for any given policy, there is no single, central point of control or authority; policy is made in numerous redundant and overlapping administrative agencies, legislative committees, and judicial bodies. Thus there are popular membership who might be able to sway the result of subsequent elections. Outcomes of policy under the elitism model generally favor wealthy, organized interests. As Charles Lindblom famously stated at the end of his seminal work, *Politics and Markets:* "The large private corporation fits oddly into democratic theory and vision. Indeed, it does not fit."[37]

Although the realities of the American political system tend to produce a bias toward wealth, that is not the only possibility. Bruce Williams and Albert Matheny, casting scientists in this light, describe scientists as members of a knowledge elite.

> If policymaking is viewed as the domain of scientific experts whose research can produce a truth upon which public policy can be ideally based, then there is no need to consider mechanisms for allowing ordinary citizens to participate in the decisions that affect them directly.[38]

In either case, whether it be wealth or scientific merit, the elite theory of policymaking produces a much less-than-democratic outcome.

Tension between pluralism and elitism appears rampant in the United States today, which suffers from a gulf in opinions between the public and the elite. Adam Finkel and Dominic Golding believe that experts and the public "hold each other in mutual contempt, with the experts thinking that the public is ignorant and not informed enough to make judgments about what to do and the public thinking that the experts are self-serving and uncaring."[39] It appears that the growing importance of expertise in policy decisions—including scientific expertise—seems to be putting limits on the democratic process.[40] Citizens are supposed to be integral to the democratic process and to the production of socially desirable results, but when scientists replace the voice of ordinary people in the policymaking process, it disempowers citizens just as much as any other elitism.[41] And, in some cases, that is exactly what has happened. For instance, Eric Herzik and John Dobra, through their documentation of the nuclear waste issue, show that the scientific community rarely speaks directly to the public, and the public is largely unaware of the views of the scientific community.[42]

Brian Silver poses a pertinent question regarding elitism: "[I]f genius is, by definition, the possession of a tiny elite, how is the average man to satisfactorily comprehend that which took genius to reveal?"[43] Anne Schneider and Helen Ingram answer this question by suggesting that the scientific complexity characterized by many policy issues often causes both political leaders and ordinary citizens to leave the policy arena to scientists.[44] Because making informed political decisions increasingly requires the expertise of scientists who are unelected, the very relationship between these experts and political decision-makers has now become a fundamental legitimacy issue within the United States democratic government.[45] Moreover, some scholars believe that environmental policy debates are not necessarily democratic but are managed by an elite transnational policy community,[46] and certainly scientists are now considered elites within our present-day political system.[47] Some even argue that this should be the case, that scientists should be autonomous from the rest of society and that the scientific community ought to be accountable only to itself.[48]

ANALYSIS OF PUBLIC POLICY

One helpful way to visualize the policymaking process is to set up a specific framework of analysis. Fortunately, several good frameworks exist today. Although there is a wide array of frameworks, from those grounded in historic-geographic and socioeconomic conditions,[49] to those which emphasize individual actors and their preferences, interests, and resources,[50] the most common framework has been to represent the policymaking process as a sequence of linearly connected stages.[51] The rationale for studying public policy in stages is that what actors do in one of the stages is largely framed by what actors have done in the earlier stages of the public policy process.[52]

The stages of the policymaking process are generally characterized as shown here.

- *Problem identification,* in which demands are made for government to solve a problem.
- *Agenda setting,* in which the policymaking body chooses a subset of issues for immediate consideration from among all the issues worthy of governmental action.
- *Policy formation* is the stage where options are considered and a plan is developed to deal with the issue.
- *Policy adoption* is when a specific alternative is chosen from among the options.
- *Implementation* occurs when the policy is put into action.
- *Evaluation* occurs after the policy has been implemented for a time; here, a judgment is made regarding the success of the policy.
- *Policy revision* occurs after evaluation, when a determination is made as to whether the policy should be continued, changed, or terminated.

An offshoot of this policy-made-in-stages approach is based on the systems approach developed by David Easton.[53] According to this approach, demands are made upon the government by society, the government reacts to these demands, and the end result is a specific policy, sometimes called a policy outcome. The societal demands involve specific types of political behavior, political culture, and ideology. Moreover, these demands are passed forward through such mechanisms as public opinion, interest groups, mass media, political parties, and community elites. The government policymaking structure is set up to view and deal with these demands within an institutional structure consisting of legislatures, elected executives, courts, and bureaucracy (including administrative agencies). Essentially, the government processes the demands to produce public policy. The end results are called policy outcomes and consist of laws, executive orders, court rulings, regulations, enforcement actions, budgets, and taxes. This type of approach focuses specifically upon institutions and political behavior both inside and outside those institutions.

Although this focus on institutions and political behavior has remained a very popular approach, there has been some criticism that viewing public policymaking through a simple sequence of stages is not sufficient to grasp the true meaning and development of public policy. In other words, the policymaking process is now viewed as much too complex to be explained in such a straightforward manner.[54] As B. Guy Peters and Jon Pierre point out: "The study of public policy is a very complex topic, and any attempt to force policy into any narrow theoretical frame should be considered with some skepticism."[55]

The conceptual frameworks of John Kingdon (1995), Paul Sabatier and Hank Jenkins-Smith (1993), Frank Baumgartner and Bryan Jones (1993), and Elinor Ostrom (1990) are currently recognized as some of the more advanced approaches to the study of public policy, each, in their own way, addressing the complexities of public policymaking.[56] The frameworks of Kingdon, Sabatier and Jenkins-Smith, and Baumgartner and Jones are grounded in the idea that policy is made through a series of complex interactions among participants, across time, and at multiple levels of government. Ostrom's framework challenges the more conventional approaches and posits that communities rely on institutions that resemble neither the state nor the market but are based on voluntary coopera-tion.[57] Furthermore, as delineated in the following paragraphs, these scholars por-tray their particular public policy constructs in a way that emphasizes a particular aspect of how policy changes over time.

The Kingdon Approach

Kingdon's approach is a framework for explaining agenda-setting, that is, how issues rise from being part of a broad set of issues that merit governmental atten-tion to an issue that will be considered for immediate action.[58] Kingdon's approach differs from a pluralistic approach because he does not view agenda-setting as a linear sequence in which the public makes demands on interest groups who make demands on government who then create policy. Rather, Kingdon argues that both problems and solutions are widely known, and that an issue rises on the agenda as a result of three possible dynamics:

1. A *focusing event* or crisis. This can include natural or environmental disasters.
2. A *major change in the political coalitions* that influence government. This can come about due to elections or a change in leadership in the executive or parts of the legislature.
3. The work of a *policy entrepreneur,* who joins together a particular problem with a solution and also builds a political coalition.

Kingdon analyzes agenda-setting by exploring three dynamic streams (the problem stream, policy stream, and political stream); when those streams merge at certain points in time, Kingdon sees a "window of opportunity" that may stimulate the production of a specific public policy. The problem stream consists of various existing problems. These do not rise on the agenda until some mechanism brings that problem to the attention of decision-makers. One such mechanism is the focusing event, which includes disasters, crises, personal experiences, and galvanizing symbols. Focusing events need to be understood within the context of preexisting perceptions, especially about past governmental actions. It is important

to note that government officials do not address all problems. Hence, how problems are defined and under what conditions they are defined help determine their
status in the problem stream.

For Kingdon, the key to the public policymaking process is understanding how
particular problems get joined to particular solutions and how a proper political
environment allows action on the problems and leads to a solution. Why some
issues make it onto the public policy agenda and others do not can be explained
by the confluence of the process streams of problems, solutions, and politics. On
occasion, problems become so pressing (for example, the energy crisis) that they
move easily to the governmental agenda on their own merit. More often, though,
problems do not move alone but emerge when changes in the constraints of the
political stream allow them to emerge. That is, problems are greatly affected by
such things as public opinion, the national mood, legislative turnover, and
interest-group pressure.

Often in the United States we see situations in which an issue remains on the
broad list of problems that concern government, but for years it fails to rise to the
decision agenda where action is imminent. Examples include acid rain in the 1980s
and universal health care in the 1990s and 2000s. Kingdon reminds us that to move
up to the decision agenda, problems usually must be linked to a politically acceptable solution. But in both of these cases, several such solutions existed. In such situations, it is often a major electoral shift (the election of Bill Clinton or Barack
Obama on health care) or the removal of important legislators who can block legislation (Senator Robert Byrd on acid rain) that lead to action on the issue.

A final way to open policy windows can occur when a person who is highly
involved in the policy process is able to join the streams through his or her own
efforts. Such a person is dubbed a policy entrepreneur. Examples from the United
States include Ralph Nader on auto safety in the 1960s and 1970s, and Al Gore on
climate change in the 2000s. Entrepreneurs join a particular problem with a politically acceptable solution, and then build a political coalition to support it.

For Kingdon, problems and solutions are floating around in problem and policy streams; actors backing particular solutions search for appropriate problems
and/or political conditions to increase the likelihood of adoption of those solutions. Within these streams, constant adjustment and adaptation of problems,
solutions, and politics occur as a result of the actions of those involved in the policy process. Issues rise on the agenda when actors sense the joining of the streams,
and are thus willing to devote time and energy to these issues.

The Sabatier and Jenkins-Smith Approach

The Sabatier and Jenkins-Smith approach centers on advocacy coalitions as the
primary determinants of public policy.[59] Advocacy coalitions are defined as
groups of actors from both private and public organizations at all levels of
government who share a common set of values or beliefs. Instead of examining
stages, the policy process is viewed as a whole within a framework in which these
advocacy coalitions attempt to manipulate the rules of government to bring about

change that coincides with their beliefs. This activity takes place within the basic social structure and in accordance with the constitutional rules of the system.

One of the founding assumptions of the advocacy coalition framework is that although most policymaking occurs among specialists within a policy subsystem, these specialists are also influenced by factors in the broader political and social economic system. Specialization is predominant within the policymaking system because modern societies are simply too complex, forcing individuals to narrow their expertise if they have any hope of providing meaningful input into the policy process. At the same time, changes in the broader social and economic system (e.g., regime change or disasters) have the ability to shift agendas and focus public attention. In addition, policy-oriented learning by all participants in the policy process can also bring about policy change.

The Baumgartner and Jones Approach

The Baumgartner and Jones approach, founded within the agenda-setting process, is structured around the principle that political systems are never in general equilibrium.[60] Baumgartner and Jones depict the policy consequences of agenda-setting as dramatic reversals rather than marginal revisions to the status quo. The generation of new ideas is said to create an atmosphere such that policy monopolies (defined as structural arrangements that are supported by powerful ideas) are unstable over time. Policy is made with fits and starts, slowly, then rapidly, rather than in a linear, smooth way. Existing political institutions and issue definitions are presented as key to the policymaking process, with issue definition, because of its potential for mobilizing the disinterested, cast as the driving force in the policymaking process, affecting both stability and instability.

Although crises do occur in American public policymaking, the status quo more typically characterizes most policy areas. Still, large-scale changes in public policy do take place, and existing problems are redefined and reshaped, sometimes dramatically. To this end, the purpose of "punctuated-equilibrium theory" is to seek to explain the occasional large departures from political processes that are generally characterized by stability and incrementalism.

The Ostrom Approach

The Ostrom approach is founded within political economy and rational choice theories, portraying policy within a framework in which decision-makers repeatedly have to make decisions constrained by a set of collective-choice rules.[61] Because of this, their perspective on the policymaking process brings a focus on the rules of decision-making within policymaking bodies. Decision-makers have incomplete knowledge of the issue and of other players' strategies; they constantly adjust their own understanding and strategies by trial and error and learning from their mistakes. Policy emerges as individual policymakers try to act as rationally as possible in a political environment.

It is important to note that Ostrom's approach focuses on the development of particular types of solutions to policy problems. Ostrom explains that her framework is designed to "shatter the convictions of many policy analysts that the only way to solve [common-pool resource] problems is for external authorities to impose full property rights or centralized regulation."[62] Through her critique of three conventional approaches (privatization, central regulation, and management by interested parties), Ostrom offers a picture of policymaking in which communities voluntarily develop policy rules, a commitment to collective benefits, and successful mutual monitoring.[63]

The Stone Approach

The approaches to the study of public policymaking outlined earlier vary from looking at public policy as a linear process that takes place in definable stages, to the notion that it is the complex interaction of policy streams or policy subsystems that determine where we are going, to the notion that viable policy solutions exist outside mainstream approaches such as privatization and centralized government. Although these conceptualizations are significant to the study of public policy, it still remains helpful to understand that the heart of policymaking lies in behavior that takes place within our policy institutions (legislatures, the presidency, courts, interest groups, administrative agencies, local governments, and political parties) and in behavior that takes place outside these political institutions (public opinion, voting, political culture, and political socialization).

With this in mind, we provide one additional approach to policymaking: Deborah Stone's insights into what she labels as the policy paradox.[64] In her work, Stone emphasizes the power of symbols and establishes the dominance of politics. The words of Stone are instructive in describing the difference between policy and politics.

> Policy is potentially a sphere of rational analysis, objectivity, allegiance to truth, and pursuit of the well being of society as a whole. Politics is the sphere of emotion and passion, irrationality, self-interest, shortsightedness, and raw power.[65]

Within this world of policymaking, Stone makes it clear that politics trumps policy; that reasoned analysis is necessarily political, and that the key to success in the policy world lies in the *problem definition* stage and the ways that issues are framed. She argues that there is no such thing as apolitical problem definition, that problems are defined with the sole purpose of mobilizing support to accomplish political goals.

Stone examines problem definition using both narratives (stories characterized by metaphor and analogy that catch the imagination of the public) and numbers (to count something is to assert that it is an identifiable entity with clear boundaries). She contends that interpretation of facts is more important than the facts themselves, and if one is looking for the wise course of action, one should not focus on the objective consequences of the action but on how the interpretation of those actions will play out. Because of this, Stone contrasts the scientific world, where interpretation of events should remain constant, unambiguous, and entirely unaffected by the observer, with the political world, where ambiguity rules.

Stone finds support for her ideas from others who study the policymaking process. Sheila Jasanoff and Mark Rushefsky both agree that problem perception and definition are absolutely vital to understanding American public policy.[66] In this regard, Rushefsky specifically highlights the fact that different people perceive events differently and that knowing who is doing the perceiving and who is doing the defining of issues offers insight into how policies are formulated in the American system of policymaking. In addition, Roger Pielke, Jr. makes the argument that successful public policymaking requires issues to be appropriately framed and presented to those with the authority and ability to act.[67]

THE POLICY PROCESS AND THE ROLE OF SCIENTISTS

Scientists, Democracy, and Public Policy

Science policy issues are different than other policy questions. They are different because the pace of technological change is rapid, complex, and difficult for both the public and policymakers to grasp, and because new developments carry irreversible consequences, challenging deeply held social, moral, and religious values.[68] Fitting all the characteristics of democracy into the public policymaking process, and then integrating science into this mix, is a challenge because the United States, as a representative democracy, fosters both a reliance on a pluralist conception of civil society and a vision of science as an independent but politically relevant enterprise.[69] As Richard Sclove notes, science poses all kinds of problems for a functioning democracy.

> Scientific leaders have no monopoly on expertise, nor do they have a privileged ethical standpoint for evaluating the social consequences of science. . . . Elite only approaches are antithetical to the open, vigorous, and creative public debate on which democracy, policymaking, and science all thrive.[70]

Seen in this light, one comes to understand that scientists are not the only force capable of impacting government and everyday life on a grand scale. For example, it is certainly clear that public participation now plays a large role with respect to policymaking, especially environmental policymaking.[71] Advocacy groups, through strategic maneuvering (defining issues, managing actors, and shifting policy venues), have the ability to shape the scope of policy conflicts to their interests.[72] Yet in some cases, broad citizen support is not enough to legitimate decisions that do not command the respect of the scientific community.[73] Furthermore, there appears to be a serious disconnect between scientists and the American public on many topics, including environmental issues, critical to our nation and the world.[74]

These tensions between scientists, the public, and policymakers bear witness to the complex nature of the interactions that take place within American public policymaking. One thing, however, is certain: Science and scientists are now integrated into every corner of modern culture, ensuring that they are now a major force with respect to participatory government and everyday life.[75]

Scientists as Hidden Participants

Because different definitions pose conflicting policy implications, and because scientists are almost always involved in defining environmental problems and issues, scientists play a crucial role in environmental policymaking.[76] However, that role may not be as obvious as one might think. Scientists are described by John Kingdon as belonging among the hidden participants who play a significant part in the public policymaking process by working behind the scenes, generating alternatives, proposals, and solutions that pave the way for successful public policy formulation.[77] In this regard, scientists are viewed as key actors in loosely knit communities of specialists where, "Ideas bubble around [and people] try out proposals in a variety of ways: through speeches, bill introductions, congressional hearings, leaks to the press, circulation of papers, conversations, and lunches. They float their ideas, criticize one another's work, hone and revise their ideas, and float new versions."[78]

Although scientists may not be responsible for the prominence of problems on the agenda, they play a key role in framing problems within a unique issue context and in setting alternative solutions to those problems. Kingdon describes a policy process in which scientists, through the gradual accumulation of knowledge or the occurrence of scientific discovery, help create a general climate of ideas that affects policymakers' thinking. Kingdon alludes to this particular aspect of the policy process as the "long process of softening up the system."[79]

In short, Kingdon's ideas offer a way to illustrate the tensions between science and policy. If the central questions about the science–policy linkage have to do with when, where, and why scientists enter the policy process and what effect they have, then the Kingdon model provides a framework to guide the search for answers to those questions. When and how scientists can most usefully intervene is a question that can be answered in several places—at the stages of problem formation, solution formation, linkage of problem and solution, creation of political forces necessary to move the problem up the ladder on the agenda, and when linking problem, solution, and politics together is necessary to advance the policy process.

Science, Citizenship, and the American Public

Integrating science into the American public policymaking process presents a particularly difficult dilemma because it forces us to weigh the specialized expertise of scientists against the views of citizens who do not possess such a knowledge base.[80] Walter Baber and Robert Bartlett suggest that it is not scientists, but citizens—through open participatory processes—that legitimize public policy decisions.[81] They argue that democracy and environmental protection are connected by the fact that neither is possible unless citizens move past their own narrow interests. This stand is supported by other scholars, who claim that the only way to get action on issues such as global warming is for the public to get angry; in the end, it is the American people, acting within the democratic process, who will make the final policy decisions.[82]

But Baber and Bartlett also point out that it may be asking too much of citizens to "play the role of critical auditor of the social and political meaning of scientific and technological advances."[83] Paralleling this view, Dorothy Nelkin points out that the very power of citizens to participate in policymaking decisions exhibiting the complexities of science is threatened because of public ambivalence toward such issues.[84] In addition, it is a generally accepted observation that the public knows little about how government, politics, and public policymaking actually works.[85] The fact of the matter is that people can be moved in specific directions by skilled politicos. As Evan Goldstein explains, because "human beings are lazy, busy, impulsive, inert, and irrational creatures highly susceptible to predictable biases and errors . . . they can be nudged in socially desirable directions."[86]

Considering that scientists are also citizens makes them a target for the influence of politicos as well. This is further complicated by the fact that scientists, acting through their role as citizens in a democracy, have every right to seek to influence the making of public policy.[87] However, when this occurs, more often than not, the science melds into ideological positions, and is often obscured by political considerations.[88] Still, if one wants to share the optimism generated by the idea that citizens can make a meaningful contribution to the democratic process—especially within a democracy based on the concept of pluralism—it is important for scientists, as citizens, to speak out publicly.[89] To be sure, scientists in no way abdicate the rights and duties of citizenship simply because of their particular professional activities.

Use of Science in the World of Politics

A commonly accepted belief is that science produces knowledge more likely to be effective than personal opinion, political ideology, or other sources of information.[90] However, policy decisions often cannot wait for scientists to produce such conclusive evidence.[91] The question of whether policymakers know enough to act is inherently a policy question, not a scientific one, because policy choices involve subjective values about which science has little or nothing to say.[92] Political players on opposing sides of a controversy often exploit scientific uncertainty to legitimate their respective policy positions[93] or simply to support the status quo.[94] Where the problem lies is not in requesting more relevant information but in the presumption that we should not act until we have all the relevant information available. Wade Robison does a good job of explaining how this works.

> By nature of the case, public policy issues present us with an epistemological short-fall: The scientific situations are too complex, and our own ignorance is too vast, for us ever to be able to reject as inappropriate on epistemological grounds the request for more information . . . it is politically advantageous to refuse to act out when it is epistemologically appropriate to ask for more information. It always looks reasonable to refuse to act on the grounds that "not all the information is in." Decision-making is then delayed.[95]

Along these lines, Sheila Jasanoff and Marybeth Long Martello document the use of waiting for "better" science as a stalling tactic on a range of environmental issues, from acid rain to climate change.[96] George E. Brown cites the current debate over global warming to cast doubt on science's ability to deliver what is needed to make good environmental policy. He argues that the "very benefits that science promises to deliver may be withheld from us because it is easier—politically, economically, socially, scientifically—to support more research than it is to change ourselves."[97]

Policymakers often use the neutrality of science to enhance and legitimize their policy positions.[98] Scientific findings are often taken out of their original context by policymakers, reinterpreted to support a specific policy position.[99] As a matter of practical politics, public officials will use scientific evidence to not only legitimize their particular policy position but to deflect criticism away from themselves, emphasizing the point that these types of decisions are so complex that they should be made by scientists, not policymakers.[100] Because the stakes are so high, in many cases, there is enormous pressure for actors in the public policy-making process "to present evidence selectively, to misrepresent the position of their opponents, to coerce and discredit opponents, and generally to distort the situation to their advantage."[101] Although this may prove fruitful for the short term or even for the specific policy position in question, there exists evidence that this type of distortion damages the presentation of good science by creating a climate of mistrust between scientists, policymakers, and the public in general.[102] The inflamed rhetoric surrounding the current policy debates about global warming and health care policy in the United States are prime examples of such distortion and mistrust.

MOVING ON TO ENVIRONMENTAL ISSUES

Our foundation for exploring the science–politics dimension of environmental issues is now set. We can now move on to a description of environmental policy-making as it exists in the United States today. As readers continue the journey through this book, they should keep in mind the major concepts and ideas presented. Look for connections to such things as Stone's emphasis on how issues are framed, and Kingdon's view of how scientists fit into the policymaking process. Ask yourself whether particular aspects of the science–policy relationship fit best with a pluralistic or elitist perspective of government. Finally, question the behavior of scientists and policymakers alike to determine if science is used correctly in our efforts to solve the major environmental problems that we face today.

REFLECTIVE QUESTIONS

Question 2-1

Barry Rabe (*Review of Policy Research,* 2008), citing California as the prime example, argues that there is a recent trend toward state-driven policy with respect to the issue of climate change.

a. Discuss the federal influence on state policymaking and state influence on federal policymaking.
b. What characteristics does California possess that makes it an especially relevant player in U.S. environmental policymaking? Cite several historical examples supporting your view.

Question 2-2

H. Josef Hebert (*Idaho Statesman,* June 4, 2008) describes how the State of Nevada is opposed to the opening of Yucca Mountain as the national repository for highly radioactive nuclear waste. He explains that the Bush administration submitted the formal application with the Nuclear Regulatory Commission for a license to build the storage site, but that Nevada officials—including the governor, U.S. senators, and U.S. House members—all pledged to fight the opening of the waste dump because it threatens "the life and safety of the people of Nevada."

a. Explain how the concept of federalism fits into the controversy surrounding the opening of the Yucca Mountain repository. Include an evaluation of when national concerns should take precedence over states' rights.
b. The Nevada officials who are opposing the opening of Yucca Mountain as a nuclear waste repository belong to both major political parties. Provide other examples of environmental policy in the United States in which geography overrides political ideology.

Question 2-3

Margot Roosevelt and Kenneth Weiss (*Los Angeles Times,* May 30, 2008) reported that President Bush's top science advisors issued a comprehensive report that for the first time endorses what most scientific experts have long asserted: that greenhouse gases from fossil fuel combustion "are very likely the single largest cause" of Earth's warming.

a. Use this event to discuss the power of the president (and executive branch) to either move policy issues forward or hold them back. In your answer, delineate the most powerful resources a president has to influence policy issues.
b. In this same article, Roosevelt and Weiss point out that—according to administration scientists—the people most vulnerable to climate change are the young, elderly, frail, and poor. Explain the advantages of making this claim for the initiation of government actions that deal with environmental problems.

Question 2-4

Charles Krauthammer (*Idaho Statesman,* June 1, 2008) offers the following critique of a class society in the United States: "For a century, an ambitious, arrogant, unscrupulous knowledge class—social planners, scientists, intellectuals, experts, and their left-wing political allies—arrogated to themselves the right to rule either in the name of the oppressed working class (communism) or, in its more benign form, by virtue of their superior expertise in achieving the highest social progress by means of state planning (socialism)."

     a.   Explain how Krauthammer's critique fits into what you understand to be the pluralist and/or elitist models of policymaking.

     b.   What part does ideology play in Krauthammer's description?

Question 2-5

Jeff Biggers (*Washington Post National Weekly*, 2008), when describing the terminology of "clean coal," states: "Never was there an oxymoron more insidious, or more dangerous to our possible health . . . Coal ain't clean. Coal is deadly."

Discuss the power of words (and symbols) in defining environmental policy issues such as the search for clean coal.

Question 2-6

Choose one of the models listed in the "Analysis of Public Policy" section of this chapter and provide a current example that illustrates the concepts delineated in the model.

SUGGESTED READINGS

Larry N. Gerston, *Public Policymaking in a Democratic Society: A Guide to Civic Engagement* (New York: M. E. Sharpe, 2008).

John Kingdon, *Agendas, Alternatives, and Public Policies,* 2nd ed. (New York: Harper Collins College Publishers, 1995).

Mark E. Rushefsky, *Public Policy in the United States: At the Dawn of the Twenty-First Century,* 4th ed. (New York: M. E. Sharpe, 2008).

Paul A. Sabatier, *Theories of the Policy Process,* 2nd ed. (Boulder: Westview Press, 2007).

Deborah Stone, *Policy Paradox: The Art of Political Decision Making,* rev. ed. (New York: W. W. Norton & Co., 2002).

Environmental Policymaking in the United States

Environmental changes are among the greatest threats to our well-being and potentially to our long-term survival.

Paul Harris, *Politics & Policy*, 2008.

A BRIEF LOOK AT THE UNITED STATES ENVIRONMENTAL MOVEMENT

Benjamin Kline, in his book *First Along the River,* offers a brief history of the United States environmental movement.[1] Kline takes readers from the early stages of the 1400s (inhabiting a new land) and the 1800s (destroying the frontier and building an industrial nation) to the beginnings of the conservation movement (1900 through the 1930s), the prelude to the green decade (1940s through the 1960s) and to the beginning of mainstream environmentalism (1970s). Kline follows these stages with a discussion of retrenchment and public apathy in the 1990s, the institutionalism of the environmental movement in the late 1990s, up to the post-9/11 environmental world.

For our purposes, we will describe some of the environmental movement's highlights as they were articulated in the late 1960s and the early 1970s.[2] As noted by Kline, the modern environmental movement in the United States was ushered in between the publication of *Silent Spring* in 1962 and the Earth Day celebration of 1970:

> In many ways the movement was a product of the times. The rapid consumerism and dependence on science of the immediate post–World War II years (late 1940s and 1950s) was contrasted by the ever-increasing decay and devastation of the environment. It was a condition that could not be ignored for long—particularly by a people whose traditional love for nature was well established. Environmentalism was an integral part of the social protest movements of the '60s generation. . . . The foundations of the environmental movement were well laid by the beginning of the 1970s—the *Green Decade*.[3]

The 1970s brought the establishment of the National Environmental Policy Act which, in part, established the Environmental Protection Agency and created the Council on Environmental Quality. The Clean Air Act of 1970, the Clean Water Act of 1972, and Endangered Species Act of 1973 highlighted a series of environmental laws designed to protect the natural environment, including laws dealing with hazardous waste and toxic pollution. In short, the 1970s "witnessed the rise of the environmental movement in the United States, as both a political and a public issue."[4]

The 1980s and 1990s were marked by a backlash against environmentalism led by President Ronald Reagan's move to deregulate United States policy as a whole and by a complacency attributed to President Bill Clinton's moderate approach to environmental policy. Despite the lack of major domestic initiatives during this period of time, by the end of the 1990s, the environmental movement had become institutionalized, both in the United States and globally.[5] From 2000 through 2008, President George W. Bush pursued a policy similar in many ways to that of President Reagan, a policy of "deregulating and weakening environmental regulations."[6] The election of President Barack Obama has brought optimism that mainstream environmentalism will again move to the forefront of American public policy initiatives. As delineated by Norman Vig and Michael Kraft,

> The election of President Barack Obama in November 2008 brought a dramatic change in policy positions and priorities after eight years of the Bush administration, and environmentalists are likely to push for major changes in national energy policy and action on climate change, among other initiatives.[7]

Yet with this optimism comes some hesitancy and concern with where we will be regarding national and global threats to the environment in the near and far future. As made clear by Kline, "Time is the currency we are using in our gamble that the potential environmental disasters we face will wait until our debating, negotiating, and inter-species squabbles abate long enough to allow us to turn our attention to energetically dealing with these issues."[8] Simply put, only time will tell.

ENVIRONMENTALISM IN THE MAINSTREAM

Unlike years past, today it is cool to be green. For many, environmentalism is part of mainstream American life,[9] and a core American value, with most Americans considering themselves environmentalists.[10] Public support for environmental protection is viewed as vigorous and widespread.[11] W. Douglas Costain and James Lester put it this way:

> [T]he environmental movement has steadily broadened its base of support over the past one hundred years [and] has moved from being largely an elitist concern, involving scientific and government experts, to one with broad-based support including middle-class and even working-class supporters.[12]

Environmental groups at the national, state, and local levels play an important and even crucial role in a political system dominated by interest groups.[13]

Environmentalists, through direct and indirect political action, "have achieved significant results through the mobilization and exploitation of legal resources to restrain both corporate and government behavior."[14] To be sure, the environmental movement in the United States has "evolved into a mature and very typical American interest group community . . . , one with an impressive array of policy niches and potential forms of activism."[15] At the same time, the public—as a whole—is viewed as well informed about environmental problems and committed to environmental protection.[16] Moreover, it is regularly proclaimed that since the first Earth Day celebration in 1970, all indicators of environmental protection in the United States point in a positive direction; that we now live "in a time not of environmental collapse but of profound natural recovery."[17]

However, recent Gallup polls suggest something else entirely—that things are getting worse; that there has been a steady decline of concern for the environment over recent years, and that the public is ill-informed and ambivalent.[18] For instance, despite the success of former Vice President Al Gore's book and film *An Inconvenient Truth,* and his 2007 Nobel Prize, a record percentage of Americans believe the threat of global warming is exaggerated.[19] While it is true that the environmental lobby in the United States is established, sophisticated, and respected, it is also true that the environmental movement has had very limited success in recent years,[20] and it is still regularly criticized as being weak.[21] Furthermore, environmental groups are closely associated with "gloom-and-doom" fundraising appeals,[22] and they retain the tag of being "too strident, too confrontational, too narrowly focused on their own particular issues, and too litigious."[23]

Many have also observed that there is a fundamental conflict between democratic systems and the sacrifice, decisiveness, and speed with which environmental policy needs to be developed and implemented if it is to be considered effective.[24] In the United States there is a trend toward increasing pollution and toward the overuse of resources.[25] And though evidence suggests that we have made substantial gains in environmental quality since 1970, many still believe that "the American environment remains significantly degraded in critical respects,"[26] and that "the state of the earth has never been more dire."[27]

What explains this contrast between optimism and pessimism about the environment in the United States? To begin, we must understand that environmentalism is a function of the values that characterize the American social, cultural, economic, and political systems.[28] As Kai N. Lee observes, "No one acts in the natural environment without acting in the public arena."[29] In the public or political arena, environmentalism has broken down along partisan lines, with Democrats being viewed as more friendly toward the environment than Republicans.[30] Americans are polarized on this issue to a much greater extent than are the citizens of other developed countries, where issues such as climate change have never become a strict left-right debate.[31]

Despite the politicization of environmental policy, its role as an election issue has been limited. The environment has played what some consider a "decisive role" in some congressional as well as state and local elections, but it has never played a prominent role in presidential elections.[32] As an example, exit polls from the 2008 election showed that the issue most important to voters was the economy (63%), Iraq (10%), health care (9%), terrorism (9%), and energy policy (7%)[33] Even for those who said energy policy was their most important issue, Obama won their vote by 50 to 46 percent. Thus the only environmental issue mentioned (energy) helped Obama gain little more than one-tenth of one percent of the national vote—hardly a decisive margin. Still, conventional wisdom continues to proclaim that because the environmental community is now part of the national political establishment, no American president can afford to be hostile to environmental protection.[34]

In spite of the polarized political climate, we are seeing an increase in the number of alliances between groups that, in the past, we would have considered policy opponents. For instance, farmers and environmentalists have now become conservation allies, expanding the context of agricultural conservation to include environmental protection.[35] It is interesting to note that this new alliance is based predominantly on the strategic use of language to shape definitions to problems in a way that is acceptable to these two divergent clientele groups (for example, opposition to "factory farms" unites small farmers with environmentalists). Deborah Stone would be proud.

Before we leave this section, we must again emphasize the recent emergence of environmental protection as a major American value. It is the quality-of-life issue that most strongly appeals to Americans, and it is here to stay.[36] Environmental protection is one of the oldest social issues, and environmental movements have helped it become part of a new paradigm of social values, and just as important, have institutionalized environmental protection into the American policymaking process.[37] The establishment in 1970 of the National Environmental Policy Act (NEPA), environmental impact statements (EISs), the Council on Environmental Quality (CEQ), and the Environmental Protection Agency (EPA) bear witness to this fact. So we conclude that despite the conflicts we see in the political arena, environmental protection is one of the core values of American society, along with social justice, economic prosperity, national security, and democracy.[38]

UNITED STATES ENVIRONMENTAL POLICY TODAY: GLOBAL ASPECTS

Environmental protection is an issue that inherently crosses political borders. Ecosystems do not follow the lines that nations make on the map. With population growth and economic globalization, our planet has become much more inter-dependent in recent decades. The most important environmental issues today affect several countries, and these problems cannot be solved by the policies of one country alone. Thus, environmental problems and policies on issues such as cli-mate change, acid rain, geochemical flux, and control of toxic pollution are viewed more and more from a global, rather than from a state, perspective.[39]

The problem is that, unlike the domestic arena, the governance of the interna-tional arena is not at all centralized—states are independent actors that are subject only to regulations to which they voluntarily submit. The international system is anarchic—that is, there is no international government that can enforce compliance.

As states become more interdependent in this era of globalization, the anarchic system structure creates both problems and opportunities for the environment.

For some, environmental degradation is "the dark side of globalization."[40] Because poor countries need to attract foreign investment and industry, they have an economic incentive to ignore the enforcement of environmental laws, which are costly to multinational businesses. Because these businesses can play one state against another in an attempt to get the most favorable tax, environmental, and labor conditions, states engage in a "race to the bottom," meaning that they compete in lowering environmental standards in order to win business from other states and grow their economy.[41]

Advocates of environmental justice point out that this process transfers pollution from rich, mainly democratic, states to poor, less-democratic countries. And though there is a short-term boost to the economy of the poor country, some economists note that this process can create environmental problems so bad in developing countries that the pollution eventually becomes a disincentive for businesses to invest in that country. Furthermore, environmentalists argue that the neglect of the environment in developing countries can threaten the very sustainability of human livelihoods in all countries.[42]

So again we return to the global interdependence inherent in environmental problems such as climate change—problems from which no state can hide, and problems that require global solutions in which all countries participate. As a response, the global community has developed decentralized systems of governance, referred to as international regimes, which attempt to address global environmental problems within the anarchic structure of the international system. Regimes are defined as

> sets of implicit or explicit principles, norms, rules, and decision-making procedures around which actors' expectations converge in a given area of international relations.[43]

In more common terms, an environmental regime such as the climate change regime consists of treaties and written agreements among states (e.g., the Kyoto Protocol), international organizations (such as the Intergovernmental Panel on Climate Change, the IPCC), regularized meetings of states and nongovernmental organizations (such as the annual conference of parties to the Kyoto Protocol), and the principles and norms that states infer from all of these interactions (such as the principle of differential treatment of emissions from developed versus developing countries).[44] Although international regimes have made great progress on some issues such as ozone depletion, many scholars and activists believe that the existing network of global environmental regimes is "woefully inadequate to meet global environmental challenges."[45] In other words, just as a country with a weak government might not have the capacity to adequately enforce its own environmental laws, the governance system (regimes) at the international level might also not be strong enough to solve the environmental problems of the twenty-first century.

The globalization of environmental problems and their handling by global environmental regimes raises important questions about democracy. As more and more observers call for all decisions concerning the environment to become more

participatory and less exclusionary, the connection between environmental policymaking and democracy is growing more evident.[46] Some scholars claim that environmentalism is now grounded in a broader set of power and control issues aimed at transitioning all countries to democracies.[47]

Yet we often see a conflict between democratic governance at the national level and cooperation at the international level. For example, suppose a country democratically decides not to cooperate with the global climate change regime. Is the climate change regime democratic enough at the international level to legitimately demand that the state comply? Many people would argue that international regimes are not democratic (witness the protests against the international trade and finance regimes at meetings of the World Trade Organization (WTO) and the International Monetary Fund (IMF)). Should regimes place economic or other sanctions on non-complying states? Suppose that the target of sanctions was a country such as the United States, where many citizens object to *any* infringement on national sovereignty. If sanctions were placed on the United States, the public would likely become more strident in its resistance to international pressure. Therefore, it is possible that a more democratic policymaking process within a country might lead to less international cooperation and a failure to solve a global environmental problem.

At the international level, states often act in their own self-interest rather than the global interest, and political power, more than democracy, still weighs heavily in determining policy outcomes. Regimes are an attempt to overcome this pattern, but the rule of law that they promote has not yet eliminated the role of national power.

It has now been well over a decade since environmental scholars have declared that the world has entered a new era in environmental policymaking—one that now embraces a global conception of environmental degradation and a new generation of environmental problems.[48] It is easy to see that environmental issues go way beyond the concepts of environmental protection and good science.

It is certainly clear that we are now functioning in an era marked by great complexity and diversity, one in which environmentalism is now cast as "the most elaborate and segmented of our social issues."[49] Globalization is now characterized as being particularly apparent in the domain of environmental policy,[50] even to the point where it is said that we now live in an "era of global environmental politics."[51] And even though it is often pointed out that concern for global environmental protection is primarily a recent phenomenon,[52] it is also noted that in just over two decades environmental protection has become an issue of central national and international concern that transcends ideology.[53] On the downside of this move toward the internationalization of environmental policy regimes is the fact that solutions to environmental problems face many formidable obstacles, including entrenched economic interests, scientific uncertainties, technological limitations, and political timidity.[54]

UNITED STATES ENVIRONMENTAL POLICY TODAY: DOMESTIC ASPECTS

In spite of the highly publicized movement toward the internationalization of environmental issues, we realize that many of our nation's "old" environmental problems remain. Implementations of the Clean Air Act, cleanup of our federal

nuclear waste facilities, and the question of whether to open up more public lands to oil exploration all continue to be vital areas of public policy concern. In the United States, as elsewhere in the world, we are still coming to terms with such environmental problems as air and water pollution, hazardous materials, and the preservation of our public lands.[55] As a nation, we have not been able to integrate policy, science, and the law into a coherent environmental strategy,[56] nor have we been able to bring about a combination of creative new technologies, broad public participation, and appropriate behavioral changes to develop a comprehensive environmental protection strategy.[57]

Moreover, because these environmental problems are inherently political problems,[58] solutions must come from within the same complex and dynamic public policymaking process described in Chapter 2. The general pattern of decision-making includes the government attempting to solve society's problems through a process of "high-stakes politics."[59] In this case, the problems happen to be environmental in nature, and as Ronnie Lipschutz makes clear: "Only politics can save the environment."[60] It is not economists, diplomats, or scientists who will produce solutions to our environmental troubles; it will be policymakers functioning in a political world, making changes in the social structures and values of society as a whole.[61]

Environmental policymaking is inherently subject to the direct and indirect influence of those features that make American politics unique. In this regard, American federalism lies at the core of many environmental issues. Which level of government should be responsible for hazardous waste siting and nuclear waste clean up? Who should have the most say in how our national forests are managed or preserved and whether Alaskan tundra should be opened for oil exploration? Who owns the rights to the precious water that flows through our Western rivers? These questions can be answered only within a framework of intergovernmental cooperation and competition.

Environmental policy is fragmented in every sense of the word. Because administrative agencies guard their turf with much resolve, this leads to more competition than cooperation. Judges overrule executives. Executives defy regulatory directives. Redundancy and overlap abound in attempting to control our environmental heritage. Policy is anything but consistent, and innovative change occurs rarely. No environmental policy is left unscathed by the intricacies of these American political characteristics. Whether the challenge comes from within the intergovernmental realm, through conflict between branches of government, from the pressures of interest groups, or simply with our bureaucratic infrastructure, the policy outcomes reflect the structures of the American political system.

The words of Dean Mann remain an accurate description of the unique and complex aspects of environmental policymaking in America:

> That the politics of environmental policymaking is a process of dramatic advances, incomplete movement in the "right" direction, frequent and partial retrogression, sometimes illogical and contradictory combinations of policies, and often excessive cost should come as no surprise to students of American politics. Environmental policies reflect the dominant structures and values of the American political system.[62]

Thus, we are left with the task of evaluating our nation's environmental policy within the confines of an institutional structure that embodies a unique and often fractionalized political system. We are attempting to resolve age-old environmental problems (e.g., local level air and water pollution) as well as dealing with a third generation of environmental problems (e.g., acid rain, climate change) that threaten human existence. In addition, we are left with the fact that solutions to environmental problems, in the absence of fundamental institutional or constitutional change, can be resolved only through the public policymaking process as it now stands.

TENSIONS IN UNITED STATES ENVIRONMENTAL POLICYMAKING

Having accepted the idea that environmental policymaking in the United States not only reflects the dominant values of the American political system but also follows the same policymaking process that guides other governmental issues, it is time to recognize that environmental policy is unique in many aspects. Several tensions exist in the world of environmental policymaking that set it apart from other policy areas.

It is important to understand that the prominence of the environmental ethos on the American agenda is a relatively new phenomenon, essentially beginning in the late 1960s, and catapulting to the forefront during the 1970s.[63] This relatively new interest in the environment has led to several sets of competing value systems, each attempting to preserve its way of life.

Environmentalism and Economic Growth

At a philosophical level, there exists a substantial conflict between the American values of economic growth and environmental protection.[64] Many find these values incompatible. Lynton Caldwell makes the following reference to this dichotomy:

> Not all human preferences are realizable in the real world; possibilities are not infinite, and basic relationships between man and nature are not negotiable. Nature does not bargain, and the biosphere is not a marketplace.[65]

The dominant American values of capitalism and the market system revolve around the belief that humans are the center of the universe and are responsible for the management of the world around them. This value system promotes economic growth, development, and the use of technology to foster these ideals. One of the dominant aspects of American political culture is faith in a market system characterized by market efficiency that allocates scarce resources and produces socially desirable outcomes.[66] Some scholars even argue that at the global level, the scale of economic integration is so vast that democracy itself has been undermined,[67] and that economic incentives lead people to adopt dominant values that are clearly economic in nature, with little, if anything, to do with environmental protection.[68] Others believe that the economic pressures from global market integration do not automatically lead to a downgrading of environmental protection.[69]

Environmentalists, on the other hand, share a much different viewpoint. They believe that the earth has finite resources and a finite carrying capacity. They generally do not see humans as superior to nature, but rather as part of nature. Ecosystems are interdependent, and humans are dependent on ecosystems; environmentalists are skeptical that humans can successfully manage ecosystems without causing problems that eventually make things worse. Many believe that human population has already exceeded the carrying capacity of the earth, which leads them to support preservation of remaining environmental assets.

Thus, in the United States, environmentalists see a negative relationship between economic growth and environmental protection.[70] "Environmentalism sharply criticizes marketplace economics generally and capitalism particularly, and it denigrates the growth ethic, unrestrained technological optimism, and the political structures supporting these cultural phenomena."[71] Environmentalists continue to define problems in ways that allow them to challenge policies favorable to development interests and growth proponents.[72]

At a more practical level, this friction between values is apparent when examining the concept of environmental protection. American preoccupation with economic growth and resource management, developed early on in the American experience, has given way to a new set of concerns that includes quality of life issues such as the environment.[73] Although there exist degrees of conflict, when Americans are asked to choose between economic development and environmental protection, they have sometimes shown they are quite willing to be taxed and regulated on behalf of environmental quality.[74] Pervading this decision are the questions of who should control our natural resources and which value should have a higher priority, economic growth or environmental protection. Policy debates over the protection of old-growth forests in the Pacific Northwest (and the general decline of timber harvest on National Forest lands), the opening of Alaska to oil exploration, the siting of a permanent nuclear waste facility in Nevada, and whether dams should be removed to enhance the return of salmon to their spawning grounds are all representative of the larger argument between growth and environmental protection, between conservation management and preservation.

Regulation and the Marketplace

Another tension revolves around the question of which method is most appropriate for carrying out environmental policy—government regulation or a market-oriented system.[75]

Supporters of government regulation believe that because of market failures, government must intervene and impose solutions.[76] Market failures are the socially undesirable results of unregulated markets—things such as pollution and depletion. Because neither consumers nor producers pay for pollution and depletion directly, the market provides no one with incentives to reduce these sources of environmental damage. One solution is to have government impose a price on polluters, making them pay a fine if they pollute beyond a certain level.

Those backing the market-oriented system believe that the market will solve all of our problems, whereas command-and-control supporters believe that, because of market failures, we need to have government regulation.[77] Those backing the market-oriented system believe that the market will fairly and efficiently solve our environmental problems. First of all, free markets generate the wealth necessary to provide the resources to combat environmental problems. Furthermore, market-based solutions, such as emissions trading for pollutants such as sulfur dioxide (SO_2), allow individual firms to reduce emissions with the flexibility that allows a company to remain profitable while still protecting the environment. Emissions trading benefits those companies that can reduce emissions below required levels at very low costs; also, it reduces the costs to companies that, because of previous investments in plants and equipment, find it more expensive to cut emissions.

In the United States, political conflicts frequently arise over which method is most efficient and which one leads to greater environmental protection. Advocates of the market system think that the command-and-control regulatory model imposes a "one-size-fits-all" policy that hurts businesses and that is often slower to fix the problem. After the heyday of regulation in the 1970s, free market supporters began to make inroads against environmental regulation, arguing that environmental regulation is ineffective, inefficient, and out of control. Supporters of regulation counter with evidence that businesses cannot police themselves, and that because there is a profit to be made from ignoring environmental costs, a market-based system will not stop pollution.

The Science–Policy Linkage to Environmental Policymaking

The complexity of environmental problems has heightened the importance of the linkage among scientific, social, and political systems—a linkage featuring the connection of science to environmental policy, where societal values play a substantial role in decision-making.[78] Sheila Jasanoff and Marybeth Martello put it well.

> [T]he forces of environmental science and politics are making people conceive of the Earth as a single, unified, and limited habitat, calling for responsible standards of stewardship and globally accountable institutions of governance.[79]

It has been long known that science and technology have increased humans' abilities to manipulate (some say exploit) the natural world,[80] and that environmental policy is heavily dependent on science.[81] As Daniel Sarewitz and Roger Pielke, Jr., observe, "The expectation that science can help inform human decisions about societal change has been especially strong in the area of the environment."[82] It is generally understood that there can be no examination of environmental policy without an understanding of the laws and forces that drive the natural world.[83] In fact, due to the special cultural authority of scientists and the uncertainty that marks the scientific process, the scientific depiction of cause and effect has become the "primary battleground in any environmental controversy."[84]

Walter Rosenbaum puts the science–policy linkage in perspective.

> [O]ne of environmentalism's most profound impacts has been to accelerate the way in which science is transforming public policy making. Environmental science . . . is compelling policymakers to think in terms of policy problems and impacts, of the consequences of present decisions and future undertakings, and on a time scale almost unthinkable a few decades ago and unavoidable in the future. The genie of anticipatory environmental science is out of the bottle, [and] science today is providing policy makers with the intellectual tools and a scientific metric for characterizing the future impact of present public decision making that impose a responsibility quite new to public life.[85]

Rosenbaum also argues that the distinguishing feature of environmental policymaking, as opposed to all other types of policymaking, is "the extraordinary importance of science, and scientific controversy, in the policy process."[86] It is also true that conventional wisdom fosters a belief that environmental issues turn centrally on the scientific method and its applications; that policymakers cannot exercise control over environmental outcomes without recourse to scientific findings.[87] As John Carroll and his colleagues note, "the environmental question is fundamentally a question of science and technology."[88]

Expectations among the American public and United States policymakers are high—some would argue unrealistically high—that good science can produce the right answers to environmental disputes.[89] There exists a strong belief among most Americans, especially when it comes to questions about our natural environment, that doing more science will provide the answers we need to solve most of our problems.[90] Americans appear to have developed an uncritical faith in science, with both scientists and politicians portraying science as the key to a better world and the solution to our most critical societal problems.[91] This confidence in science is never more evident than when advocates ask for higher levels of funding for scientific research. This request is almost always based on "the premise and promise that more scientific knowledge and technological innovation will lead to the solution of society's most serious challenges."[92]

Yet, it is not clear that all advances in science and technology have translated into sustainable advances in the quality of life for the majority of the human race.[93] Richard Somerville squarely points out, "experience teaches us that science alone is never enough. When confronting environmental challenges, considerations of fairness, equity, and justice must also inform any successful international agreement."[94] And in making the argument that we need "every ounce of technological ingenuity and scientific understanding we can muster to pull us back from the abyss of irremediable environmental disaster," William Leiss strongly urges us not to be fooled into thinking that science and technology can, by themselves, bring about such change.[95] Perhaps Daniel Sarewitz puts it best:

> It is preposterous to imagine . . . that the environmental challenges facing humanity can possibly be addressed by increasing our knowledge of the physics, chemistry, and biology of environmental processes divorced from a commensurate advance in our understanding of human kind's interaction with and effect on those processes.[96]

THE TENETS OF SCIENCE

The next chapter will identify the tenets of science—the rules and standards that guide the scientific process as it is used to describe the natural world around us and look for the answers to society's woes, including the critical environmental problems that we face in today's ever-changing climate. To understand the tenets of the scientific method is to move toward an understanding of why it is so difficult to integrate science into the policy world.

REFLECTIVE QUESTIONS

Question 3-1

Andrew Revkin (*New York Times,* April 6, 2008) points out that leaders of the Intergovernmental Panel on Climate Change (IPCC) have emphasized a market-based approach to dealing with climate change.

     a. Explain the reason so many environmental problems have been cast as economic problems. Do you believe that the goals of environmental protection and economic progress are mutually exclusive? Provide specific support for your answer.

     b. Document an environmental policy in the United States that has been considered successful due to a market-based solution.

Question 3-2

Florida Governor Charlie Crist (*Time,* July 7, 2008), in talking about the planned $1.7 billion restoration of the Florida Everglades, stated: "If we can't solve the Everglades with an abundance of money, science, and good will behind an effort that's been hailed as a worldwide model, then what can we save?"

     a. Explain the importance of benefit-cost analysis to the attempt to restore the Everglades to what they once were.

     b. Using the Everglades restoration as an example, discuss the importance of money to scientific research.

Question 3-3

H. Josef Hebert (*Idaho Statesman,* June 2, 2008) makes the case that higher electric bills and expensive gasoline are driving the current debate over climate change. Explain how one could argue that this is a prime example of turning a complex environmental issue into a debate over the conflicting values of environmental protection and economic security.

Question 3-4

David Webber (*Review of Policy Research,* 2008) claims that a lasting facet of the 1970 Earth Day legacy is the image of environmentalism as activist-dominated and centered on crisis-driven events.

a. Describe a current incident or environmental problem that might qualify as being driven by a crisis mentality. Provide details supporting your choice.

b. Delineate the positive and negative aspects of emphasizing the catastrophic consequences of environmental problems.

Question 3-5

Use the case of Love Canal to illustrate how a policy entrepreneur can have a substantial impact on the policy outcome.

SUGGESTED READINGS

Walter Baber and Robert Bartlett, *Deliberative Environmental Politics: Democracy and Ecological Rationality* (Cambridge, MA: MIT Press, 2005).

Christopher Bosso, *Environment, Inc.: From Grassroots to Beltway* (Lawrence: University of Kansas Press, 2005).

Judith Layzer, *The Environmental Case: Translating Values Into Policy,* 2nd ed. (Washington, DC: CQ Press, 2006).

Robert Paelke and Douglas Torgereson, eds., *Managing Leviathan: Environmental Politics and the Administrative State,* 2nd ed. (Peterborough, Ontario: Broadview Press, 2005).

Zachary Smith, *The Environmental Policy Paradox* (Upper Saddle River, NJ: Pearson-Prentice Hall, 2009).

CHAPTER 4

The Power of Science

Science provides the power to understand natural phenomena, and, by virtue of that power, to expand the range of choices for management of nature and human institutions.

Eric Ginsburg and Ellis Cowling, *Environment International*, 2003.

Science is a glorious thing, but it is no substitute for wisdom, prudence or democracy.

Yuval Levin, *Washington Post National Weekly Edition*, 2009.

SCIENCE, SOCIETY, AND DEMOCRACY

Science plays a profound and formidable role in American public policymaking. This is easily demonstrated by the fact that issues related to science are omnipresent in today's society,[1] and by the fact that in today's rapidly moving society, science has been increasingly called upon to provide information to improve decision-making in public affairs.[2] Science is called upon in this manner because it is conveniently designed to inform social policy; it serves as a language and reference point that allows for informed discourse about the nature and seriousness of societal risks.[3] Whether it involves the present-day focus on energy independence, nuclear waste disposal, and the related emphasis on reducing greenhouse emissions, or the enduring questions involving biotechnology and genetic engineering, science mixes quite extensively with the everyday decisions of citizens and policymakers in our democratic society.

There appear to be no limits to the influence that science wields. The scientific process is cast as the most powerful instrument created by human mind,[4] with an enormously powerful impact on our culture and society.[5] Scholars suggest that science is "man's greatest intellectual adventure,"[6] one that has the power to determine the success or failure of all human purposes.[7] Science and technology have also been described as a possible remedy for the inadequacies of participatory democracy,[8] even though science does not work through any sort of democratic consensus.[9] The idea that science is not just the best approach, but is the *only*

49

approach to addressing issues involving the natural world—which by definition includes concerns about environmental protection—is pervasive throughout the scholarly literature.

Francis Collins characterizes science as being able to generate profound insights into material existence as well as being "the only reliable way to understand the natural world."[10] William Leiss observes that science possesses "superiority over every earlier human approach to the investigation of natural forces."[11] Deborah Stone regards science as one of the most powerful social institutions for determining cause and legitimating claims about harms, insisting that science commands "enormous cultural authority as the arbiter of empirical questions."[12] In short, science is considered modernity's preeminent instrument of legitimation,[13] the best process we have for validating research.[14]

THE DEFINITION AND CHARACTERIZATIONS OF SCIENCE

Over the years, science has proven to be a very difficult concept to explain or describe in a straightforward manner. Paul Sabatier speaks of "the bewildering complexity" of the phenomena surrounding the concept of science,[15] and Karen Litfin puts the difficulty of defining science into the following perspective.

> "Science" covers too much ground to be defined concisely. It is a product of research, employing characteristic methods; it is a body of knowledge and means of solving problems; it is a social institution and a source of social legitimacy.[16]

Having said all that, one has to start somewhere in getting a handle on exactly what we mean when we talk about science. Kenneth Hoover and Todd Donovan give us an excellent starting point.

> Science as a way of thought and investigation is best conceived of as existing not in books, machinery, or reports containing numbers but rather in that invisible world of the mind. Science has to do with the way questions are formulated and answered; it is a set of rules and forms for inquiry and observation created by people who want verifiable answers. . . . Science is a process of thinking and asking questions, not a body of knowledge. It is one of several ways of claiming that we know something. In one sense, the scientific method is a set of criteria for deciding how conflicts about differing views of reality can be resolved. It offers a strategy that researchers can use when approaching a question. It offers consumers of research the ability to critically assess how evidence has been developed and used in reaching a conclusion.[17]

Note that Hoover and Donovan specifically define science as a *process*. More to the point, scientific knowledge can only be obtained by following the scientific process and the assumptions that underlie its foundation. Alan Isaak provides us with a listing of these underlying assumptions.[18] Science's first basic assumption is that of *determinism* or *causation*, the idea that "Nothing in the universe just happens." In more technical terms, determinism means that if we want knowledge of the world, we have to assume that the world is coherent, and that there are certain causal relationships that can be expressed in such forms as "If A occurs, B occurs." Moreover, it is the search for these causal relationships that defines the work of scientists.

The second assumption is that of *empiricism,* the idea that if the world is what we are interested in, then it is the world we must examine. In short, all descriptions and explanations have to be based on what can be observed (directly and indirectly) in the world we live in. The third assumption is that of *objectivity,* the idea that science is value-free. This assumes that scientists can separate their professional judgments from their personal values and beliefs. Isaak notes that some find the idea of objectivity a bit too unrealistic because no scientist can be perfectly objective. Hence, some replace objectivity with the assumption of intersubjectivity, whose simple meaning centers on the belief that biases can be identified and weeded out. The fourth assumption is that of *replication,* the idea that all proposed scientific facts are open to inspection and the procedures used to arrive at these facts are described clearly enough so as to be repeatable.

Isaak also provides us with a careful and concise definition of the scientific process itself.

> The scientist takes his observations and attempts to classify and analyze them. His first objective is to formulate useful *empirical concepts* that organize the phenomena that interest him. Then, starting with the assumption of determinism, he attempts to find relationships between these concepts. If successful, he discovers a scientific *law* or *generalization.* Further systematization of empirical knowledge is achieved by the construction of *theories,* which are collections of logically related generalizations. Finally, the scientist uses his laws and theories to *explain* events and situations that have occurred or exist and to *predict* future happenings. It can thus be said that the scientist's attempts to systemize are all leading to this ultimate objective, to explain and predict—to show why things were, are, or will be.[19]

Paul Sabatier, in his second edition of *Theories of the Policy Process,* provides another way to look at the meaning of science. Sabatier delineates what Darwin considered to be the four critical characteristics of science:[20]

- Methods of data acquisition and analysis should be presented in a sufficiently public manner that they can be replicated by others.
- Concepts and propositions should be clearly defined and logically consistent and should give rise to empirically falsifiable hypotheses.
- Propositions should be as general as possible and should explicitly address relevant uncertainties.
- Methods and concepts should be self-consciously subjected to criticism and evaluation by experts in that field.

Sabatier summarizes these characteristics with the statement that science should be "clear enough to be proven wrong," and designed to be "self-consciously error seeking, and thus self-correcting."[21] This self-correcting aspect of science goes right to the heart of what makes the scientific process such a profound and valuable way of knowing: science "frequently stumbles, but it gets up and carries on."[22] In less colloquial terminology, science is perhaps the only human activity in which errors are systematically criticized and, in time, corrected.[23] A more recent definition of science is provided by the National Academy of Sciences (NAS).

> Science is a particular way of knowing about the world. In science, explanations are limited to those based on observations and experiments that can be sustained by other scientists. Explanations that cannot be based on empirical evidence are not a part of science.[24]

Accordingly, following the scientific method is a dynamic process that "does not reveal 'truth,' so much as produce the best available or most likely explanation of natural phenomena."[25] The scientific method is described as possessing two crucial characteristics: (1) a transparent approach in which both new and old data are available to all parties, and (2) a continuing effort to update data, and therefore modify, and even reject, previously accepted hypotheses in light of new information.[26]

Others follow the lead of the academy by emphasizing the importance of transparency in a democracy dependent on the active participation of citizens in the production of knowledge.[27] In fact, some see transparency as the key to science's ability to improve the human condition, with scientists having the independence to confirm, refute, or improve upon findings of a specific course of inquiry.[28] The words of H. Sterling Burnett are appropriate here.

> The transparency of scientific data and methods is key to science's ability to improve the human condition . . . [T]he integrity of scientific research . . . depends upon a sharing of access to scientific data, [which] is critical to policy-makers and the public alike.[29]

Bill Joy also promotes the value of openness to the scientific process,[30] as does the United States General Accounting Office when it calls for scientific research to be made available with "open and timely access."[31] Science is supposed to be a fair process in which there is "adequate opportunity for presentation and discussion of the data, their relevance for society, and the underlying values and preferences of the participants regarding the use of the data or findings."[32] In recent times, with the events of September 11 bringing forth a focus on control of information and secrecy, the concepts of transparency and openness have become a rallying cry for scholars who are now calling for the "unfettered ability of our scientific community to collaborate openly and move forward rapidly in the conduct of scientific research."[33]

Many other characterizations of science exist. For instance, Arild Underdal suggests that confidence in scientists and their findings rests on the competence and integrity of scientists. Confidence exists in the competence of scientists as producers and custodians of advanced and reliable knowledge and in scientists as truth-seekers, strongly committed to collecting and analyzing evidence independent of any substantive interests.[34] Richard Somerville is convinced that if science aspires to be helpful to society, it must include ethics and equity as an integral part of its research agenda.[35] David Guston puts it this way: "If the public cannot trust science to have integrity, what can it trust?"[36]

THE ROLE OF THEORY

Many policymakers have an unscientific understanding of the relationship between scientific theory and truth. In the United States we encounter this most often regarding debates about the theory of evolution and creationism. Because of the concept of falsifiability, the only thing that scientists can ever know for sure is when they are wrong. Scientists make a hypothesis and test it. If the data do not support the hypothesis, then the scientist rejects the hypothesis as clearly wrong. However, if the data do support the hypothesis, this does *not* mean that the hypothesis, or the underlying theory which generated it, is right or true. It simply means that the current theory or hypothesis *has not yet been proven false.*

This emphasis on falsifiable hypotheses is central to the scientific method, and it produces a situation in which scientific theory slowly approaches truth, but never quite attains it.[37] As an example, for years scientists believed that Newtonian physics was the best theory to describe the relationship between forces and matter (recall the equation $F = ma$, or force equals mass times acceleration). Newton's equations worked very well to explain the world, but they were never perfect. Over time, some anomalies appeared—situations in which Newton's formulas did not perfectly predict things. For instance, the orbit of the planet Mercury was observed to be not quite as Newtonian theory predicted. When a theory generates minor anomalies but still explains most of the world, it tends to maintain its dominant role in a discipline.[38]

However, as anomalies build up over time, others try to develop new theories that explain all that the old theory explained *plus* some of the anomalies.[39] In 1905, Albert Einstein deduced the theory of relativity, which produced a new set of equations (the most famous of which, $e = mc^2$, is known to all) that superseded Newton. At that point, the discipline of physics went through what philosopher of science Thomas Kuhn called a paradigm shift. Einstein's theory replaced Newton's as the dominant theory. However, even Einstein did not achieve a final truth. Relativity does not explain everything we observe. Physics continues to progress, and one day a new theory will supersede Einstein's theory.[40]

The fact that science never achieves a final truth creates uncertainty that policymakers and the public are often unable to grasp. Darwin's theory of evolution does not explain everything; for scientists this is normal, but when the public hears of an anomaly, they make take it to mean that Darwin was wrong. Similarly, climate change theory, while well developed, cannot explain all deviations from normal climate. This makes it easy for the public, when confronted with a summer of cool weather, to reject the whole theory of climate change.

SCIENCE AND ENVIRONMENTAL POLICYMAKING

Clearly, science is connected to environmental policymaking in a profound and meaningful way. Some go so far as to declare that at the foundation of *every* environmental problem lays a profound reality: science is the prime mover of most environmental issues.[41] There exists recognition that changes in the natural world are the result of advances in environmental science that shed light on both the nature of the problem and the directions of solutions.[42] Some things, such as the urgency of the atmospheric problems that confront humanity and the clues needed to address them effectively, simply would not be known or discernible except through the means of science.[43] While science alone cannot definitively resolve environmental controversies, it plays a part in every major issue by defining the boundaries of the technically feasible and the politically acceptable.[44] Nowhere is this better illustrated than by President Barack Obama's appointment of the eminent scientist Steven Chu to the Cabinet post of Energy Secretary, as Chu extols a strong belief that technology and innovation are the key to solving our energy and climate problems.[45]

According to Zachary Smith, the idea that science and technology will provide solutions for our problems with nature is built into the very fabric of the American social paradigm.[46] Smith is not alone in this observation. There now exists a strong consensus among environmental scholars that we have moved into the realm where we are no longer just observing nature but attempting to control the future of nature and its interactions with the human race through the power of science.[47]

However, we should not get too far ahead of ourselves in accepting science as the singular driving force regarding environmental policymaking. While it is alluring to think that science can simplify environmental policymaking by creating a clearer picture of the future, this dimension of science is deeply problematic.[48] There are still many who feel that the expectations of science are "excessive and unrealistic,"[49] as well as "impossible."[50] Those who caution against such high expectations point to the severe limitations on scientists' ability to resolve public controversies.[51] These doubters submit that scientific research can actually produce such ambiguous, fragmentary, or contradictory data concerning the existence of an environmental problem, that it completely frustrates the task of fashioning and evaluating environmental policy.[52] In these terms, science is accused of being ill suited to the needs of a truly democratic society.[53]

More and better science is not viewed as the answer. It does not lead to quicker or more certain policy decisions, nor does it have the ability to silence political controversy.[54] Science alone is viewed as not enough to stimulate a response to a policy problem,[55] and as having only a marginal influence over policy decisions.[56] Roger Pielke, Jr., summarizes this view of science.

> [T]he conception that scientific information is sufficient for policymaking persists. Perhaps because it is easy for policymakers to rationalize inaction in terms of the expectation of clarifying information, and for scientists to justify accepting substantial research funding. . . . From such perspectives, policymakers tend to view science as a panacea, instead of as a component to be integrated with the broader decision process.[57]

In attempting to get at how science can best be used to solve our environmental problems, William Leiss provides an excellent overview of the connection between good science and environmental policymaking.[58] In this regard, Leiss comments on the call for science-driven solutions to environmental problems; that is, he focuses on the idea that good policies ought to be rooted in good science.[59] It is here, however, that Leiss questions whether ecosystem science can or ought to be the primary driver of environmental policymaking. Leiss cites three basic factors in this regard.

- Policy requires yes/no decisions, whereas science often is continually evolving from one level of uncertainty to another;
- Environmental policymaking is often driven in a political context by just those issues for which we have at the time the most imperfect scientific understanding;
- Environmental issues usually lack immediacy in that they are based on long-term trends, whereas the political world is driven by immediacy. Hence, the inevitable scientific uncertainties coupled with the immediacy of the political world make environmental policy doomed to disappointment or crippling compromise.[60]

In summary, Leiss does not posit that science is necessarily irrelevant to the environmental policymaking process, but that the factors listed illuminate the tendency for science to become entangled within the institutional inertia of interest-group politics, often engulfed by policy warfare. In the end, what communities decide about when they make policy is meaning, not matter, and science cannot settle questions of meaning.[61] Karen Litfin puts this belief into perspective.

> The faith in the power of science . . . runs deep [but] because science deals with the world of facts, not values, and because values are ultimately what informs our actions, we cannot expect science to save us. . . . The political impact of scientific knowledge is determined far more by its incorporation into larger discursive practices than by either its validity or the degree to which it is accepted by scientists.[62]

At the same time, there are those who argue that it is possible to successfully integrate science and policy if we meet a specific set of criteria, including: clarity of objectives, processes, and desired outcomes; clarity of roles and responsibilities of scientists, policymakers, and the public; quality control through open peer and public review; and effective communication and involvement of stakeholders throughout the environmental policymaking process.[63]

It would be an understatement to note that meeting these criteria would be an extremely difficult task. However, there should be no doubt that there does exist a strong link between the consensus process supported by peer review and effective policymaking.[64] There exists, especially within the scientific community, a strong faith in the peer-reviewed system to deliver trustworthy assessments.[65] As Arild Underdal suggests, although individual scientists may fail to meet the high standards set by the scientific process, we can still have confidence in the ability of the community of scholars through its pluralistic, competitive structure, and procedures of critical peer review to provide us with reliable knowledge.[66] The key to providing good science appears to be for scientists to carefully follow the peer review process that is at the heart of the scientific method.

GOOD SCIENCE

We often come across the term "good" science or "sound" science. In fact, there are those who speculate that science described in this manner is "a buzzword in almost all policy debates."[67] Others, however, proclaim that the phrases "sound science" and "peer review" are words that are only used by those in the political world as a means of justifying predetermined political conclusions.[68] Still others suggest that policymakers really do not want to know the truths that science can provide, but often abuse science by using it to legitimize set ideological positions rather than to meaningfully inform policy.[69] Alternatively, Radford Byerly and Roger Pielke, Jr., posit that good science is a necessary but not sufficient condition for successful policymaking in a democratic society and that science needs to be associated with a societal goal if there is to be democratic accountability.[70]

Others contend that in order to improve the use of sound science, we have to start by understanding the difference between scientific analysis and values, and that openness is the key to making good science happen. Viewed in this light, scientific analysis should be "an open market for facts and ideas and that no one opinion is inherently superior or inferior to any other—they should all be held up to scientific testing and scrutiny."[71] Science needs discussion; it needs the criticism of other scientists.[72] In the end, however, scientific information is deemed appropriate only under certain conditions: if it helps in the clarification of values (or goals), describes trends with respect to those goals, accounts for observed trends, or projects a realistic range of scenarios from which action alternatives might be developed.[73]

A final way to define "good" science is to contrast it with "bad" science. The most common forms of bad science that find their ways into policy debates have one or more of the following characteristics:

1. The research is funded by a party that has a major interest in the outcome of the project. For example, a tobacco company might fund studies showing that second hand smoke is not a health hazard; the coal industry funds studies that show climate change to be trivial. If this type of research is subject to peer review, it can become acceptable to the scientific community.
2. The research is not peer reviewed, though it may be ideologically screened. Many reports have not been published in a peer-reviewed journal or as a book by a press that requires peer review. Often legislators see reports from ideologically oriented think-tanks that are commissioned and published by the think-tank itself, and not subject to outside critiques. For instance, reports published by the CATO Institute (a libertarian think-tank) always promote market solutions to any environmental problem.
3. The research makes claims that are not based on objective data or evidence. This is easy to spot when one reads critically. Sometimes authors refer to data without citation, or claim to possess data that is not publicly available.
4. The research uses inappropriate methods to make the data conform to the hypothesis. This is hard for the non-expert to catch but occurs all the time with survey research, in which question wording, sampling methods, and other seemingly minor factors can produce wide shifts in the results.

THE ROLE OF SCIENTISTS IN THE ENVIRONMENTAL POLICYMAKING PROCESS

Scientists' Conundrum

As you can see in the following, Walter Rosenbaum's description of environmental policymaking not only points out the essential details of the science–policy conundrum, it speaks to what some believe to be the key to solving that conundrum: determining what part scientists and science should play in the development of environmental policymaking.

> Environmental policymaking is a volatile mixture of politics and science that readily erupts into controversy among politicians, bureaucrats, and scientists over their appropriate roles in the process as well as over the proper interpretation and use of scientific data in policy questions.[74]

It has been demonstrated quite conclusively that over the past several decades, scientists have been critical actors in the environmental policymaking process, serving as entrepreneurs, introducing, popularizing, and elevating environmental ideas onto national and international agendas.[75] It was scientists who played the pivotal roles in discovering and publicizing many of the environmental problems that sit on our domestic and global agendas today. Scientists were the earliest and most powerful proponents of policies to address climate change, biodiversity, DNA research, and ozone depletion.[76] Surely, scientists have proven to be a major influence, some would say the "principal lever,"[77] in changing attitudes about the environment, helping to reduce the influence of self-serving private and public interests.[78]

Despite these claims in support of science's strong influence, there are still some who argue that the role that science and scientists play in policymaking, while important, is really quite modest.[79] This question of influence turns on what is considered, as noted earlier, one of the great tensions in the environmental policymaking world (and most all other public policy, too): the question of how science is to be represented in the policymaking process. It is asserted by both scientists and policymakers alike that getting the science right is the first step in forging a political consensus.[80] But what does getting it right mean, and how exactly should the science fit into the policymaking process?

This critical question concerns the mode of presentation of scientific data: Should scientists participate directly in the political process or not? Dorothy Nelkin describes two very different positions regarding this question.[81] One position advocates that scientists must directly participate in the political process (or risk making their science irrelevant). The other position threatens scientists with the loss of their scientific credibility if they do take a policy position. With respect to the first position, many argue that scientists, to preserve the integrity of their science, must fully participate in the political debates that involve their expertise. If scientists stay silent about issues, if they do not learn the politician's language, if they do not take the time to see the world from the politician's viewpoint so that they can meaningfully participate in the policymaking process, it signals to the general public and policymakers alike that there is little to worry about regarding environmental concerns.[82] The argument here is that scientists must not only make a concerted effort to understand the difficulties of integrating science into public policymaking, they must actually participate in the integration of their science into the policymaking process. If scientists fail to do so, then the nonscientific criteria will prevail.[83] Roger Pielke, Jr., summarizes this point of view.

> The scientific community has a responsibility for assessing the significance of science for policy [and] through such a process scientists themselves can work to limit the negative effects of the politicization of science and contribute to a more effective understanding of the limits of science in political debate.[84]

Yet when scientists do participate in the political side of a debate by taking policy stands, they are often accused of providing "junk science," or science that is politically rather than scientifically driven. This criticism is powerful, for research that is not value-free violates a core tenet of the scientific method. It has been shown that when scientists do actively participate in public policy debates by advocating specific policy positions, their public image as scientists suffers.[85]

Scientific Uncertainty

Another crucial aspect of the science–policy linkage is represented by the scientific uncertainty that underlies most environmental issues. In this regard, scientific uncertainty is directly linked to environmental protection because environmental policy decisions are frequently made on the basis of imperfect information.[86] The scientific complexity of environmental issues often confuses and mystifies both policymakers and the public alike.[87] In the complex world of American policymaking, scientists cannot provide all the answers to solving our environmental problems.[88] Some problems are simply not solvable within the deterministic framework of science.[89] And just because scientific knowledge is critical to environmental policymaking does not mean that scientists themselves are the driving force in the policy realm. Once the scientific knowledge is produced, many other actors have the potential to influence the direction the policy follows,[90] and it has been shown that scientific assessments often do not demonstrate significant influence on decisions affecting environmental quality.[91]

Sheila Jasanoff contends that one must accept the messiness and complexity of the science–politics linkage as being the way that the processes of decision-making work in a democracy; that the scientific uncertainty surrounding most environmental policy issues essentially leads to a forced marriage between science and politics.[92] So, what are scientists to do? Research findings do not speak for themselves. They have to be filtered through the particular lens of policymakers within the decision-making process, and the scientific uncertainty surrounding environmental controversies often allows policymakers to dismiss scientific contributions that do not line up with their political ideals.[93]

Furthermore, the omnipresent uncertainty that surrounds all scientific findings sometimes appears to lead us in the wrong direction. Specifically, some observers now charge that we have allowed scientific uncertainty to postpone controls on dangerous activities, thus causing severe environmental problems.[94]

Scientific uncertainty used in this manner is especially magnified because both the public and policymakers alike are often confused about what is good science and easily misled.[95]

More often than not, science and scientific advice leads to political controversy rather than political accord.[96] Scientists themselves, by excluding pertinent scientific information related to particular policy disputes over method and interpretation, can inadvertently become involved in a censorship that threatens good environmental policymaking.[97] On the other hand, the existence of uncertainty is sometimes "managed" by both scientists and politicians in ways that allow them to justify action (or inaction) and build authority, reinforcing the dominance of science in a debate such that both scientists and politicians benefit.[98] Brian Silver puts it this way: "In racing and in science there are no 'sure things,' only odds-on favorites."[99]

We are now operating during a period of time when scientists are supposed to present the "best available science" to help solve environmental policy issues; a time when scientists are asked to provide a discussion of the value of science to society.[100] Science is viewed as being universal in nature,[101] and as "inspiring and noble, and its pursuit an enchanting mission."[102] Yet no rational framework exists for addressing science and technology throughout all of our governmental institutions,[103] and if science is to be preserved as a universal search for knowledge, the emphasis must be on the integrity of its processes and procedures.[104] To be sure, science has often proven to be ambiguous and capable of posing more questions than answers.[105] Along these lines, it is understood that science-based analysis does not necessarily determine a policy choice nor reduce political conflict.[106] Even among the scientific community, a minority sometimes rejects the weight of the evidence.[107] Moreover, scientific uncertainty, coupled with excessive social dislocations, has created an even greater demand for increased levels of rationality in policymaking.[108]

We are left with the fact that scientific information "typically 'disappears' into the complex mix of diverse forms of reasoning and types of information considered simultaneously by decision-makers responsible for formulating public policy."[109] Once again we conclude that scientists (and science) cannot deliver solutions to environmental problems—it is just too much to ask of science. The idea that scientists, through additional research, can resolve both scientific and policy conflicts is not confirmed by experience.[110] Instead, environmental policy decisions must be guided by conventional political structures and some notion of social welfare and normative decision-rules.[111] Ultimately, mastery of scientific knowledge is not sufficient to make policy decisions about environmental issues because those types of judgments are preeminently political in nature.[112]

SCIENTISTS AS CITIZENS AND HUMAN BEINGS

Scientists, like philosophers, attempt to interpret the universe and understand it for what it really is.[113] Scientists also attempt to impart the wisdom of those interpretations to the greater society in hopes of bringing about meaningful discourse. Yet because we live in a representative democracy, all policy decisions end up being political decisions that are filtered through the American policymaking process in the public sphere.[114] And therein lies the problem: some (maybe most) public policy decisions involve complexities that go beyond the intellectual and practical capabilities of the public in general and policymakers in particular. The vastness of the knowledge required, the technicality of the subject, and scientific uncertainties all contribute to limitations in understanding for the very people who must provide input into the policy process and who must ultimately make the final policy decisions. As noted by Roger Masters, science appears mysterious and threatening to the public at large, with scientific explanations of the world often appearing to be unrelated to the concerns of the average citizen.[115]

Bruce Williams and Albert Matheny describe the complex nature of the linkage of science to public policymaking in general and to citizens in particular.

> When policies involve issues suffused with the complex scientific and technical questions posed by social regulation, it is impossible to exclude experts entirely from a role in the policy process. A central problem in such policies is how this information can be incorporated into the calculations used by citizens to define their self-interest and constitute themselves as engaged publics.[116]

In short, at some point in time, most policy solutions are going to require input from scientists in one form or another. Scientists not only possess the expertise, training, and knowledge required to provide such input, they possess the authority, legitimacy, and high social prestige to make such input valuable and meaningful.[117] Simply put, scientists have the ability to illuminate connections between choices and political outcomes and to shape the public dialogue.[118] Still, we must remember that scientists are human beings and that science is not a separate entity, remote from society and the lives of people.[119] As put so eloquently by Arild Underdal, we do not expect scientists to be "devoted exclusively to the pursuit of 'eternal truth'—in splendid isolation from the mundane concerns that plague governments and all other segments of society."[120] In the democratic society in which we live today, there exists a basic need to have scientific methods that are built around the experiences of people in living environments, as opposed to the closed environment of laboratory instruments.[121]

It is important to keep in mind that scientists are not just scholars but are also citizens who are as free as anyone else in society to express their political preferences,[122] and to find their own unique way of influencing society within the framework of the American democratic system.[123] Some scholars take this assertion a step further, arguing that scientists, as citizens, have an obligation to do whatever is possible to realize more fully the democratic ideals of society.[124] To be sure, scientists have both a duty to explain their work to the best of their ability and a right to be open about the potential, limitations, and practices of science.[125]

MOVING TOWARD THE LINKAGE OF SCIENCE TO POLICY

The next chapter illuminates the different perspectives that guide the work of scientists on the one hand, and policymakers on the other. Many scholars fear that because scientists and policymakers work in two completely different and separate worlds, linking science to environmental policymaking in a meaningful way is a difficult, if not impossible, task. Other scholars hold out hope that this connection not only can be made, it must be made for the sake of maintaining some semblance of environmental quality and sustainability in a rapidly deteriorating natural world.

As we move toward a more detailed description of the science–policy interface, keep in mind the difficult position in which scientists are placed regarding when and how they should participate in the policymaking process. Is it as scientists, as citizens, as advocates, or a combination of these? In addition, think about two other intangibles. The first is that, as Brian Silver points out, scientists come in many colors, with the green of jealousy and the purple of rage being among the more fashionable.[126] The second is that, in the end, science is more than just a matter of reason; it is also a matter of luck and imagination.[127] As readers will see in the coming chapters, the allure that science, through the diligent efforts of scientists, can provide us with the "right" solutions is quite strong within the American public policymaking process. But this allure is also tainted by the fact that science is conducted by human beings, subject to all the noise and shadows that come with living in a very politically and culturally defined society. In the end, we must come to terms with the fact that linking science to policy, just as Silver describes, involves the human qualities of pride, imagination, and just plain luck.

REFLECTIVE QUESTIONS

Question 4-1

Glen Toner (*Innovation, Science, and Environment,* 2008) acknowledges the Intergovernmental Panel on Climate Change (IPCC) as the global authority on the science of climate change, mostly because of its rigorous assessment process of peer-reviewed published research. Toner even notes that the IPCC's innovative and authoritative quality of its work resulted in being awarded the 2007 Nobel Peace Prize.

Go online and find information that counters Toner's claim; that is, find literature that claims that the IPCC is not the most rigorous and scientific authority on climate change. In so doing, provide reasons why critics of the IPCC argue that their work is not representative of the "best" science available today.

Question 4-2

Deborah Stone (*Policy Paradox,* 2002) states that there is always a cost to acquiring information and that information is often deliberately kept secret. For scientists working under contractual obligations to maintain confidentiality, describe some of the possible consequences of releasing protected information. Are there also consequences for withholding such information?

Question 4-3

Andrew Ross (*Science Wars,* 1996) claims that science does not have a monopoly upon rationality. What is Ross talking about? What other ways of "knowing" can contribute to a rational discussion? In your discussion, provide a succinct definition of what the term *rational* means to you.

Question 4-4

Walter Rosenbaum (*Environmental Politics and Policy,* 2008) speaks of the relentless evolution of scientific research that frustrates, confuses, and discredits existing environmental policymaking by producing all sorts of new and unexpected discoveries. Think of one such recent discovery and describe the effects (both good and bad) it had on existing policy.

Question 4-5

Patrick Hamlett (*Understanding Technological Politics,* 1992) posits that professional and personal scientific disputes, when aired in public, diminish the authority of science. Search out and find an example that supports Hamlett's assertion.

Question 4-6

Brian Silver (*The Ascent of Science,* 1998) defends the role of scientists in the policymaking process by arguing that to discover iron is not to make swords. Explain what Silver is talking about, especially as it applies to how science connects to environmental policymaking in the United States.

Question 4-7

Al Gore (*An Inconvenient Truth,* 2006) pointedly claims that science has now "proven" beyond a doubt that the Earth's climate is changing at a much faster rate than originally feared. What would a scientist find incorrect about how Gore uses the terminology of "proven?"

SUGGESTED READINGS

Sheila Jasanoff, *The Fifth Branch: Science Advisers as Policymakers* (Cambridge, MA: Harvard University Press, 1994).

Daniel Sarewitz, *Frontiers of Illusion: Science, Technology, and the Politics of Progress* (Philadelphia: Temple University Press, 1996).

Brian Silver, *The Ascent of Science* (New York: Solomon Press, 1998).

Aaron Wildavsky, *But Is It True? A Citizen's Guide to Environmental Health and Safety Issues* (Cambridge, MA: Harvard University Press, 1995).

Edward O. Wilson, *Consilience: The Unity of Knowledge* (New York: Alfred A. Knopf, 1998).

CHAPTER 5

The Science–Policy Interface

It is sad but true that ecological science is too often ignored or misunderstood by politicians and others whose decisions affect the air we breathe, the waters we drink, and the health of all species—including us.

David Sleeper, *Hubbard Brook Research Foundation*, 2008.

SCIENCE, POLITICS, AND ENVIRONMENTAL POLICYMAKING

Within the sphere of American public policymaking and politics there exists a tension between scientific truth and the quest for a just society.[1] This tension is especially prominent in the realm of environmental policymaking, in which the role of science appears to be accentuated. In fact, the battles over what is the best approach to conducting environmental policymaking in North America, according to William Leiss, are consistently based on two unifying themes, and both are centered on the role of science: the use of science as a justification for action (or inaction), and the question of scientific credibility.[2] Leiss goes on to explain in detail what makes the environmental policy domain so special, and, to no surprise, managing science is prominent.

> Almost every policy aspect in [the environmental] area is presented to politicians and the public in the form of a more or less adequate scientific description of a state of affairs . . . and the adequacy and credibility of that description becomes a key factor—often, *the* key factor—in the policy response. In other words, a great deal of the policy response is a matter of "managing" these scientific descriptions and describing in what way they do (or do not) demand a response that will limit the ability of some social actors to do this or that in the way of creating environmental impacts.[3]

Many scholars provide support for the view of environmental policymaking as described by Leiss. Judith Layzer observes that environmental disputes are almost always defined in terms of the science.[4] Arild Underdal contends that the constructive use of input from scientific research in the making of environmental policy decisions requires a way of combining (and balancing) the integrity and autonomy of the scientific undertaking with responsiveness to the needs of decision-makers.[5] Richard Benedick maintains that the successful linkage of science to policy results in the reduction of environmental pollution.[6] And Richard Monastersky points to the global warming issue as a textbook example of how science and politics have grown intertwined, with climate science becoming "irrevocably politicized."[7]

There are, however, problems with making science meaningful to environmental policymaking. Science is often characterized as being only marginally relevant to good decision-making.[8] This characterization is exhibited in an issue of *The Environmental Professional,* whose editors bemoan the fact that the United States suffers from the lack of an independent, nonpolitical, respected source of environmental information. The editors claim that science is disconnected from decision-makers and the public, suggesting that environmental policy decisions are not based on sound science.[9] Stephen Meyer takes this argument further by declaring that what most academics would consider good science is largely antithetical to the practice of politics and plays to the particular strengths of anti-environmental forces.[10] Along this same line of thought, Walter Rosenbaum reports that environmental policies are often made (and unmade) without resort to the scientific evidence that is supposed to inform such decisions.[11] Zachary Smith summarizes this line of thought.

> There is often a presumption that in environmental policy making, decisions should not be made without all the available information at hand. Furthermore, it is argued that decisions should not be made about the environment unless the scientific evidence establishes clear causality, without uncertainty, and is direct and provable. [Yet] science is not well suited to providing this kind of evidence. The standard of uncertainty and unquestioned causality is, in fact, rarely met in science. Scientific predictions are often necessarily drawn from the probabilities of a particular outcome. Nonscientific policy makers often seem to not understand this about science and demand "hard scientific fact" before proceeding to policy conclusions.[12]

As one can surmise from the discussion, environmental policymaking is a good place to explore the science–politics linkage. Recall that the policy process in the United States is fragmented and decentralized. This gives opponents of any legislation ample opportunity to delay action. In the American system, it is always easier to block policy than to implement it. Opponents, then, can seize on the scientific uncertainty that always exists, and call for more study before taking action. They can also challenge the authority of scientific evidence because there are always competing perspectives in the world of science. Furthermore, the lack of certainty that scientists convey contrasts with opponents' ability to portray (with certainty) the costs of new regulations and policies. Therefore, environmentalists often find themselves at a big political disadvantage.

The following sections take readers through the maze of questions and problems that define the complex world of linking science to politics, with an emphasis on the importance of integrating science and politics for the betterment of the environment. As Kai N. Lee concedes:

> Environmental policy should be idealistic about science and pragmatic about politics. Idealism is necessary because knowledge is limited and rigorous science offers the best-known route to reliable knowledge.[13]

THE LINKAGE BETWEEN SCIENCE AND POLITICS

In the world of American public policymaking, it is commonly accepted that knowledge is inseparable from power. Furthermore, it is said that whenever science is implicated in policy problems, the linkage between knowledge and power becomes even stronger.[14] Hence, it should not be surprising that the interaction between scientific and political authority in the United States has been increasing at a substantial rate,[15] with an "indispensable and growing need for the contribution of scientific expertise to public policy."[16] Scientists are more actively engaged in the creation and evaluation of policy than at any time in our history.[17] One witnesses this aspect of the science–policy linkage in the work of Sheila Jasanoff, who documents the use of science in the political debate over biotechnology. Jasanoff pronounces the status of science within politics as "fundamental" and "constitutional," declaring that it "is the transcendental cognitive authority of science that most powerfully complements political authority."[18]

The common view in the United States today is that public policymaking is now actively considered to be the result of research at the frontiers of science combined with a unique collaboration between scientists and policymakers.[19] And despite the fact that the way in which scientific knowledge is transformed into decision premises is neither pure science nor pure politics,[20] most observers of the American policymaking process agree that the linkage of science to politics is simply indisputable.[21] It is now a generally accepted view that science and politics function together in a multidimensional way,[22] that there is no way to separate scientific and political contributions to the decision-making process.[23] Political battles are played out in the language of science,[24] with science and scientists playing a central role—some say "the" central role—in the development of contemporary economic and social goals.[25] Roger Pielke, Jr., outlines this view:

> It has become widely accepted by the public and policy-makers (and most scientists as well) that science shows relevance to a wide range of societal problems. Consequently, we should not view science as an activity to be kept separate from policy and politics but, instead, as a key resource for facilitating complicated decisions that involve competing interests in society. We want science to be connected to society. But how we make this connection is not always easy or obvious.[26]

Sheila Jasanoff asks one of the most studied questions of our time: How do we go about harnessing the collective expertise of the scientific community so as to advance the public interest?[27] Tim Clark offers the most basic answer to this question: "Science can contribute to the policy process by determining matters of fact, clarifying historic trends and conditions, and making projections about them."[28]

Helen Ingram and her colleagues offer a more nuanced answer. They speak of the value of science to government in terms of the legitimacy scientists provide: if an idea is strongly backed by a reputable scientist, it cannot be easily dismissed.[29]

Karen Litfin takes the idea of scientific legitimacy a step further, claiming that the cultural role of science as a key source of legitimation means that political debates are framed in scientific terms, with questions of value reframed as questions of fact, leading to the search for further scientific justification.[30] For example, debates about the regulation of toxic waste revolve around two important values: the protection of public health, and the promotion of free (unregulated) markets. Policy debates begin with people taking sides on the issue based on which of these values they most support. As science enters the discussion, empirical evidence is used to document the extent of the threat to the public health, legitimizing this value at the expense of advocates of laissez-faire economics.

Because policymakers are viewed as having little understanding of the scientific process,[31] and because there is a need for the best estimates of a wide range of plausible outcomes, policymakers consistently seek advice from scientists.[32] One of the basic reasons policymakers seek such advice from scientists is because they want information "undiluted by either party doctrine or the policy views of general administrators."[33] There exists a belief that scientific information provides an objective basis for resolving political disputes.[34] It is asserted that the reason science has historically maintained its legitimacy is only through cultivating a careful distance from politics.[35] Moreover, it is suggested that science can be the basis of objective criticism of political power because science claims no power itself. In essence, politics can afford to respect the independence of science because science does not attempt to dictate its purposes.[36]

The claim is that science should be kept separate from considerations of policy and politics,[37] and that science and policy have fundamentally different aims: science aims at truth, whereas policymaking aims at right action.[38] In the words of David Guston, "People often think of politics and science as entirely separate enterprises. Science is engaged in the high pursuit of truth, and politics is engaged in the baser pursuit of interests."[39] In short, if science is to perform its legitimating function within the American public policymaking system, it has to "stand apart from the contaminating touch of politics."[40] Put another way, it "is absolutely critical to differentiate *scientific results* from their *policy significance*."[41]

Understandably, scientists feel strongly that others should not set their basic values and objectives so rigidly that they cannot follow where their research leads them.[42] Today, there is unease among both scientists and policymakers alike for fear that science will ultimately become (if it has not already) something that policymakers will simply sift through and pick and choose from, selecting viewpoints that appeal to their own personal political preferences.[43] There is a strong commitment among scientists to keep their science separate from political influence. Accordingly, Tora Skodvin and Arild Underdal contend that it is important to draw clear boundaries between the realm of science and the realm of policy. To substantiate their beliefs, Skodvin and Underdal provide a detailed description of how the relationship between the worlds of scientists and policymakers should be carried out:

> Science and politics contribute two distinct and different systems of behavior. Some may characterize the difference as one of opposite poles, where science is everything politics is not: pure, objective, governed by rational analytic reasoning and thus not hostage to subjective biases, manipulation tactics, or coercive power—ingredients often associated with politics. . . . The ideal relationship between science and politics is seen as one where knowledge—generated by competent, truth-seeking scientists working in accordance with stringent professional standards—is communicated, undistorted, to decision makers who then utilize it as factual premises for policy decisions. In its interaction with politics, science must above all remain science and never blend with politics; any adaptation of the modes of operation that characterize politics constitutes "contamination" and will inevitably lead to the perversion of science.[44]

However, there are many who question the ability of science and scientists to be objective and free to express their ideas once they are pulled into politics.[45] Scientists, like other citizens, may hold strong policy views that can influence their evaluations.[46] Going straight to this point of contention, Karen Litfin—in her description of how scientists involved in the debate over stratospheric ozone were drawn out of their laboratories and into the negotiation process—touches on one of the most controversial aspects of a scientist's connection to public policymaking: whether scientists can provide reliable and ideological neutral data to policymakers.[47] John Zillman characterizes this aspect of the science–policy debate as "the challenge that the quickening pace of policy formulation poses to the objectivity of science."[48]

Although policymakers seek to use science to legitimate their positions, the prevailing view among scholars is that science (and scientists) cannot provide the sort of legitimacy that actors in the policy process crave.[49] For instance, Sheila Jasanoff contends that both empirical and theoretical research have effectively dismantled the idea that the scientific component of decision-making can be separated from the political component and entrusted to independent experts.[50] This viewpoint is echoed in the words of George E. Brown, Jr., a prominent member of Congress, with his observation that policymakers should dismiss any scientific viewpoint whose only motivation is to support a preferred policy outcome.[51] Along these lines, Brown argues that the culprits who have discredited the use of science in the policy process are those skeptical scientists who have rejected the conventional wisdom of valid scientific analysis and chosen instead to present their views in opinion pieces aimed at policymakers, the media, and the general public rather than their fellow scientists. Brown's solution to this problem is for the scientific community to invest a much greater amount of time and energy in educating policymakers and the public about the importance and value of the scientific process.[52]

THE DIFFERENT WORLDS OF SCIENTISTS AND POLICYMAKERS

Norman Miller posits that the need to enlist science in public policy decisions has never been greater because of the growing complexity and impact of potential problems, and the social and economic costs that may be necessary to address them. Yet in the same breath, Miller states what many believe to be an unfortunate fact—that science and public policymaking are fundamentally incompatible.[53] For all practical purposes, Miller is correct: science and policy are evaluated using completely different standards.[54] Therefore, scientists and policymakers who strive for excellence in order to maintain their self-identities and protect their sources of legitimacy will tend to misunderstand and disrespect each other.[55] Although scientists and policymakers both strive to obtain high-quality scientific data, they pursue distinctive paths toward the generation and ultimate use of such information,[56] and they often lack a basic understanding of the other's knowledge systems.[57]

In its basic form, scientific knowledge is a product generated by a process external and quite different from the policy process.[58] There exist two systems of behavior, "an imminent tension between impartiality and objectivity on one hand, and strategic reasoning and tactical maneuvers to promote particular interests on the other."[59] In this regard, Walter Rosenbaum notes substantial differences between scientists and policymakers, especially with respect to what policymakers want and scientists can produce. According to Rosenbaum, policymakers want accurate and credible data and they want it immediately. Yet scientists often cannot produce this type of information in a timely manner, if they can produce it at all.[60] Zachary Smith puts it this way:

> Politics is about bargaining, compromise, and the balancing of interests. Science, on the other hand, tries to deal with "truth" or, to the extent possible, absolutes. The scientifically correct answer to a problem may not be politically viable.[61]

One reason for misunderstandings between scientists and policymakers is that they typically ask different questions.[62] Scientists deal with facts and observations, whereas policymakers seek to affect how the world "ought to" or "should" be.[63] Science is viewed as subject to the "transcendental norm of truth-telling, while the institutions of constitutional government guard against abuses of power by the state."[64] Yet scientists and policymakers are often drawn into each other's worlds, and science simply cannot be thought of as external to the political process.[65] Environmental issues especially appear to lure scientists into entangled policy conflicts in which they are asked to perform functions for which they have had no decent training or experiential background.[66] Walter Rosenbaum labels this the "treacherous zone between science and politics," where public officials are asked to make scientific judgments and scientists are asked to resolve policy issues when neither has been trained to do so.[67]

MANAGING THE SCIENCE–POLICY LINKAGE

Many observers, however, do not believe in the notion that a straightforward linkage between science and politics or between scientists and policymakers exists. Karen Litfin, for instance, portrays a more complex policy world in which knowledge and power must be understood as interactive and where science and politics function together in a multidimensional way.[68] Litfin makes the case that it is scientific knowledge, rather than the scientists themselves, that proves crucial to environmental policymaking; that is, once scientific knowledge is produced, it becomes available for a host of political actors to exploit in ways that promote certain policies:

> Scientists may join together in an epistemic community to influence the course of policy, but their power is circumscribed by a host of contextual factors. Policymakers may co-opt or manipulate the scientists, or they may simply ignore what the scientists have to say. Whether or not the voices of scientists are audible may depend upon seemingly extraneous contingencies beyond the control of either scientists or policymakers. Furthermore, the scientists may deliberately refrain from addressing the policy implications of their research.[69]

Much has been written about the tension between science and politics, with most agreeing that there is no clear line between science and politics.[70] The relationship between science and politics is viewed as complex and precarious, "vulnerable to various kinds of observations and perversions on either side."[71] Furthermore, the increasing politicization of science reflects that times have changed,[72] and that there is no clear separation between science and its relationship to society.[73] And, contrary to what many want to believe, science does not inherently serve humanity; what makes science serve a cause—other than the search for knowledge—is politics.[74]

Because scientists are often politically naïve, they sometimes fail to see that policy is not made solely on the basis of scientific results.[75] Science is still conceived by many scientists as a realm of objective facts, divorced from political considerations. Scientists are encouraged by their disciplines to avoid politics, policy, and value discussions at all costs because such involvement tends to corrupt objective science.[76] Hence, scientists often fail to distinguish the political power they possess from their socially accepted competence as interpreters of reality.[77] This is why some scientists assume that policy should simply follow from good science, and are astonished when it does not.

Tora Skodvin and Arild Underdal, characterizing the science–politics interaction in terms of a tension between impartiality and objectivity on the one hand, and strategic reasoning and tactical maneuvers to promote particular interests on the other, offer insight into how the science–policy linkage could be managed:

> What we are looking for is an arena where scientists and policy-makers together can work effectively towards a consensual interpretation of relevant knowledge with reference to a particular policy problem . . . such arenas will be more effective if they are constructed as buffers—coupling scientific knowledge with the concerns of policy-makers without penetrating and impairing the internal mode of operation of either system.[78]

THE BOUNDARY BETWEEN SCIENCE AND POLITICS

More and more, scientists are being asked to keep their findings and determinations open to examination and challenge. Yet it appears that many scientists do not want to be part of the policy world. They shy away from the disorderly mixture revealed by science in action and prefer the orderly pattern of scientific method and rationality.[79] However, it is often difficult to remain on one side or the other of the science–policy boundary.

Though it is regularly accepted that policymakers and scientists inhabit different worlds and speak different languages, it is also true that there exists a very high degree of interaction between these two distinct professions. This interaction takes place within "complex networks of power, with the authority of each group being highly circumscribed by the authority of the other, [where] interpreting and framing knowledge become crucial political problems as information is mustered to achieve policy objectives."[80] Although individual scientists may attempt to avoid interaction with the other world, their work is inherently affected by those of their colleagues who do interact with the policy world. This intersection, where science and politics come together, is referred to as a "fine, bright line,"[81] and "interface between two cultures."[82]

> To one side is the rough and tumble, the horse trading and pork barreling, the colorful bustle of politics. To the other side is the ivory-towered, rational contemplation and methodological pursuit of truth.[83]

Many scholars cite a need for increasing the quality of the interactions between scientists and policymakers.[84] Surprisingly, the burden of improving that relationship is put on scientists, who are criticized for not reaching out to policymakers and for failing to identify the specific needs of decision-makers.[85] Analysts complain about scientists' failure to recognize the political dimensions of their work.[86] At the same time, it is often difficult for scientists to accept the fact that science is inextricably linked with nonscientific elements of society: politics, history, economics, emotion, and luck.[87] In addition, scientists are criticized for their long-standing aversion to politics, and for viewing politics as an unseemly activity that compromises their credibility.[88] Political leaders seek quick answers. When those answers are not forthcoming, the tendency is to blame scientists for being on opposite sides of controversies, generating public skepticism about scientific evidence.[89] In the end, scientists are asked to develop a clearer understanding of the interface between science and policy, as well as a better understanding of the appropriate roles for science, scientists, and the public in differentiating between personal values and policy preferences.[90]

However, for scientists, it is a complicated task to make the transition across the science–politics boundary, to provide scientific expertise to policymakers, and to bridge the gap between those who conduct research and those who govern. The central problem is identified as "the on-going struggle between the plausibly corrupting influence of politics as usual and the potentially unaccountable self-governance of an authoritative professional community."[91] Notwithstanding the enormity of solving this problem, policymaking must go on. But this is no easy task. Despite continuing calls for bridging the gap between science and policy, there is little consensus on just how this is to be accomplished,[92] and an apparent lack of people who can provide such a linkage—as those with an understanding of both the science and policy worlds are quite scarce.[93]

Some believe that the solution to the science–policy dilemma is as simple as creating a more explicitly permeable boundary between the laboratory and the surrounding world.[94] Others find this solution problematic because of the difficulty of distinguishing scientific facts from political values.[95] One cannot get away from the idea that science, with its arguments crafted in ambiguities and paradoxes, remains a creature of politics.[96] The dilemma scientists face in dealing with the idea that there is a separation between science and policy finds scientists continually searching for a way to bridge the gap between their world and the world of policymakers.[97]

SCIENCE IS NOT THE SOLUTION

The belief in the power of science to improve human life is perhaps the quintessential hallmark of the modern era.[98] An example of this success is the establishment and implementation of the Montreal Protocol of 1986 that phased out the use of the ozone-layer-depleting chlorofluorocarbons in manufacturing, and is credited with solving the problem of the ozone "hole." The success of the Montreal Protocol is portrayed as the result of research at the frontiers of science combined with a unique collaboration between scientists and policymakers.[99] Still, many examples exist of the failure of more or better science to solve policy disputes, especially regarding environmental problems. Global warming, also cast as climate change policy, is widely viewed as such an example. As Judith Layzer asserts, improved scientific understanding of climate change did not translate into policy; rather, it prompted the mobilization of powerful interests opposed to international climate change policy.[100] Toward this end, the movement toward a policy on climate change, sometimes called a textbook example of how politics and science have grown intertwined, is referred to as "a surreal example of how the results of research can be stretched and distorted when they get politicized."[101]

Policy disputes have less to do with science than with broad political issues and questions of power, responsibility, and accountability.[102] Moreover, scientific competence alone is not viewed as a sufficient basis for policy influence,[103] and scientists have always had serious concerns about the difficulty of quantifying the human experience.[104] Thus, efforts to translate scientific information directly into wise and sensible policy decisions are likely doomed to failure.[105]

The question of the value of science is not a scientific subject, and scientists know that they do not have any magic formulas for solving social problems and no special insights into how to make better public policy.[106] Wade Robison explains these ideas.

> Scientists are no better off than the rest of us in facing a situation in which there is a great deal of which we are ignorant, in which what we think we know we may not know, and in which we must act cautiously, given the harm that may occur from our present acts and omissions. Scientists can presumably understand the scientific issues better than someone without scientific training, but that competency to

comprehend part of what is at issue does not create a competence to comprehend all that ought to be happening. . . . These judgments are pre-eminently political.[107]

Still, there exists a belief that science can transcend politics. As a society, we are beguiled by a faith in the ability of science to make politics more rational and cooperative.[108] But most observers agree that science is rarely a sufficient basis for selecting among alternative courses of action because desired outcomes invariably involve differing conceptions of the sort of world we want in the future.[109] There exists a "futility of calling on science to cut short a policy controversy before the groundwork has been laid for accord among disparate social and political values."[110] In other words,

> science cannot tell us what to do. Deciding what to do occurs through a political process of bargaining, negotiation, and compromise . . . whenever one invokes science . . . as a justification for selecting one course of action over others, then one is "politicizing" science. From this perspective, the politicization of science is a natural and, indeed, essential part of the political process. [In the end, however,] science has exceedingly little capacity to reconcile differences in values.[111]

Some contend that the information needed by policymakers to resolve major conflicts is precisely the type of information scientists are least likely to authoritatively deliver.[112] Policy generally moves faster than science, and the capacity of scientists to provide information may require more time than policymakers are willing to accept, especially for politically hot issues.[113] Because of this, scientists have been criticized for not providing the "right" information to policymakers or for providing too much information that goes underutilized.[114] Scientists quite often do not have reliable answers to the questions decision-makers wrestle with, and sometimes the answers scientists think they have turn out to be wrong, leaving decision-makers to regret that they ever listened.[115] In reality, all science can offer is probabilities, and hence scientists have become just one more partner in a broad-based decision-making process that involves anybody with a stake in the outcome.[116]

In general terms, science can either solve our policy problems for us or stand aside from them. That is why the scientific community and the policymakers are constantly being asked to develop the clearest possible idea of the working rules that govern their relationship.[117] Some continue to look at science as an ideal, like democracy, justice, and freedom; an ideal toward which our aspirations are aimed.[118] Yet a more realistic way to look at science is not as providing a prescription for solving problems, but as a tool for effectively alerting society to potential problems.[119] Accordingly, Daniel Sarewitz believes that scientific research should be viewed as a process that can help constrain the terms of political debate and delineate boundaries within which policy decisions make sense.[120] Science can contribute basic facts that are relatively noncontroversial components of broader issues and define or illuminate new realms of ethical debate by enlarging society's world view. To be sure, the most authoritative component of political debate is not science but the matrix of cultural values that guide society in its struggle to advance.[121]

THE CHALLENGE FOR SCIENTISTS: STANDING APART FROM POLITICS

Despite their best efforts, scientists are unable to stand apart from the policy, or political, world. Science is viewed as always being politicized.[122] To the extent that scientists suppress uncertainties, they are in effect constructing a political decision for which they are not accountable.[123] Yet because policymakers will inevitably use their information, scientists cannot avoid being drawn in one form or another into the policymaking process and hence, becoming directly involved with controversies that are not scientific but political.[124]

Because scientific knowledge is used in policy debates, public activity leads scientists to consider normative principles and moral issues.[125]

> Environmental issues frequently place scientists in a highly charged political atmosphere in which impartiality and objectivity, among the most highly esteemed scientific virtues, are severely tested and sometimes fail. Scientists are consulted by public officials in good part because the scientists' presumed objectivity, as well as their technical expertise, makes them trustworthy advisers. But impartiality can be an early casualty in highly partisan and polarizing policy conflict.[126]

Perhaps scientists no longer have the luxury of remaining above the fray when it comes to the American public policymaking process.[127] The tension between the political side (what ought to be done) and the scientific side (the consequences of what is done or not done) clearly poses a dilemma for scientists that draws them into the arena of public decision-making.[128] Stephen Meyer makes the case that scientists who attempt to remove themselves from politics are naïve:

> Scientists have an obligation to inform public policy, and that means being political players. Specifically, it is time to drop the idealized—but ridiculous—belief that "pure science" is not political. Although the initial pursuit of scientific knowledge may seem largely apolitical, the results of scientific research and their use in policymaking are often highly political, regardless of what the scientists think. . . . Any study that holds the potential to shift policy, redistribute resources, and influence the relative power of advocates and opponents of environmental protection, is fundamentally political. . . . For scientists to pretend to be above the political fray is to consign science to irrelevance in policy making.[129]

Following this same pattern of thought, some view the neutrality portion of the scientific code as only camouflage for special interests, a way to hide the moral and political from the realm of scientific discourse itself.[130] If neutrality is viewed as an impossibility, then it should be acknowledged that every participant, expert or not, is a political actor with interests and values.[131] Kathryn Harrison and George Hoberg assert that those who make policy decisions, including politicians, bureaucrats, and scientists, must involve their own values in choosing among a number of scientifically plausible alternatives, thus enmeshing science and policy into the same sphere of decision-making.[132] Further, they argue that by acknowledging that this is the case—that policy and scientific judgments are both made at each step of the policy process—we encourage scientists and political decision-makers "to make explicit the basis for their decisions so that we can explore the boundary where scientific advice ends and value judgments begin."[133] This is more in line with some schools of thought in the social sciences, which argue that since research is not value-free, scientists should reveal their values and biases and make them transparent so that their work can be fairly evaluated.

But the allure and power of policy-neutral science is still a very potent force in the policymaking process. There are those who continue to classify science into separate realms, characterizing science as policy-neutral if it is transparent, reproducible, and independent, and classifying science as normative if it conveys an implied policy preference.[134] As the scientific community is asked to play a greater role in environmental policy matters, scientists are also asked to remain objective and not slant their results according to personal prejudices.[135] Scientists are cast as the "apolitical elite,"[136] and as ethically and politically neutral.[137] It is claimed that if science loses its rational, objective, truth-seeking nature, then science also loses its role as the ultimate arbiter of nature.[138] Indeed, if the scientific community wishes to claim independence from partisan politics, then with this comes an obligation to provide independent guidance on the significance of science for a wide scope of policy alternatives.[139]

In a contradictory manner, scientists often claim to be focused only on science while also making the case that their science is central to resolving political conflict in one specific direction or another.[140] But they cannot have it both ways. If scientists complain that their advice is ignored or distorted during the policymaking process,[141] then they must acknowledge that, like other citizens, they may hold strong policy views that can influence their evaluations.[142] To be sure, the simple fact that many natural scientists pursue their occupation because they want to contribute to "the greater good" is illustrative of the tension between following the tenets of the scientific process at the same time as pursuing societal values.[143] The question becomes: If science in the policy setting is always colored by values, then what role should scientists, who are professionally committed to impartiality, expect to play in decisionmaking? Perhaps the correct response is for scientists to inject their own political values into science.[144]

Adding to this complexity, scientists often portray themselves as outside the political process and as poorly understood by politicians.[145] They complain that the objectively determined best solutions as revealed by science seldom carry much political weight. Scientists maintain that even when they receive a hearing, their views are distorted by the press and misinterpreted by political actors. However, the scholarly literature in political science and public policy presents a contrary view. Researchers find that scientists wield a great deal more influence than they admit to having, especially in environmental policy.[146]

Research has also shown that scientists have a long-standing aversion to politics and are reluctant to become politically active for fear of compromising their reputation for scientific objectivity.[147] Many scientists want to see themselves as standing apart from the world of politics—reticent to participate in the political process for fear of having their credibility compromised by policymakers who are not only scientifically illiterate but intolerant of uncertainty and unappreciative of the concept of probability.[148] In this regard, scientists are even criticized by their peers for publicly discussing issues with high degrees of uncertainty because most citizens (including policymakers) are not competent to assess scientific complexities.[149]

Yet other scientists argue that the ideal of objectivity portrayed by many scientists is fiction. These scientists believe that they must take a proactive approach—coming out of their laboratories to take an active and personal involvement in public decision-making.[150] If this is so, the burden is put on scientists to learn the politician's language and to see the world from the politician's point of view.[151] From this perspective, scientists must give up the unrealistic view that science is not connected to the social and political environment,[152] and accept science as a "profoundly human endeavor, a product not of disembodied minds but of actual people in social interaction."[153] In other words, scientists can no longer "simply do [their] science and not worry about these ethical issues."[154]

IMPROVING THE SCIENCE–POLICY LINKAGE

It has never been easy to translate the findings of science into reasonable environmental public policies. As explained above, scientists and policymakers operate in worlds so different that little communication takes place across the barriers of language, culture, and preconception.[155] However, some scholarly work centered on environmental policymaking suggests that a respectful social attitude of scientists and policymakers toward each other in their working relationship may be more important than any differences in orientation that might otherwise divide them.[156]

The suggestion that the education of policymakers by scientists will make the science–policy linkage more effective is one that has received a lot of support. Gretchen Daily claims that the lack of understanding of the character and value of natural ecosystems traces ultimately to a failure of the scientific community to effectively convey the necessary information to the public,[157] and Sheila Jasanoff speaks of an unspoken presumption—by both policymakers and the public alike—that better scientific characterization of a problem will lead to better policymaking.[158] Jane Gregory and Steve Miller contend that scientists have now been delivered a new commandment: communicate better with the public.[159]

Given the tensions and complexities of the science–politics linkage, it is not likely that simply improving communication between scientists and the public and scientists and decision-makers will solve the dilemma of providing good science to policymakers. The challenges are much greater. One of those challenges is to find a way for scientists and policymakers alike to come to grips with the fallacy of policy-neutral science. The following chapter will attempt to bring the science–policy interface into focus with an exploration of why it is so difficult to let go of an ideal that has been the bedrock of the scientific process since the beginning of time.

REFLECTIVE QUESTIONS

Question 5-1

Chris Mooney (*environment 360,* July 7, 2008) reports that the George W. Bush administration placed politics over science when it came to environmental policymaking and that the new administration needs to "strive more broadly to bolster the role of science in environmental and other types of agency decision-making, so that the best available information once again drives policy."

    a. Find two examples used by critics of the Bush administration to illustrate why they believed politics was placed above science with respect to environmental policymaking.

    b. Once again, we see the use of the terminology "best available" information. What does that phrase mean to you? Provide a specific definition of what this would mean in the scientific world.

    c. Based on your readings, was there ever a time in American public policymaking when "the best available information" drove policy? If so, cite that time period and explain how this was so.

Question 5-2

Charles Krauthammer (*Idaho Statesman,* June 1, 2008) offers the following critique of scientific models: Predictions of catastrophe depend on models. Models depend on assumptions about complex planetary systems—from ocean currents to cloud formation—which no one fully understands, and which is why the models are inherently flawed. The doomsday scenarios posit a couple of events, each with a certain probability. The multiple improbability of their simultaneous occurrence renders all such predictions entirely speculative. Yet on the basis of this speculation, environmental activists, attended by compliant scientists and opportunistic politicians, are advocating radical economic and social regulation.

    a. Provide a critique of Krauthammer's argument. Do you agree or disagree with his main premise? Explain why or why not.

    b. What do you think Krauthammer means by the terms "compliant scientists" and "opportunistic politicians"? Is he using terms in a negative or positive manner? To what effect?

    c. How does Krauthammer portray the role of probability as it relates to development of environmental policy? As a scientist, how would you explain the notion of probability and why it is inherent in all scientific research?

Question 5-3

There appears to be widespread satisfaction with the appointment of Steven Chu as Secretary to the Department of Energy (Steven Mufson, *Washington Post National Weekly,* 2009). The satisfaction appears to stem from the fact that Chu is a scientist first, and not a policymaker.

Discuss the advantages and disadvantages of Chu's training as a scientist as he enters into the world of American public policymaking.

SUGGESTED READINGS

Stephen Bocking, *Ecologists and Environmental Politics: A History of Contemporary Ecology* (New Haven, CT: Yale University Press, 1997).

David Collingridge and Colin Reeve, *Science Speaks to Power: The Role of Experts in Policy Making* (New York: St. Martin's Press, 1986).

Karen Greif and Jon Merz, *Current Controversies in the Biological Sciences: Case Studies of Policy Challenges from New Technologies* (Cambridge, MA: MIT Press, 2007).

Philip Kitcher, *Science, Truth, and Democracy* (New York: Oxford University Press, 2001).

Bruce Williams and Albert Matheny, *Democracy, Dialogue, and Environmental Disputes: The Contested Languages of Social Regulation* (New Haven, CT: Yale University Press, 1995).

CHAPTER 6

The Ideal of Objectivity

Enthusiasts for the sciences write books and articles that proclaim the search for objective knowledge as one of the crowning achievements of our species. Detractors deny objectivity of the sciences, question our ability to attain truth and knowledge, and conclude that the sciences are instruments of oppression.

Philip Kitcher, *Science, Truth, and Democracy*, 2001.

OBJECTIVITY AND THE PUBLIC POLICYMAKING PROCESS

Science, at its finest, is meant "to provide value-free application of inductive reasoning to the material world that is distinguishable in its essence from the morally charged revelations of oracles, prophets, and politicians."[1] Traditionally, scientists—among others—have promoted this value-free nature of scientists as the "neutral, disinterested, and objective expert . . . the rational and authoritative arbiter of public disputes."[2] Those that support this view cultivate the image of objectivity,[3] often heralding science as an objective enterprise populated by an apolitical elite.[4] The words of Mark Tercek, president and chief executive officer of *The Nature Conservancy*, are typical of this view.

> Science is at the heart of the Nature Conservancy's mission. It guides where and how we work and assures those with whom we collaborate that our conduct is consistent and sound. Science ensures that we are not driven by the whims of politics, personalities, or opportunism. It is one reason we have maintained our respected reputation over nearly six decades.[5]

When looking at the American public policymaking process and the linkage of science to policy, one must always keep in mind that there exists a single overriding belief that appears to transcend all other beliefs—the belief that science is objective and value-free, whereas political life is ideological and value-laden.[6] Science is characterized as being grounded in a deterministic universe in which all effects come inexorably from previous physical causes with no room for morality. It is a universe with facts but not values.[7] It is an ideal expressed by the words and thoughts of President Barack Obama in one of his early expressions of how he wants his administration run: "We make scientific decisions based on facts, not ideology."[8]

The authority and influence of scientific expertise rests on the assumptions of scientific neutrality and objective truth,[9] and on the general tenet that science provides reliable and ideologically neutral data.[10] For science to be pure, scientists tell us, science must be value neutral.[11] In fact, some observers argue that for the sake of the democratic process itself, great care needs to be taken to avoid invasion of objectivity by strongly held moral or political views.[12] There is even a call to restore a space for objective knowledge within the messy heart of political deliberation such that science "produced in this discursively purified space can then be drawn upon as authoritative enough to legitimate the most controversial decisions of state."[13]

The vision of decision-making as driven by rationality—that is, driven by rational thought and processes—has increased the authority wielded by scientists, reflecting the presumption that the methods employed by such experts are objective and as such will permit the assessment of costs and benefits without bias.[14] It is believed that effective policymaking requires just what scientists believe they have to offer: objective sifting of the facts, balanced visions, thoughtful reflection, and the mobilization of the best wisdom and highest competence.[15] Scientists are trained to discover how things work or why they happen, not what is good or bad,[16] and there still exists a strong resentment by some against scientists who take policy positions unrelated to their fields of expert knowledge.[17]

Scholars such as Helen Ingram argue that repeated involvement in politics may very well harm a scientist's objectivity.[18] The idea is that scientists should be free from assumptions about human purposes and values, protecting themselves from the temptations of power and the dangers of political control.[19] Politics, policy, and value discussions are to be avoided at all costs because they corrupt objective science and professionalism.[20] In these instances, some argue that instead of becoming more entrenched in the policy side, scientists should be shielded from political, economic, and social pressures and restricted only by their own abilities and imagination.[21] Those following this view believe that science is founded on the integrity and honesty of scientists,[22] and that moral, political, and religious judgments should not enter into the scientific process.[23] In brief, scientists are to be "totally apolitical,"[24] providing "sound, impartial advice."[25]

Objectivity, or at least the illusion of objectivity, is a source of strength for scientists.[26] Phyllis Coontz puts it this way: "While one may argue whether a value-free science is possible, objectivity continues to be the *sine qua non* of science, and according to such a view, scientific findings should be nonmoral in their application."[27] Bruce Bimber concisely describes this vision of the science–policy ideal: "The idealized image of the scientific expert involves not only simply knowledge but also a large element of objectivity, of being above politics and partisanship."[28] Bimber goes on to suggest that it is this ability to appeal to nonpolitical standards that provides legitimacy in the policymaking process. To label someone a scientist is to acknowledge the legitimacy of the scientific ideal.[29]

Scientists must protect themselves from the vagaries of values and must maintain their status as an invaluable social reservoir of disinterested, impartial, methodical inquiry, bowing only to the authority of reason in its unrelenting pursuit of truth.[30] They are considered "neutral" actors with sufficient knowledge of the issue and experience to assemble a balanced perspective.[31] An ideal world is one in which scientists strive for a detached objectivity, an impartiality that is thought to facilitate the generation and interpretation of information in a neutral way.[32] Robert Proctor describes how "neutral" science is differentiated from the values of society:

> The principle of neutral science, together with the doctrine of subjective value, constitutes the fundamental political ideology of modern science. Science in this view is neutral and public; values are subjective and private. Science is the realm of public reason, values the realm of personal whim. . . . [t]he scientist discovers, society applies.[33]

The allure of neutral science, unaffected by the influence of politics, remains strong today. It is certainly true that "the ideal of value-free science retains its firm hold on the national imagination, of cheerleaders as well as skeptics."[34] President Obama, in one of his first radio addresses, illustrated this belief. He observed that promoting science meant much more than just providing money; it meant ensuring that facts and evidence are never twisted or obscured by politics or ideology.[35]

THE FALLACY OF NEUTRAL SCIENCE

On the surface, it might appear that science can be completely objective and neutral. However, most observers now believe that the assumption that scientific and technical knowledge can provide an objective body of facts from which policy can be rationally generated is pure fallacy.[36] The expectation that politics can be legitimated by appeal to an autonomous, freestanding "independent" science has proven to be untenable.[37] So long as priorities of science are shaped by larger social priorities, the ideal of the "neutrality of science" confronts the reality of the politics of knowledge.[38] As Deborah Stone observes, "facts do not exist independent of interpretive lenses."[39] The fact of the matter is that, within American public policymaking today, the more commonly accepted view is that scientific objectivity is an illusion, a myth that reinforces the idealistic perception of science.[40] As Sheila Jasanoff states,

> The notion that the scientific component of decisionmaking can be separated from the political and entrusted to independent experts has been effectively dismantled . . . the idea that scientists can speak truth to power in a value-free market has emerged as a myth without correlates in reality.[41]

Bruce Williams and Albert Matheny also describe this illusion, or what they call the myth that science produces truth.[42] They argue that scientific inquiries are always shaped by social values; that not only the questions, but also the answers, are shaped by the social context in which science takes place. Philip Kitcher is even more direct. He claims that the ideal of objectivity is fiction, that all scientists believe what they want to believe, and that truth has little or nothing to do with what scientists believe.[43]

Some scholars maintain that science cannot protect itself from the influence of social values shared by the whole community, and that the remoteness of scientific knowledge from the social and physical environments in which it is measured and used is as irrational as anything we might imagine, and downright hazardous.[44] Stated another way, what poses for scientific truth is influenced by the degree to which the scientific community is open or closed to diverse views and perspectives.[45] Accordingly, Michael Shermer describes scientific truth in the following terms:

> Although we dislike the notion that truths, especially scientific truths, might be strongly influenced by who is doing the truth telling as much as by the quality of the evidence, the fact is that who you are and who you know sometimes matters as much as the consistency of your arguments or the quality of your evidence. Integrity, trust, reputation, fame, society memberships, and institution affiliations all converge to construct the validity of a claimant, and thus his or her claim. When Einstein spoke, people listened—no matter what he said.[46]

Put in a straightforward manner, science is simply not unimpeachable.[47] There can be no perfect, objectively verifiable truth.

> The most one can hope for is a serviceable truth: a state of knowledge that satisfies tests of scientific acceptability and supports reasoned decision making, but also assures those exposed to risk that their interests have not been sacrificed on the altar of an impossible scientific certainty.[48]

In today's society, words like *truth, rationality,* and *objectivity* only inspire unrealistic hopes for what science can accomplish;[49] unrealistic hopes in "a godlike objectivity" that can never be achieved by human beings moved by passion and subject to bias.[50] In reality, scientists often have personal values that influence (consciously or unconsciously) the questions they ask, the models or experiments used, the assumptions made, and the interpretation of the results of an experiment.[51] Scientific judgment is almost certainly influenced by one's belief about how government should regulate the economy, by one's institutional affiliation, or by other social and political attributes.[52]

In the end, all science "must be understood in the context of a particular group with particular practical interests and with a particular history."[53] K. C. Cole puts it more simply: "Like the rest of us, scientists tend to see what they expect to see. . . . Scientific objectivity is inevitably blurred by the biases built into human perception."[54] Nicholas Ashford offers a more detailed analysis:

> Science . . . insists that things are either true or untrue and, by marshalling established scientific conventions as the tests, encourages us to believe that no value judgment ever attends the establishment of truth. It is, however, clear that those who undertake scientific inquiry today, in fact, hold strong value-laden views concerning the use of their science. . . . There are also many ways to frame the scientific question

and to choose which data to collect and analyze. . . . By either speaking out about those values or by remaining silent, scientists exercise a value judgment about the way science [is] used.[55]

OBJECTIVITY AS A MATTER OF DEGREE

Walter Rosenbaum provides a good description of the attempt to insulate science from politics:

> Social and political bias can be particularly pernicious when not recognized or admitted by the experts. It is now evident that many technical controversies in policy making may not be resolvable by resort to scientific evidence and argument because scientific solutions will be permeated with social, political, and economic bias. Indeed, political controversy often subverts scientific inquiry. Experts can be readily, even unintentionally, caught up in the emotionally and politically polarizing atmosphere of such disputes, their judgment compromised. . . . Yet no barrier can be contrived to wholly insulate science from the contagion of social and economic bias.[56]

As is signaled in Rosenbaum's description, there is now a greater awareness that scientific advice is far from being independent input; that it is shaped by its own history and by its institutional and political contexts.[57] Scientific research is not carried out in isolation from the rest of society: "[S]erendipity and the expectation of intellectual autonomy cannot liberate the research system from the influence of societal norms."[58] Most observers now view science as a socially constructed process,[59] value laden,[60] and conceived in an arena that is based on deeply contested values in American society.[61] Science is a human construct that is influenced by personal biases even though it attempts to minimize them.[62] As Daniel Sarewitz makes clear, the search for truth is not independent from social, political, economic, or moral suasion: "The question at hand is not whether scientists search for truth but which truths they search for and how the directions of their search emerge from, and influence, culture."[63]

Scientists who perceive their own work as value-free and do not see themselves as seeking power can easily delude themselves about their own political involvement.[64] However, most scientists now understand that if science is conducted according to the rules established outside the profession, it can no longer be considered objective or free from bias.[65] Scientific evidence is interpreted through theories and hypotheses, and these are shaped by nonscientific factors.[66]

The old understanding assumed good science produced truth and that scientists deserved a special place in politics. The new understanding treats scientific knowledge as "a negotiated product of human inquiry, formed not only via interaction among scientists but also by research patrons and regulatory adversaries."[67] For the most part, scholars are now quite consistent in their recognition that scientific activities do not generate absolute or final "truth." Instead, it is understood that scientific activities produce contingent knowledge that is always subject to recall;[68] that science is a profoundly human endeavor, a product not of embodied minds but of actual people in social interaction.[69]

In the world of American public policymaking, scientists are sometimes portrayed as naïve, positing simple answers to complex problems.[70] Scientists' institutional contexts and scientific training, as well as the political culture prevalent in their particular country, influence the choices that they make.[71] In essence, the interaction of political culture, disciplinary priorities, and personal research ambitions influence the work of scientists as do scientists' individual backgrounds, observations, ambitions, and the constraints and opportunities provided by their scientific disciplines.[72] Stephen Bocking provides an example of such an instance when he documents how the personal concern of biologists for the protection of the environment led directly to their public call for research to be directed to benefit society.[73]

In sum, objectivity is now viewed as a matter of degree.[74] Accordingly, the science that is chosen to inform policy decisions is a reflection of society's prevailing cultural values and political milieu.[75] Scientists are no longer viewed as "very intelligent, deliberation people, looking for answers to the woes of society, unrestrained in their search for new problems and new solutions."[76] Scientists are human beings trying to exert some control over their lives.[77] Social interests and relationships "are every bit as critical in the formation of scientific consensus as in any other domain of human activity."[78] Not only cannot science deliver truth, but scientists, either tacitly or explicitly, "arrive at their verdict by considering what fits best with their view of the good or the beautiful or what will bring them happiness."[79]

THE SEARCH FOR A USEFUL TRUTH: LIMITED OBJECTIVITY

Those who have studied the science–policy linkage in the American public policymaking process offer ways for scientists to cope with the myriad problems they face in protecting the integrity of their work. One of the most prominent suggestions is for scientists to accept the fact that as human beings and citizens, they possess values and views that influence their work.[80] Scientists are asked to gain a deeper understanding of how science intersects with policy and to acknowledge the fact that isolating objective truths from human values and capturing what is most important about public life with science shape experts' attempts to inform policymaking.[81] In this regard, scientists—as the potency of science and technology grows and the global interdependence of society deepens—must now view progress more in terms of its human context.[82]

In a democratic setting, this means scientists should improve their understanding of the interplay of their own and other peoples' values in the policy process.[83] Simply put, if scientists are to be true to the scientific method, the claim that pure science is (and ought to be) value-free cannot be placed above critical inquiry.[84] One example of how science has begun to recognize and regulate the role of values in research is the now mandatory requirement that research be preapproved by human and animal subjects review boards. Any university scientist using a human or animal subject in research must submit their plans to a board comprised of peers from many disciplines. The research is evaluated ethically, with a goal of preventing abusive research practices.

Although the ultimate purpose and rationale of science is to enhance our knowledge and understanding of nature, humanity, and society, scientists should come to terms with their own private concerns and professional interests.[85] Scientists, to be effective, must speak to power in a political and bureaucratic context, and must speak a "useful truth," a truth that is always to be viewed in light of scientists' relationship with power.[86] If the facts tell the story, then the recommendation is that the scientific community be completely open about the lack of a consensus and explain the scientific reasons for it.[87] The specific values to be protected and advanced through policy research should not be hidden under a cloak of objectivity. Instead, they should be clarified openly by scientists in consultation and collaboration with others in particular decision contexts.[88]

Scientists must come to understand that although their scientific inquiry may claim to be value neutral, the uses of scientific information in policymaking are not.[89] There simply are no effective strategies for protecting science or scientists against the subversion of values.[90] Everyone connected to the policymaking process, including scientists, must come to grips with the understanding that the power of science rests in the very thing that leads naïve critics to attack it: the obligation of scientists to change their views as new data are found and hypotheses are tested. While scientists cannot control the use of their science, they can be more active in publicizing the importance of the scientific method and the process that makes it so valuable—checking and rechecking, verification and replication, and attempts to falsify claims.[91] The more the public and policymakers know about the way scientists go about their business, the better chance scientists have in establishing credibility in the policy world.

In completing their research according to the principles of the scientific method, scientists are not encouraged to become self-reflective.[92] Instead, scientists are simply asked to conduct their research in a value-free manner.[93] However, according to Aaron Wildavsky, what we need is not objectivity in the sense of having no views but a willingness to consider different hypotheses and, when considering each, to be guided by evidence.

> What is wanted is not scientific neuters but scientists with differing points of view and similar scientific standards. . . . The integrity of science as a process of seeking knowledge does not depend on the honesty or even the capability of individual scientists. . . . Instead, science depends on institutions that maintain competition among scientists and scientific groups who are numerous, dispersed, and independent.[94]

It is certainly clear that the abutment of science with moral values is straining the relationship between science and society.[95] And, while most scientists recognize that science is not carried out in a sociological vacuum, few scientists would admit that their work bears the traces of their philosophical or religious convictions.[96] Among many scientists there remains a strong commitment to an unbiased search for answers.[97] Scientists bridle at the thought that their research must conform to standards of "political correctness,"[98] and believe that they are in a good position to detect and weed out partisanship and the loss of credibility that comes with such bias.[99]

However, as Wildavsky noted, the crucial steps for achieving at least a limited objectivity take place in disciplinary institutions, not in the minds of scientists. If scientific fields become so narrow that the possibility of blind review of research is eliminated, then the social connections and personal reputation of scientists can easily become more important than the quality of research. So scientists in a subfield must be sufficiently numerous. They should also be dispersed—if all the research in an area is conducted in one or two labs, then along with the loss of anonymity in the review process, we also generate a kind of inbreeding of ideas that can lead to lack of creativity and unwillingness to challenge conventional wisdom. Finally, independence means that scientists are not beholden to such a small number of funding outlets that they have too much incentive to alter their research to fit the funding agency's desires.

Scientists are often perceived publicly as being a humble group of truth-seekers. But the reality is sometimes different.[100] The question we are interested in is: When scientists are drawn into the pulling and hauling of politics, is their freedom and objectivity instantaneously and completely lost?[101] We argue that it is not, and that limited objectivity is an achievable goal. But the goal cannot be achieved by individual scientists alone. Scientists consider themselves able to cope with client demands and at the same time able to maintain the scientific validity of their work by persuading clients that the judgment of the scientific community is important.[102] While that may be true in many cases, it is important to have the possibility of many clients/funding agencies (government and private), and the institution of academic tenure, to provide scientists with the independence to resist the pressures of clients.

Still, many scientists continue to distance their work from questions of values or politics,[103] and continue to honor the ideal of objectivity.[104] The scientific community, as a whole, maintains its stubborn insistence that scientific research can be carried out objectively regardless of the source of funding.[105] Many scientists acknowledge the relevance of values but argue that just because science is not value-free, because it is a human enterprise, does not make all science normative.[106] Through this acknowledgment, scientists show a certain amount of support for the idea of limited objectivity. Still, some—like Edward O. Wilson— aspire to the ideal of complete and untainted objectivity:

> Can we devise a universal litmus test for scientific statements and with it eventually attain the grail of objective truth? Current opinion holds that we cannot and never will. Scientists and philosophers have largely abandoned the search for absolute objectivity and are content to ply their trade elsewhere. I think otherwise and will risk heresy: The answer could well be yes. Criteria of objective truth might be attainable through empirical investigation. . . . No one should suppose that objective truth is impossible to attain, even when the most committed philosophers urge us to acknowledge that incapacity. In particular, it is too early for scientists, the foot soldiers of epistemology, to yield ground so vital to their mission. Although seemingly chimerical at times, no intellectual vision is more important and daunting than that of objective truth based on scientific understanding.[107]

In the end, however, the motives of individual scientists probably do not affect the quest for limited objectivity, as long as institutions are in place to protect it. Brian Silver argues that it does not matter if scientists' motivations spring predominantly from irrational sources or that their work is not the result of "completely unprejudiced searchers-after-knowledge, floating free of established dogma."[108] In support of this contention, Silver offers up the examples of Newton and Boyle, two outstanding scientists whose findings stood the test of time even though they both saw their science as the means to reveal God's creation. In short, according to Silver, "A scientist's beliefs and actions may be as strange as any other man's, but what drives a scientist is almost irrelevant to those of his discoveries that stand the test of time."[109]

MAKING THE TRANSITION TO ADVOCACY

Despite the skepticism of policymakers and other scholars, many scientists continue to honor the ideal of objectivity, at least in its limited form. At one time the responsibility for the integrity and productivity of science was assigned to the scientists themselves without realizing that there were interests within science.[110] That is not true today. In most disciplines, scientists are numerous and dispersed; institutions of peer review remain anonymous, review boards prevent abuse of subjects, and academic tenure protects the independence of the researcher.

However, modern pressures on scientists to play a greater part in the policy process put added strain on the attempt to achieve some form of objectivity, even if it is a limited objectivity. Nonetheless, scientists are learning to cope. As readers will see in the next chapter, scientists are learning the ways of the policy world, participating as scientists, citizens, and advocates. But, in some cases, the costs are high. Science is being used in ways that some consider not only unethical but also immoral. On the other hand, the role of the scientist as an advocate in the policy arena might also have beneficial effects. We will explore these ideas of scientific advocacy in the following chapter.

REFLECTIVE QUESTIONS

Question 6-1

According to Associated Press reporter Rebecca Boone (*Idaho Statesman,* June 6, 2008), in one of his decisions U.S. District Magistrate Judge Mike Williams stated that the Fish and Wildlife Service wrongly downplayed scientific evidence and emphasized uncertainties in findings rather than relying on "the best scientific data available."

a. Explain what you understand to be the meaning of "the best scientific data available."
b. Discuss the part that expertise plays in making such rulings. In other words, what kind of expertise must the parties (judge, Fish and Wildlife Service, scientists) bring to the table?

Question 6-2

Dr. James Hansen is known to have said: "What I am an advocate for is the scientific process."

   a. Describe how you would explain the difference between a scientist and an advocate. Do you think it is possible to be both an advocate and a scientist? Explain why you believe what you do.
   b. What are the major assumptions and major tenets of the scientific process that some say would protect a scientist from societal bias?

SUGGESTED READINGS

Patrick Hamlett, *Understanding Technological Politics: A Decision-Making Approach* (Englewood Cliffs, NJ: Prentice Hall, 1992).

Sheila Jasanoff and Marybeth Long Martello, eds., *Earthly Politics: Local and Global in Environmental Governance* (Cambridge, MA: MIT Press, 2004).

Roger Masters, *Beyond Relativism: Science and Human Values* (Hanover, NH: University of New England Press, 1993).

David Orrell, *Apollo's Arrow: The Science of Prediction and the Future of Everything* (Toronto: Harper Collins, 2007).

Don Price, *The Scientific Estate* (Cambridge, MA: Harvard University Press, 1965).

CHAPTER 7

Advocacy

Objectivity, and the willingness to consider new scientific or scholarly evidence on its merits, are among the few things that distinguish scientists, engineers, and other scholars from lay-persons in society. For this reason, scientists who become advocates for social or political causes do so at some peril of losing both their objectivity and their credibility.

Ellis Cowling, North Carolina State University, *Seminar on Ethics*, 1988.

SCIENTISTS UNDER ATTACK

As described in the last chapter, scientists face a very difficult task in balancing the tenets of the scientific method with the desire to participate in a value-laden public policymaking process. Two things come to mind. The first deals with the idea that science, and scientists, can make things better. Take, for example, the words of Mark Tercek—the president and chief executive officer of *The Nature Conservancy*—who, as quoted earlier, describes the importance of scientific objectivity to the vision of the conservancy's mission. Yet later, in speaking of the conservancy's priorities, Tercek offers this thought: "I believe our scientific expertise and research should do more than inform our own actions; we have the ability to influence those forces that have the power to disrupt—or protect—our most valuable land and waters."[1] As explained by Tercek, the faith in science's ability to inform policy is strong, and, to be more specific, there is nothing inherently contentious about the same people providing both good science and good policy. It is simply the way things are done. But, we know that linking science to policy is a very difficult proposition. Whether we like it or not, complications arise when scientists enter the public policymaking process.

The second thing that comes to mind illustrates one of the most uncomfortable complications of the science–policy linkage. When a scientist does speak outside the confines of the scientific process, he or she is often subject to an enormous negative backlash. A good example of this is provided by a quote from

Karen Wright in a 1991 *New York Times Magazine* article that is cited by Mark Bowen in his book *Censoring Science*. In the article, Wright offers the following description of James Hansen, one of the most prominent—if not the most prominent—scientists exploring the climate change issue.

> It's not his science that gets Jim Hansen in trouble—it's his style. Hansen has all the moves of a hustler but none of the guile. Backed by a body of exhaustive and universally respected research, he routinely flouts his profession's tacit restrictions on categorical and unauthorized statements while maintaining the pacific innocence of a curious child.[2]

Clearly, the ability of scientists to effectively participate in the policy process and still retain their scientific credibility comes into doubt. Scientists have always had the ability to mobilize public support because they enjoy "considerable public prestige and trust."[3] Now they are being asked to use that trust to impact the world of environmental policymaking, to forgo the rules of good science in favor of advocacy.[4]

The question we are interested in exploring is a very straightforward one: Do scientists serve the nation best when they function as an "apolitical elite," or are they more effective when they recognize that they are "in the battle rather than above it?"[5] Given the circumstances within which they must operate, scientists find themselves in a very precarious position. When scientists enter the policymaking world there is never an explicit mention of values, although most everyone accepts the fact that it is often a deep difference in values and interests that motivates actors in the policy process, including scientists.[6] It is certainly understood by scientists that, at best, it may be inappropriate to publicly discuss policy ideas that possess a high degree of uncertainty,[7] and at worst, seeking political victories through science diminishes the constructive role that scientific expertise can play in the policy process.[8]

The very essence of science—the ability to produce objective results—is at risk because scientists are coming under immense pressure to provide more definitive answers than their current research can sustain.[9] One set of scholars summarizes this dilemma as follows:

> There has been concern that the close advisory role that scientists have come to play in government has meant that scientists too often lend their reputation for objectivity to legitimize positions and policies determined by government for reasons other than science. It may also be the case that the scientist's reputation for objectivity may be used to legitimize the special interests of some subfields or some scientific networks. In their zeal to obtain what they view as their fair share of attention, science advocates may exaggerate the significance of their findings. In the long run, such exaggeration may damage the overall status of the scientific community as well as distort the overall balance of effort directed to the many important science questions needing answers.[10]

WHAT POLICYMAKERS WANT FROM SCIENTISTS

In the American public policymaking process the relationship between knowledge and power has proven to be more contentious than ever.[11] Policy debates require factual information about the likely costs and consequences of political action or inaction. Much like a courtroom, the policymaking environment is often adversarial, and opposing parties want to marshal as much evidence as possible for their preferred position. In a courtroom, the most credible witnesses are those who are bright, objective, and who have no personal or ideological interest in the outcome. In the policy arena, scientists fit this description perfectly.

So policymakers want scientists to provide the evidence that they possess. Yet the technical complexity of their evidence means that unlike judges and jurors in a courtroom, ordinary policymakers and the media are usually unequipped to make accurate interpretations of that evidence. Therefore, policymakers want scientists to explain what interpretation should be given to scientific findings, rather than just the science itself.[12] And to provide added credibility, policymakers want scientists to actively participate in this interpretation,[13] insisting that scientists have a responsibility to provide such advice and to discuss the policy implications of their work.[14] But tensions arise from such demands.

One of the most unsettling demands for scientists is the frequent request by policymakers to provide scientific findings that support specific ideological beliefs.[15] Of course, policymakers want to claim that science supports their decisions. But often, this use of science is disingenuous, with politicians purposely ignoring credible data because it does not support their political views.[16] When scientists participate in this sort of open advocacy, it not only affects scientific objectivity, it undermines the relationship between scientists and policymakers.

Another problem can arise when scientists are not simply independent, disinterested participants in the policy process but, due to the nature of the policy under consideration, might actually stand to profit personally should government authorize more support for their type of research. In such cases, scientists are sometimes pushed into the position of advocating, of using "technological magic in order to dazzle the vulgar voter into letting them have millions for the advancement of scientific truth."[17] In such cases, scientists who participate put their reputation with their fellow scientists on the line; policymakers are taking no such risk, adding further strains to the science–policy relationship.

These tensions and strains in the relationship between scientists and policymakers accumulate over time, and create a situation in which policymakers (and the public) cannot differentiate between when scientists are presenting their scientific findings and when scientists are advocating for a particular policy position.[18] Not knowing the difference corrupts both the scientific enterprise and the policy process.[19] If public policymakers come to believe that scientific findings are simply an expression of a scientist's political beliefs, and not based on the scientific method, then over time scientific information will play a diminishing role in policymaking.[20]

INCREASE IN ADVOCACY: THE CALL TO SPEAK OUT

Emerging environmental issues have led to an increase in using scientists as policy advocates.[21] Indeed, the idea that scientists—especially those concerned with the environment—should leave their idealized world of detachment and objectivity to become full-fledged participants in the policy process appears to be gaining strength. Although many scientists continue to maintain a professional tradition of "political neutrality toward social causes," more and more scientists are taking public positions.[22]

Scientists are often viewed as the only ones with the knowledge and ability to translate the rapid deterioration of the global environment into terms that will prompt outrage from the general public and action from policymakers.[23] Those who fear ecological destruction argue that scientists have an obligation to inform public policy, an obligation to become political players in the environmental policymaking process.

It is suggested that science has moved into a new era, one requiring thought beyond just solving nature's puzzle.

> The most important problems science must now address, including those related to sustainability, can no longer be seen as reducible to mechanistic explanation, because they are frequently embedded in complex systems with inherently unpredictable properties that involve global events or trends and have global implications that affect every person, indeed every creature, on the planet.[24]

In this new era, scientists can be chastised for refusing to advocate. Scientists have been called irresponsible if they do not to speak out in defense of environmental protection.[25] Academic scientists, in particular, have been chastised for remaining on the sidelines while the White House and Congress have ignored them or made controversial decisions that ran counter to their conclusions.[26] In contrast, other scientists have been cast by environmental activists as bold for taking a public stance in favor of environmental protection.[27]

So in the end, scientists face a dilemma. Their peers argue against advocacy while activists and policymakers demand it. Some observers complain that the failure of scientists to educate Americans about the dangers of ecological destruction is the primary reason for policy failure, and contend that scientists need to stop pretending to be above the political fray or they will be consigned to irrelevance in policymaking.[28] We are struck by the irony that the risk either way—whether scientists become advocates or not—is that the long-term relevance of science in policymaking will be diminished.

FEARS OF THE SCIENTIFIC COMMUNITY

Many scientists are reluctant to become politically active, fearing that doing so would compromise their reputation for objectivity as scientists.[29] Many scientists also tend not to speak out because the flavor of the debate is so political.[30] A scientist's political capital is his or her professional reputation for providing objective information.[31] Many scientists believe that their status with other scientists is a good deal more important than their public image. The more a scientist becomes identified with one end of the environmental spectrum, the more he or she is likely to be referred to as an environmentalist rather than a scientist.[32]

Scientists are often ill equipped "to negotiate safely the quicksands of policy development."[33] In many instances, science has become little more than a mechanism for marketing competing political agendas, and scientists have become leading members of advertising campaigns. The uproar over the publication of *The Skeptical Environmentalist* in 2001—condemned by environmentalists for being extremely optimistic about claims that the environment was not getting worse—is a good example of a heated controversy about the environment that "spilled over from the environmental community onto the pages of leading newspapers and magazines around the world," resulting in a contentious public debate among scientists that was carried out in the broader societal setting.[34] In this type of environment, scientists have a legitimate fear of being "burned" if they bring their findings forward into the public policymaking world.[35] Scientists become "loath to leave their laboratories and get involved in the public arena" as it is unlikely to contribute to their professional careers because public outreach is not counted as an "important, positive element of high-caliber professional behavior."[36]

At the same time, it is naïve to think that scientists are not cognizant of how their advice shapes their individual fortunes as well as how it shapes public policy.[37] And, in the end, it is the scientists themselves who decide whether to participate in public affairs or avoid such responsibilities.[38] They can choose if, how, and when to become actively engaged in policy and politics.[39]

For those scientists who do choose to publicly advocate for policy positions, there is danger. Government scientists have been fired for publicly supporting scientific hypotheses that fly in the face of prevailing political dogma; others have been forced to publicly support political positions that conflict with their own scientific convictions.[40]

Lapses in the process of scientific self-regulation have "called into question the capacity of scientists to vouch for the integrity of their published findings."[41] Scientists can be labeled a "hired gun" for an organization, promoting the interests of and acting as advocates for the policies of the organization.[42] There exists a good chance that scientists could very easily end up being viewed as just another political, rather than scientific, advocate.[43]

ADVERSARIAL SCIENCE AND SKEPTICAL SCIENTISTS

The trend in environmental policymaking appears to be moving away from the goal of achieving scientific consensus and toward a more adversarial use of science in which scientific experts are used to support opposing sides of conflicts.[44] Policymakers who oppose certain scientific output question the data and the interpretation of the data, selecting a rival scientific finding more in keeping with their own political interests.

> The result is embarrassment and frustration for all: policy actors feel cheated because their experts have failed to put together a watertight case, immune from the skepticism of the opposition, and the scientists are injured by what they see as the gross insensitivity of the policy process . . . to the finely-balanced machinery of the scientific method.[45]

The end result is that the "capacity of scientific expertise to contribute to dispute resolution is therefore negated, and claims to authoritativeness must collapse, as political adversaries call upon highly credentialed and well-respected experts to bolster conflicting political positions."[46]

In today's adversarial science–policy model, both sides in technological disputes try to discredit the scientific expertise of the other side, thereby "reducing the influence of expertise in general and casting doubt on the ability to find unbiased, reliable scientific or technical advice."[47] Zachary Smith delineates the tactics used by those seeking to limit or discredit the use of scientific opinions. They include: (1) suppressing analysis and data; (2) conducting scientific proceedings in private; (3) putting scientists sympathetic to certain ideological positions on boards; (4) magnifying or manufacturing uncertainty; (5) punishing or ridiculing whistleblowers who expose misuse of science; and (6) equating fringe scientific opinion with mainstream scientific opinion, thus giving the public the perception that there is serious disagreement in the scientific community when there is very little disagreement among respected scientists.[48]

Because of the predominance of this adversarial science mode of policymaking, the public assumes that for any scientific issue there will always be some scientists who are in agreement and some in disagreement, as well as others who will invariably change their minds.[49] If so, then science is no more than a strategic and tactical resource in ideological debates in which advocates offer a particular "spin," "cherry pick," or even misuse information to present their preferred action.[50] Scientists view this as the perversion of science by politics.[51]

An especially pernicious problem for scientists is the professional skeptic scientist. These are people who may have scientific credentials, but who have crossed over to become full-time ideologically motivated advocates. Scientists are warned to never debate an ideologue because they are bound by the limits of their data, whereas ideologues are not.[52] It is the extreme arguments of hired-gun skeptics (also called contrarians[53]) that almost always appear more authoritative in a public arena because these "debunkers of science tend to be better communicators."[54] As all good politicians have learned, the "sound bite" is more persuasive than a long, technical argument. And sound bites tend to win political debates— once reported, the time and space required to expose and refute the lies cannot compete with glib quips about how trees and volcanoes cause smog.[55]

The arguments of skeptical scientists put the scientific community in a conundrum because the scientific process puts great faith in disagreement among scientists. In fact, such disagreement is valued as a healthy sign of a policy process in which rival views are pitched against one another.[56] But by acting as an ideological "hired gun," the skeptical scientist is acting in bad faith, outside the norms of scientific inquiry. The temptation, then, is for traditional scientists to criticize the skeptic and to challenge his or her very credentials. However, in an adversarial policy environment, this tactic tends to backfire. Skeptical scientists and their financial backers will only turn the table and criticize the credibility (and perhaps the personal life) of the traditional scientist. By engaging in confrontation, the traditional scientist provokes actions that wind up making all scientists look like politicians.

It appears to be a no-win situation for scientists.[57] If scientists accept the challenge to debate, they may inadvertently give substance to the bogus ideas of their opponents, and provoke counterattacks on their own credibility. If scientists decline to debate, the implication is that the scientific debate is closed when in fact it is just beginning. Scientists react badly to demands like this in part because the word "debate" is a rather poor description of the way disagreements get hashed out in science. Science is a deliberative, yet still competitive, enterprise, in which each side is duty bound to fairly consider all arguments and data that bear on the matter at hand. In the war of sound bites, the people who feel free to lie and distort can always win.[58]

Although most scientists generally try to limit their advice to scientific issues within their expertise or at least clearly distinguish between science and personal opinion, skeptic scientists frequently fail to abide by this standard in their publications. Skeptic scientists are often perceived as more credible precisely because their views conflict with the consensus of peer-reviewed science. Their testimony is accepted as proof that the peer review process has failed and that unsound science is being used for major decisions.[59] A frequently voiced example of such use is the Bush administration's lack of movement regarding global warming, in which skeptics are cited in support of the view that scientists still are not sure exactly how the processes take place.[60]

WHAT SHOULD SCIENTISTS PROVIDE?

Objectivity, Citizenship, and Accessibility

It is typical to ask all entities impacting policymaking to exhibit some very basic characteristics. They should be accurate, trustworthy, objective, timely, and accessible.[61] As depicted throughout this work, for scientists, the ideal of objectivity stands out. Some maintain that the only way for lowering the risk to scientists and the temptation of policymakers to interfere with the conduct of science is to maintain an indirect linkage between science and policy.[62] For good policymaking to take place there must be a dividing line between science (based on facts) and advocacy (based on values) such that facts remain the province of scientists and values remain the province of policymakers.[63] Society has developed ways to sort out the difference between facts and values by using the scientific method and certification by peer review.[64]

Scientists are directed to avoid the trap of mixing personal policy preferences and judgments with scientific information and expression. However, some argue that it is important to distinguish between scientists as experts and scientists as citizens.[65] In the role of expert, the scientist is the person whom we consult for facts and logic. In the role of citizen, the scientist is a concerned individual trying to influence decisions.

> Scientists should be free to investigate the natural and social worlds as they see fit . . . they have a duty to communicate more than just the "bare facts" of science. As responsible citizens, they should be prepared to bring out the social implications of their own work and their colleagues' work, voicing their optimism and enthusiasm where appropriate and their concerns and reservations where they have them.[66]

The boundary between scientist and citizen, however, is often ill-defined, especially because research can be intensely political in nature. Scientists compromise their reputation as scientists when they do not know how to separate their role as citizens, in which they have the right to express any opinion, and their role as scientists, in which their opinions should be based on well-established facts.[67]

Of course, we have seen that reaching the ideal of absolute objectivity is quite problematic. In contrast, accessibility—in the form of transparency—appears to be a much more realistic goal. George E. Brown makes this case. He suggests that the scientific community

> needs to make a concerted effort to counter the skeptic scientists by scrupulously ensuring that scientific assessments are open to all scientifically credible views, educating policymakers on the role of scientific peer review, and responding clearly and cogently to the scientific and technical criticisms raised by their critics. The scientific community has a civic duty to directly and actively rebut any inaccurate, misleading, or distorted scientific claims that are made in the public arena.[68]

One straightforward way for scientists to exhibit this openness is simply by announcing when they have stepped out of a scientific role and into the role of political advocate.[69] Another way is for scientists to do a better job of communicating more realistic and appropriate expectations about what science can and cannot do.[70]

Better Communication and Better Education

In recent years social scientists have documented a loud and clear call for scientists to better communicate with both the public and policymakers alike, to better tell their story,[71] to structure and present scientific research activities in a manner that helps serve both societal goals and the goals of science.[72] This call came about because of poor communication by scientists about the state of scientific knowledge and its significance to decision-makers and the public, as well as an inadequate integration of research results into environmental decision-making.[73] One set of observers describes the quandary for scientists.

> Scientists excel at research; creating knowledge is their forte. But presenting this knowledge to the public is something else altogether. It's here that scientists and their allies are stumbling in our information-overloaded society—even as scientific information itself is being yanked to center stage in high-profile debates. Scientists have traditionally communicated with the rest of us by inundating the public with facts; but data dumps often don't work. So in today's America, those seeking a broader public acceptance of science must rethink their strategies for conveying knowledge.[74]

This call for scientists to better communicate has taken several forms. Scientists are warned that effective communication of complex scientific findings requires simplification and a better vocabulary for discussing science with laypeople.[75] Scientists must get away from their "mystifying jargon" and "bewildering models."[76] Scientists are asked to communicate their research results in a more straightforward manner, one that helps the public (and policymakers) better understand and interpret complex environmental issues.[77]

However, it is not easy for scientists to communicate information to the public in a meaningful way.[78] Scientists generally have no formal training whatsoever in communication. They often have developed their communication skills only among the community of scientists, or, in some cases, with university students. In both cases the jargon of science need not be greatly altered to get the message across. When the audience is the public, the media, and policymakers, however, the stereotypes of the "mad scientist" or "absent-minded professor" are much easier for scientists to fulfill than to portray themselves as astute communicators.

Scientists must improve their understanding of the policy process and take more seriously the act of communicating within the American public policymaking system.[79] Scientists need to put aside their fear of damaging their careers and communicate directly with the public about their work.[80] To start the process of improved communication, scientists must first gain a better understanding of what the public knows about science, and how public attitudes are formed and expressed through the political participation system.[81] The next step is to help the public and policymakers to better understand how the scientific process works; to effectively communicate the notion that science based on doubt and uncertainty is not to be feared but welcomed as part of both the scientific and policymaking processes.[82] So scientists need to educate themselves, learning policy and communication skills, so that they can educate policymakers and the general public.[83] Alan Leshner summarizes this view:

> Instead of simply increasing public understanding of science, scientists need to have a real dialogue with members of the public, listening to their concerns, their priorities, and the questions they would like us to help answer. . . . Scientists are learning that a respectful dialogue with the public is much more effective in finding common ground than a more traditional, instructional monologue. [Engaging with the public] should bring scientists into closer proximity with their fellow citizens, which in turn should give each group a far better understanding and greater empathy for the perspective of the other.[84]

Some critics of the way scientific information is communicated speak directly to the marketing, or selling, of science—the need for more effective packaging and presentation of scientific results,[85] or "thoughtful public relations to convert the dull, scientific knowledge into interesting, convincing public knowledge."[86] There is, however, a disdain among scientists to do such marketing. (It's not enjoyable work for them, and not what they were trained to do.) All in all, despite their misgivings, scientists are being asked to learn how to communicate scientific findings in a "sound-bite oriented, media-dominated world."[87]

More and more scientific organizations are now encouraging their members to do such marketing, to better communicate with the public. And scientists are responding. There are indications that an increasing number of scientists are becoming active, good communicators.[88] In recent times, scientists are doing a better job of producing summaries of their research findings that are written in plain English,[89] and creating feasible lines of communication between themselves, policymakers, and other users of scientific information.[90] However, this type of action does not necessarily alleviate the fear of some scientists who still perceive this type of communication as publicity seeking, whereas others simply believe that communicating with nonscientific audiences is not worth the effort because the scientific reward system does not value such efforts.[91] John Myers and Joshua Reichert voice this fear:

> there is a vital need to translate [scientific] information to the general public as well as policymakers, in ways that prompt action needed to preserve what remains of the planet's natural resources. This is not a traditional role for scientists and it is not an easy one for them to play. It calls on men and women who have typically defined themselves as observers and analysts to become more actively engaged in advocating the protection of those systems that are the object of their study . . . scientists have generally avoided becoming involved in the rather messy process of shaping public policy [and] have often been criticized by their peers and penalized within their disciplines for such involvement.[92]

It is often observed that both the public and policymakers lack an accurate understanding of science, especially when it comes to understanding the science surrounding environmental problems.[93] The claim is that most citizens and leaders find scientific matters "forbiddingly difficult if not terrifying."[94] The best answer to this deficiency is fairly straightforward: citizens and policymakers need to receive a good portion of science education.[95] However, since the days of Sputnik this has been attempted in the United States, without noticeable improvement. Hence, the initiative is left to scientists.

So, the scientific community needs to invest much greater time and energy in educating members of Congress and the public about the functions and characteristics of science, including providing guidance on the proper linkages between science and policy.[96] The scientific community could do a better job of raising the public's scientific literacy.[97] It is even suggested that by raising scientific literacy among the public, scientists can bring about more open and democratic controls on the use of technology.[98]

If science literacy is an important goal, then it is up to scientists to demystify science by explaining how science is connected to the ever-changing social and political realities of scientific research.[99] We conclude that educating the public is an integral part of every scientist's career. As stated by one pair of scientists, "If those of us who are most familiar with the beauty and intricacy of nature, and its essential role in supporting humanity, will not come to nature's—and thus humanity's—defense, who will?"[100]

Consensus

As noted in the introductory chapter, there is a great deal of faith put in the idea of reaching scientific consensus. When the scientific community reaches such consensus on environmental issues, then action is not only recommended, it is required.[101] Moreover, as the prospect of scientific consensus increases so does the likelihood of more effective policymaking.[102] Scientific consensus on the cause and existence of the ozone hole over Antarctica is given a large amount of credit for developing an effective policy to phase out the production and consumption of chlorofluorocarbons (CFCs).[103] And if one looks at the current movement toward a sustainable policy on climate change, one also witnesses the fact that this movement is—at least partially— based on a general acceptance of the growing scientific consensus about anthropogenic changes to the global climatic system.[104]

Yet reaching scientific consensus on questions that are more than marginally relevant to policy is—just like the possibility of objectivity—an ideal, a myth, and a nearly impossible task.[105] Because of the need to initiate and formulate policy in a timely nature, as opposed to the long-term nature that characterizes the scientific process, it is simply unreasonable to expect policymakers to wait for scientific consensus before acting.[106]

To illustrate the complexities of achieving scientific consensus, let us look more closely at the issue of global warming, a prominent—maybe the most prominent—issue on the environmental front today. On this issue we have a mechanism for consensus that the scientific community does not ordinarily possess—the International Panel on Climate Change (IPCC). This United Nations panel employs hundreds of scientists who meet at regular intervals to evaluate current research and describe what consensus exists to policymakers.[107] Despite this, some argue that what is needed is "a more visible and increasingly certain international scientific consensus about humans' impact on the global climate."[108] But the nature of the scientific method will not produce true consensus until long after the findings are desired by policymakers. In a field as broad as climate research, the number of scientists and their disciplinary diversity means that it takes a long time for research to be evaluated by the field, and especially for competing views to be convincingly evaluated by empirical evidence. This is normal science, and normal science usually has debates, not consensus.

Still, one would hope that the IPCC, after all its diverse input and lengthy deliberations, could accurately convey the state of consensus on climate change. However, more than 400 prominent scientists from more than two dozen countries recently voiced significant objections to major aspects of the so-called "consensus on manmade global warming."[109] In fact, some even argue that there is no scientific consensus on global warming, as advocates often claim, and even if there was, consensus would not be all that important: "Galileo may have been the only man of his day who believed the Earth revolved around the sun, but he was right!"[110]

The lack of a scientific consensus, which is a normal situation, does matter.[111] In the absence of scientific consensus there will always be legitimate scientific experts available to support the opposing sides in any conflict, and, hence, the capacity of scientific expertise to contribute to dispute resolution is negated. In the end, most observers note that scientific consensus is only one of the factors needed for achieving political consensus on environmental issues,[112] and that scientific consensus—even when it exists—does not necessarily generate political consensus.[113]

> [T]he optimistic view that consensus within the scientific community on "facts" will foster consensus among decision-makers on policy is somewhat naïve. . . . [T]here is no straightforward method of "deriving" policy from knowledge, there is no simple, linear relationship between the state of knowledge in a particular issue area and consensus on substantive policy measures. Research-based knowledge may in various ways inform policy decisions, but neither the scientific method nor the conclusions it produces can ever *resolve* conflicts over interests or values.[114]

Media

One of the driving forces behind the public politics of environmentalism is adroit media manipulation,[115] an organized force admiringly described as the "media juggernaut."[116] From the perspective of scientists, the influence of science in public policy is sharply limited by media misunderstanding and distortion.[117] It is certainly true that through the interpretation and presentation of scientific findings to the public, journalists can skillfully shape public perception, and these journalists often operate without full knowledge of the scientific research.[118] Furthermore, what the media usually cares about most are "catchy" stories, not scientific results.[119]

One source of the problem is the professional requirement within the media to present both sides of issues. However, the need to present an opposing viewpoint—any opposing viewpoint—sometimes results in legitimacy given to the views of a minority fringe. When this occurs in some contexts—for instance, when a small group of 20 counter-protesters are quoted to balance the coverage of the views of the 100,000 protesters—regular people can evaluate this fairly. But for technical scientific issues this is impossible. For example, in the global warming debate, one critic argues that the media has largely ignored mainstream scientists, as "this soap opera is kept alive by a dwindling number of deniers constantly tapped for interviews by journalists who pretend to look for balance."[120] But even if journalists are not biased, their professional obligation to seek balance will keep the skeptical scientists in business.

Perhaps out of frustration with inaccurate media coverage, or because of self-ish desires to manipulate it, there has been a growing willingness on the part of scientists to sidestep traditional checks and balances by releasing premature scientific findings. This practice detracts from the quality of the scientific information the public receives and, at the same time, erodes public confidence in society's experts.[121] Scientists are charged with ignoring conventional scientific processes to present their views in opinion pieces aimed at policymaking, the media, and the general public rather than their fellow scientists. This action not only tarnishes scientists' reputations, it undermines the functioning of good science.[122]

Scientists are warned that for the good of science they must show restraint when interpreting their findings and not go to the media before the publication of the results.[123] Despite their assumptions to the contrary, media coverage of controversies may not necessarily be improved by better dissemination of scientific information,[124] especially if the quality of that information is suspect. The media have their own requirements for balance, and use their own judgment for what is salient and what will "sell." When members of the scientific community participate in the politicization of science through the media, both the scientists and the policy process are likely to be discredited.[125]

One of the more confounding problems faced by scientists is responding to the compromising effects on their credibility and objectivity when attacks are made in the media about industry-funded research findings. Debates in the media about such research are common and polarizing. A good example of one such recent debate is the one between chemical industry-based scientists and those scientists critical of industry-sponsored research findings being accepted as valid science. The critics of industry-funded research point to the dominant and sometimes improper role that industry-funded scientists play on committees and panels that make recommendations about public policy that directly relates to the industry that employs the scientists.[126] Industry-based scientists Craig Barrow and James Conrad, on the other hand, propose that such criticism is "mistaken and counterproductive to societal interests." [127] They further argue that mechanisms such as disclosure of funding, peer review, and the scientific process itself, provide effective safeguards against biased science.[128] Other scientists are not so convinced. One such scientist is Jennifer Sass, who documents several examples of what she refers to as biased industry science findings that were reported in the scientific literature: a 1993 Environmental Protection Agency (EPA) study that shows selection bias by industry scientists; a 2004 submission to the EPA by industry that exhibited bias due to financial sponsorship; and the well-documented tobacco industry efforts in 2001 to obscure the contribution of second-hand smoke to disease by using what they considered "sound science."[129]

These public debates, carried out in the media and involving industry-based scientists, touch all scientists because they focus attention on the fact that both the public and policymakers have a difficult time differentiating good (unbiased) science from bad (biased) science, and scientists are often asked to respond to such uncertainty through the media, by explaining the meaning of such terms as "peer review" and "sound science." Along these lines, Chris Mooney argues that calls for peer review and sound science are sometimes used by industry-friendly scientists to stall efforts to protect the environment.[130] A specific recent example of such action is the ethanol manufacturers' call for slowing down the rush to judgment on ethanol's climate impact because the science has not been "adequately proven or even quantified."[131]

The way scientists are supposed to respond to such public debates and attacks on their credibility is by becoming more active in the public side of the debate, managing their results and responses in a way that better educates the public and policymakers alike, and doing so through media outlets. In this regard, Mooney and Matthew Nisbet call on scientists to "package their research to resonate with specific elements of the public,"[132] and Jane Lubchenco suggests that it is critically important for scientists to "speak the language of lay people when talking to non-scientists."[133] Once again, we are looking at the idea of framing issues to better inform policy, and in this case, it is a question of whether scientists are up to the task of doing a more effective job—especially through the media—of explaining, defending, and protecting the ideals of the scientific process.

WHAT DO SCIENTISTS THINK?

The simple truth is that while it may be a scientist's responsibility to engage in sociopolitical reflection, in the end, it is policymakers who must make the final decisions.[134] Scientists, like all interested parties, are just one part of the policymaking equation, asked to provide input but not responsible for the ultimate outcome. Hence, scientists must understand that they are more than welcome to participate as both scientists and citizens in the environmental policymaking process. Having said that, the dangers of advocating for particular policy solutions are clearly illustrated. No matter how you look at it, crossing the boundary between science and policymaking is an inherently difficult and complicated process, and one that should never be taken lightly.

As noted earlier, it is the scientists themselves who must decide when, if, and to what degree they enter the policymaking process. Scientists do think about how their world links to policymaking, and they have some very strong beliefs about how that should work. With this in mind, the following chapter highlights how scientists view their special connection to the environmental policymaking process.

REFLECTIVE QUESTIONS

Question 7-1

Juliet Eilperin (*Washington Post National Weekly*, 2008) talks about "high-profile skeptics such as University of Virginia professor emeritus S. Fred Singer and Virginia state climatologist Patrick J. Michaels" in the context of scientists who are challenging the idea that a scientific consensus exists on climate change.

    a. Define what scientific consensus means to you. In other words, how do we know when scientific consensus exists?
    b. Make the argument that we need to have skeptics (some use the term contrarians) if the scientific process is going to work according to its tenets.
    c. Discuss why critics accuse such skeptics as Professor Singer as denigrating the scientific process and disrupting the transfer of legitimate science into the policymaking process.

Question 7-2

Eric Ginsburg and Ellis Cowling (*Environment International*, 2003) argue that policymakers should refrain from asking and scientists should refrain from answering such questions as: "What do you think our society or agency or company ought to do?" Instead, in order that scientists can legitimately answer, the questions should be of the form, "If *this* management option were selected, then *that* is what I would expect to be the outcome."

Discuss the positive and negative aspects of restricting scientists to the form of questioning proposed by Ginsburg and Ellis. In addition, discuss if (and how) you would restrict testimony by scientists.

SUGGESTED READING

Bruce Bimber, *The Politics of Expertise in Congress: The Rise and Fall of the Office of Technology Assessment* (Albany: State University of New York, 1996).

Mark Bowen, *Censoring Science: Inside the Political Attack on Dr. James Hansen and the Truth of Global Warming* (New York: Dutton, 2008).

Paul Ehrlich and Anne Ehrlich, *Betrayal of Science and Reason: How Anti-Environmental Rhetoric Threatens Our Future* (Washington, DC: Island Press, 1996).

Janc Gregory and Steve Miller, *Science in Public: Communication, Culture, and Credibility* (New York: Plenum Press, 1998),

Bruce Smith, *The Advisors: Scientists in the Policy Process* (Washington, DC: Brookings Institution, 1992).

CHAPTER 8

Transcending Disciplines and Borders: Science, Canada, and the United States

To the extent that the gaps between the great branches of learning can be narrowed, diversity and depth of knowledge will increase.

Edward O. Wilson, *Consilience*, 1998.

SCIENCE AS A UNIVERSAL LANGUAGE

Science is often portrayed as a universal language that transcends all political and cultural differences between countries. As Edward O. Wilson states, "The laws of physics are in fact so accurate as to transcend cultural differences."[1] However, scientists working across national or disciplinary boundaries frequently discover that their assessments of causes and consequences differ from those of their counterparts in other countries and fields. And more likely than not, the difference in assessments is the result of differences in historical perspectives, intellectual priorities, and standards of proof or definitions.[2] As we discussed in an earlier chapter, objectivity has its limits, even for the most conscientious scientists.

This chapter explores how scientists themselves view the science–policy linkage. Given the vigor with which scientists debate scientific findings, it should come as no surprise that we find a diversity of views on the tensions that exist between science and policy. In this regard, Sheila Jasanoff makes an important point regarding the study of science across borders:

Setting the experiences of one country against another's offers salutary reminders of the degree to which even the homogeneous West is not univocal in its response to science and technology. Democracy, too, is not a single form of life but a common human urge to self-rule that finds expression in many different institutional and cultural arrangements.[3]

Because culture and the policy environment differ across national lines, our exploration of scientists' views compares scientists in the United States with those in Canada. In addition, we will highlight the most important disciplinary division among scientists by comparing natural scientists with social scientists.

More often than not, the tendency in studying environmental policymaking has been to focus on the political side: how policymakers, interest groups, or the media influence the way policy is formulated and implemented. Furthermore, most writing and interpretation on this subject matter has come from social scientists, with little input from natural scientists. And, at least in the United States, the tendency has been (for the most part) to focus exclusively on the American point of view. The results that will follow expand the critique of how science connects to environmental policymaking by incorporating Canadian and American natural and social scientists into the analysis of the dynamics surrounding the science–policy linkage.

BRIDGING DISCIPLINARY AND CULTURAL DIFFERENCES

Exploring how differences between natural scientists and social scientists affect environmental policymaking is important because scientists live and work in a society that is defined by complexity and influenced by a larger set of political, economic, historical, social, and scientific interactions.[4] There is simply no way that scientific communities can escape the influence of politics.[5] As one observer of the science–policy linkage submits, "Environmental problems are considered to be the social aspects of natural problems, and the natural aspects of social problems."[6] Natural scientists are important to environmental policymaking because they are called upon to communicate scientific facts and uncertainties and to describe the expected outcomes, following the best scientific methodologies. Social scientists are important because they shed light on the way the science–policy linkage actually works, through their own scientific studies.

Exploring how scientists in two different countries view the science–policy linkage is of interest because there is a general tendency to believe that the tenets of science are in conflict with the political and cultural factors that make up nationalism. Scientists must balance two different responsibilities: loyalty to their countries and loyalty to humanity.[7] Often, scientists are viewed as citizens who do not generally relinquish their national identities.[8] Despite their commitment to objectivity, scientists feel pressure to assist the government by providing testimony and support for scientific programs preferred by the government. Additionally, governments are far more likely to pay attention to studies done within their own borders than to those from other countries.[9] In short, nationalism matters:

> [T]he belief engine that drives our perceptions is so powerful that, with rare exceptions, it is almost impossible to step outside one's culture, to shed the belief baggage that comes with residence in a community of believers, to filter knowledge through the belief engine in order to see the evidence for what it really is—whether that be truth or hoax.[10]

The policy process dealing with science and technology and the interests that lobby them remain predominantly national, even if progress in science and technology inexorably moves toward international and global effects.[11] International negotiations relating to the environment are dominated by consideration of the likely impact on the domestic politics of each of the participants, rather than by some form of consensual scientific results.[12]

REVIEW OF PREVIOUS STUDIES ON THE NATURAL SCIENCE–SOCIAL SCIENCE DICHOTOMY

Science and Specialization

There is strong evidence to suggest that scientists' disciplinary backgrounds influence their approaches to research questions and how evidence is presented, leading to divergent interpretations of data and different ways of combining information.[13] Specifically, it has been shown that single-discipline training tends to produce scientists who view problems narrowly, from the perspective of their discipline, rather than from a more integrated, holistic view.[14] In short, the way in which one perceives how science interacts with public policymaking has a lot to do with whether one is trained as a natural scientist or social scientist,[15] with natural scientists delineated as those in fields of study such as physics, chemistry, biology, astronomy, and earth science, and social scientists delineated as those in fields of study such as political science, economics, sociology, psychology, anthropology, geography, and history, as well as interdisciplinary fields such as policy science, human ecology, and management.[16]

It should be no surprise to readers that a knowledge gap exists between natural scientists and social scientists.[17] There also exists a striking cultural divide between natural and social scientists,[18] with neither natural scientists nor social scientists able to speak or understand each other's language.[19] Knowledge in the natural sciences is more consensual than in the social sciences.[20] Natural scientists operate within a clearly defined and accepted framework of rules, while social scientists do not have such a structure in place.[21] Furthermore, natural and social scientists tend to regard each other with suspicion or hostility; to the extent that they regard each other at all. Few formal mechanisms exist to promote cooperation between the two.[22] Social scientists are not known to communicate well with natural scientists, and sometimes not even across their own disciplines.[23] Social scientists, insecure about their scientific status and aspiring to replicate the "scientific" success achieved by the physical sciences, are generally not accorded by government or the public the same (high) status as natural scientists.[24]

Natural scientists appear to possess a benign indifference toward social scientists, barely aware of the existence or content of social science studies, as these are considered irrelevant to the practice of the natural sciences.[25] This is deflating to many social scientists, who feel they have a lot to offer in solving our most pressing quality-of-life and global environmental problems; after all, they study human behavior.[26] Also, social scientists who apply a positivist methodological approach argue that they are using the same method as their colleagues in the physical and biological sciences.[27]

However, some natural scientists (or critics of social science) argue that despite their interest in explaining variation in human behavior, social scientists have paid little attention to the foundations of human nature,[28] and social science research has not succeeded in making politics appreciably more rational, political debates more intelligent, or policies more certain of success:[29]

> When outsiders look into the subject matter of other sciences, their jaws drop in awe of nature's beauty and power. They are justifiably impressed by those who work hard to uncover nature's amazing secrets. By contrast, when outsiders look into the subject matter of political science they see ideological battles, demagoguery, and scandal. . . . The promise of the natural sciences is that we can improve our existence by using them to uncover the properties and mechanics of forces that are fundamental to our lives. The promise of political science is no different. . . . The trouble with politics is that its subject matter is ugly and that talking about it causes all kinds of personal discomfort.[30]

The "ugliness" of the subject matter might better be described as complexity; and that complexity is central to the reply of social scientists to their critics.

Lynton Caldwell, in comparing the natural sciences to social sciences, states: "The behavior of humans, individually and socially, is the most complex of these and the least amenable to objective investigation."[31] Similarly, natural scientists like Eville Gorham proclaim "the relative simplicity of the physical sciences and the extreme complexity of the social sciences,"[32] and Edward O. Wilson observes that the social sciences are hypercomplex, "inherently far more difficult than physics and chemistry."[33]

In sum, significant cultural differences exist between social and natural sciences, grounded in part on the differences in their subject matter. Natural scientists have more prestige, more research funding, more dramatic and useful findings, but a simpler subject matter. Social scientists apply similar methodologies to more challenging questions; their results are less impressive, but they would like more respect.

Hope for Integrating Disciplinary Knowledge: Consilience and Collaboration

Because environmental problems combine strong human elements with physical and biological processes, lasting solutions to these problems require collaboration between natural scientists and social scientists. This presents a huge incentive for cooperation across disciplines. Wilson offers his perspective on reaching across disciplines:

> It is to view the boundary between the scientific and literary cultures not as a territorial line but as a broad and mostly unexplored terrain awaiting cooperative entry from both sides. The misunderstandings arise from ignorance of the terrain, not from a fundamental difference in mentality. The two cultures share the following challenge. We know that virtually all of human behavior is transmitted by culture. We also know that biology has an important effect on the origin of culture and its transmission. The question remaining is how biology and culture interact, and in particular how they interact across all societies to create the commonalities of human nature.[34]

Wilson asserts that if the social and natural sciences are to be united—his concept of consilience—the disciplines of both will need to be defined by the scales of time and space they individually encompass and not just by subject matter. Wilson speaks of "borderlands" between disciplines,[35] and promotes the proposition that "only fluency across disciplinary boundaries will provide a clear view of the world as it really is."[36] However, at least in one direction, Wilson holds out hope. He points out that the natural sciences, as represented by the environmental sciences, by their own swift expansion in subject matter, are drawing closer and closer to the social sciences.[37]

Since at least the atomic bombing of Hiroshima, there have been calls for natural scientists to expand their education and training so that they become aware of how their science influences the political world around them; that is, scientists are asked to see social responsibility as part of their intellectual culture.[38] One step toward achieving this is closer collaboration between natural scientists and social scientists,[39] the goal being to accept social scientists as full partners in the process of focusing science on social problems.[40] To this end, environmental scientists should act as cultural diplomats, using their own knowledge and viewpoints to encourage discussions between scientists from other countries and other disciplines.[41] Yet, scientists are not especially well organized to participate in such a manner.[42]

The good news is that the boundaries between physical and social sciences appear to be blurring, or at least overlapping,[43] and there is hope that a paradigm will emerge that will lead social scientists of all stripes to common perceptions of social existence without requiring them to surrender their unique identities or risk being swallowed by the natural scientists.[44] We will now consider the comparison of Canadian and American natural and social scientists as an illustration of how this blurring may be taking place.

REVIEW OF PREVIOUS STUDIES ON CANADA–UNITED STATES DIFFERENCES

Canada and the United States as Distinct Countries

Canada and the United States are often viewed as being indelibly linked by commonalities but as following distinctly different paths.[45] On the one hand, Canada and the United States share a relatively large number of common institutional linkages and common cultural characteristics.[46] On the other hand, a certain asymmetry of power, economic development, and population size has always distinguished the United States–Canadian bilateral relationship.[47]

Canada and the United States have two distinct forms of democratic political systems with differing founding values, historical experiences, and political institutions,[48] with these differences leading to divergent domestic policy priorities.[49] Canada's parliamentary system, founded in Westminster-style government, is markedly different than the United States' presidential system of separation of powers and checks and balances.[50] Canada is a "model of extreme decentralization among Western democracies [where] Canadian provincial governments are more powerful, more independent, and more influential than are American state governments in most issues of environmental policy."[51] The United States' system of government is fragmented, providing multiple points of access that typically result in ongoing contention and debate in the policy process. The Canadian system has limited protection of individual rights and limited access to the decision-making process, resulting in a more controlled and consultative policy process than in the United States.[52]

Canada and the United States have both set high standards for environmental protection and have displayed strong environmental leadership domestically and internationally.[53] Americans and Canadians support environmental protection in general as a high priority,[54] while salience for particular environmental issues remains low.[55] Still, the Canadian environmental policymaking process is less pluralistic, less open, less adversarial, and more influential than that of the United States,[56] with provincial governments having extensive authority over natural resources and environmental policy.[57]

Canadians, as a whole, are more sympathetic to environmental protection than are Americans, and are more supportive of environmental regulation,[58] with a tendency toward seeking multilateral consensus and universally binding treaties, conventions, and norms.[59] Canadians are more socially liberal, skeptical of national-level authority, and supportive of cooperative approaches. Americans are more socially conservative, deferential to authority at the national level, and inclined toward an individualistic "survival of the fittest" view of the world.[60] Canadians are more collective and supportive of governmental institutions at the provincial level, whereas Americans are more individualistic and while deferential, still suspicious of government institutions at all levels.[61]

Being members of the less populous and less powerful of the two countries, Canadians are more aware of the border and how transboundary issues affect their country.[62] In this regard, there is a tendency on the part of Americans to take Canada for granted, whereas Canadians continue to push the United States toward recognition of the uniqueness of the Canada–United States relationship.[63] The asymmetry that defines the Canada–United States relationship often puts Canadian policymakers "largely at the mercy of American domestic political outcomes."[64]

Although many Americans do not know it, not only are there differences between the historical perspectives of Canada and the United States, but there are also substantial differences between the countries' political cultures and environmental regulatory regimes. These differences reflect on scientific viewpoints and perspectives.[65]

Canada and the United States: Different Perspectives on Science

There exist stark and definitive differences between how Canadians and Americans view the linkage of science to environmental policy.[66] Environmental policymaking in the United States, as opposed to Canada, is not only more adversarial; it exacerbates the tendency for scientific information and scientists themselves to become embroiled in political debate.[67] In the United States, scientists face the challenge of resolving political conflicts and maintaining professional integrity while providing scientific input in an adversarial policy environment.[68] One example is that of wetland policy, where the scientific findings were more easily politicized in the adversarial setting in the United States than in the more cooperative policy environment in Canada. The development of criteria in the United States has followed a trend in public decision-making toward lengthy reviews and debates of scientific information and a tendency to cite scientific evidence as a compelling reason for policy formulation.[69]

There is a preference in the United States for having a large number of federal-level government scientists engaged in formal research to solve environmental problems, while Canada uses a more centralized and autonomous decision-making process.[70] In fact, Canada's relatively closed bureaucratic decision-making system has led to less emphasis on peer-reviewed, policy-oriented science,[71] and a reliance on government scientists, rather than the more independently minded university scientists.[72] Additionally, government technical specialists in non-research roles in Canada play a more important scientific role in comparison to the United States, because of the lack of critical mass of agency scientists in the provinces. In Canada, scientific consensus is sought among government scientists and provided to policymakers through working papers.[73] American science frequently assumes a major, often dominating, role in western scientific undertakings,[74] while Canadian science—at least over the past decade—has been somewhat isolated.[75] There even exist charges that Environment Canada's scientists are an underutilized resource who are kept in the dark and are often very poorly managed.[76]

TALKING TO SCIENTISTS

Up to this point in the book, we have relied on scholarly work and journalistic writings to describe and explain how science gets linked to policy. Now it is time to hear from the scientists themselves. Over the past two decades, Professor Leslie R. Alm has interviewed hundreds of scientists regarding the importance of science to the environmental policymaking process. There is no claim here that those interviewed represent a purely random sample from a comprehensive population. However, we believe that it is a sample quite representative of scientists whose expertise lies in the environmental arena. Alm chose scientists to interview based on their published works relating to environmental issues. Over sixty percent of the interviews were conducted in person. The rest were conducted by phone, and in a few cases, via email messaging. All of the interviews were conducted solely by one of the authors, and all interviewed scientists were granted confidentiality.

Scientists from both the United States and Canada were interviewed: scientists who worked for universities, governments, or the private sector, and who had extensive environmental work-related experience. Specific results from these interviews (other than those conducted in 2008 and 2009) have been published elsewhere, and it is not our intention to simply rehash those findings. Instead, we are using the knowledge and information gleaned from these interviews to provide an overview of how the science–policy linkage is perceived from the standpoint of scientists.

The questions asked in the interviews were understood to be very large and philosophical in nature, with scientists asked to explain their views in detail based on their personal and professional experience. The questions were open-ended, allowing scientists to talk about the science–policy linkage from their point of view. The interviews centered on four major questions: Do policymakers listen to scientists? Is it possible to separate science from policymaking? Is it possible for scientists to be objective? Should scientists advocate policy positions?

We make no attempt here to reduce the results to a numerical format. Instead, we make broad generalizations based on our review of the interview results, and we provide specific quotes from the scientists themselves. We do this in hopes of spurring both contemplation and discussion among the readers. Hearing these thoughts and ideas from scientists directly involved in the environmental policy-making process is an excellent way to explore the complications, tensions, and complexities of attempting to link science to policy.

Overall Perceptions of the Science–Policy Linkage

Following are the results of the interviews, with direct quotes from scientists explaining their perceptions regarding the science–policy linkage.

Listening to Scientists. As a whole, the interviews show only slight differences between natural scientists and social scientists when it comes to the influence of science (and scientists) on the environmental policymaking process. However, this difference comes with an intervening variable—country. In the United States, natural scientists are more skeptical about the influence of science, while in Canada it is the social scientists, as a whole, who are more skeptical about the influence of science.

As anticipated, the interview results indicate that scientists continue to struggle with their relationship to policymakers. The vast majority of the interviewed scientists support the view that scientists do not wield a great deal of influence with policymakers, and that science plays a subordinate role in a policymaking process that is dominated by political considerations. A scientist with the California Air Resources Board stated what he believed was obvious:

> The science is not getting through. There is a problem because scientists are not appointed to decision-making positions. They are political appointments, not based on their scientific knowledge. They are appointees who do not know or understand the science.

A research scientist with an international natural resources agency made the following argument:

> The science does not matter. It is all political. You can amass data all day long. Have you ever heard of studying the issue to death? More study is just a political ploy. If you can't beat them, just ask for a study, and it works very well. It gives you a way to beat them. In most cases the science is just too complex, and it has very little to do with the decision. It is just used by both sides to justify their positions, and I think the scientific community has been a bit naïve about further study really mattering.

However, a North Carolina State University scientist offered the following (more nuanced) description of the science–policy linkage:

> Let me tell you a story. A policymaker from Georgia introduced himself to a scientist who was working on ozone research by saying, "I just want to make good policy, to do good government." But without an adequate understanding of how the science works with respect to ozone, we can't do good government. Now, it is the responsibility of policymakers to deliver good government, but they can't do that if they don't know enough about ozone to improve the air quality. To be successful, we have to have better science. As LBJ used to say, we need to "reason together." "Let us reason together." Now that is an example of a decision-maker introducing a scientist to the policymaking world in a way that says "You have to help me by providing good science so we can do good government."

As anticipated from the scholarly literature, there exists a strong perception among scientists that policymakers "shop" for science and scientists, and that much of the best science goes unheard because policymakers tend to listen only to those scientists who support their views. A Forest Service scientist put it this way: "If policymakers find a scientist who agrees with their preconceived notions, then they become their champion and seek to minimize, and are critical of, anyone who disagrees." In this regard, there exists a genuine frustration in the scientific community about the way in which the worth of science is degraded by the policymaking process. There is a feeling not only that politics is dominant but that the only science getting through to policymakers is the science that supports particular ideological views. As a scientist at an environmental research institute observed, "What policymakers want is science that is palatable. I hate to say it, but it is true. Science has to be politically palatable."

Along these same lines of thought, a research scientist with the National Acid Precipitation Assessment Program and a policy analyst with the United States Geological Survey show their frustration with the way scientists are treated by policymakers:

> I am a trained scientist using the scientific method. But politicians realize that scientists have a hard time making up their minds because of the demand for certainty. The politicians are using scientists' training against them as a delaying tactic. Wouldn't it be nice to know the final scientific results? Isn't that the purpose of science, to provide the best information to allow people to make the final decision?
>
> The big problem, I think, is a deep lack of trust: some political decision-makers believe that the science they get is not objective but is geared toward a predetermined conclusion, while some scientists believe that no matter what evidence they provide, a politically motivated course of action will be selected.

The interviewed scientists also believe that there exists a major lack of communication between scientists and policymakers. A research scientist with the Environmental Protection Agency explained the difficulty of communicating with policymakers:

> Scientists want to explain why and explain the complexities. Policymakers want yes or no answers with no doubts. They want you to screen the evidence and give them

an answer. They do not want caveats. It was an eye-opener to me when I testified, and it was very frustrating. They wanted everything to look black and white.

Some scientists believe that the poor communication between policymakers and scientists is due to policymakers' lack of understanding of science and what science can provide. Scientists with the National Acid Precipitation Assessment Program and the Environmental Protection Agency detail this view:

> Policymakers just do not know any better. They think science should tell them the answer. They can't fathom what science is and don't realize that science is always challenging its own consensus. That is what science is all about. There never is just one opinion, and there never is perfect knowledge. There are no simple answers.
>
> Congressmen do not understand the science, and the public does not either. This has political implications because it is the policymakers who guide us, not the science. It is not the science that calls the shots, but the politics.

A scientist with the University of Minnesota conveys the struggle scientists have in communicating, especially as it relates to their passion for studying the natural world:

> I am a pure scientist interested in studying practical problems, and it took me a long time to understand that I had a responsibility to communicate my views to policymakers. I would go even further. I'm very suspicious of people who take up ecology with the claim they are going to save the lakes. They cannot do their best work unless they are most interested, have a joy, a strong intellectual curiosity about the natural processes as well.

On the other hand, a scientist who works for the Department of Energy suggests that the burden of successful communication between scientists and policymakers falls mostly to the scientific community:

> Some scientists are just better at explaining the science than others. Taking complex scientific ideas and translating them takes good scientific communication skills. We need to encourage such scientists to be spokesmen. But we do not. Other scientists look down upon these communicators. The scientific community needs to recognize the value of these people and their kinds of skills. But we should not ask them to go beyond the science.

A scientist working for a national clean air coalition also puts the burden on scientists to make the connection to policymakers:

> If the definition of scientific research is to create simple sentences, then, to tell the truth, it is the job of scientists to formulate a carefully phrased statement that represents the truth, which is consistent with all the empirical evidence and is not contradicted by any existing evidence. That is how we have to do science. As scientists, we argue with each other about things and eventually reach a consensus view among persons with very different perspectives.

But easing this burden is not (and will not be) an easy task. The thoughts of a scientist with the California Air Resources Board make this clear:

It is very difficult to switch from science mode to philosophical mode. It's not like, at 2 PM, now I will switch. There is only so much you can squeeze out of us, and it takes a lot of effort because the policymakers speak a strange language. You have to understand the science and simplify it so policymakers see your argument. You have to learn a whole new culture, and if you do, you must undertake an entirely new profession, and then your scientific credibility goes and your peers begin to question you. You have to remember that a person is in science for a reason, and it is their fundamental nature.

Separating Science from Policymaking. In Chapter 7 we argued that scientists have difficulty making the connection to policymakers because scientists and policymakers operate from two completely different points of view, both philosophically and professionally. The interviews did not elicit a single, overriding finding on this question of separation. Instead, the interviews suggest that in both the United States and Canada, there are major differences between the way natural scientists and social scientists perceive this separation.

As a whole, natural scientists are much more inclined to believe that it is possible to separate science from policy. Natural scientists, one from the University of Vermont and a senior scientist with the Pew Center, make the case for separation:

It is perfectly possible to separate science from policy. Scientific study can be completely isolated, assuming you get the dollars. Scientists can do basic research and communicate their findings through peer-reviewed research and let others, the public and policymakers, attach value to it.

When I talk, I create a discernible firewall. I say "Here is the science, and this is what the science says." I do not discuss the policy options. That is not my job. That is for other people to do. People listen to me because they know I do not push policy positions. I just provide the science and answer questions about the science.

A social scientist from York University makes the case that one cannot really separate science from policy:

Both science and policymaking are located in a broader puddle. They are part of an overall culture where normative ideas are good, real, and possible. But we still have political expediency. There's a certain kind of research that is funded, and certain policies are supported. Science and policy are tied together in this culture.

A social scientist from North Carolina State University uses his experience in testifying in front of Congress to express why he believes the separation between science and policy is a tenuous one:

I've had the [. . .] experience of testifying in the United States Congress on thirteen occasions and served on a half-dozen national committees, and I must begin by stating that scientists are their own worst enemy. In general, the entire scientific profession has long basked in the notion that we are separate, above the common folks, and even if I take the time to talk and explain to you in layman's terms, you are too stupid or you will probably twist what I am saying to fit your perspective because, as a scientist, I am credible. You will use me to back up your preconceived notions. It is a two-edged sword. Scientists who are truly scientists are supposed to bask in the holy tabernacle of empirical wisdom, providing no opinions, even on my own data; that I have no obligation to explain what my data means or to describe my feelings about my observations. I call these people technicians, not scientists. I believe scientists have the responsibility to say what they think and what their data means. These technicians say, "Do I look like a politician?" Policymakers view scientists as naïve fools, having their proverbial heads in the sand, and not having any idea what the real world is about, sequestered in their own special place.

And, as mentioned in Chapter 7, natural scientists believe that mixing science with policy creates grave dangers regarding scientific credibility. Carefully consider the words of a political scientist from the University of Northern British Columbia as he attempts to clarify the boundary between science and policy:

> The biggest danger with mixing science with policy is that you lose your credibility, trustworthiness, and reliability as a scientist, though not necessarily as a caring human being. To me it is fine to get drawn into the emotional part; one can't help it. But, again, you have to figure out the boundary. In the environmental/sustainability field the boundary is shifting toward acceptance of stronger advocacy by scientists and will likely continue to do so as these problems continue to get worse.

Objective Science. The interviews suggest that in both the United States and Canada, there are major differences between the way natural scientists and social scientists perceive the ability of scientists to complete bias-free research. The vast majority of natural scientists asserted that it was possible to be objective in completing their research, while the vast majority of social scientists asserted that it was not possible.

A social scientist from a major U.S. university put forth the general view of social scientists:

> It is abundantly clear that science has political implications. Science is not neutral. There is no such thing as neutral knowledge. Science is political, with its funding, choices of topics, how knowledge is dispersed, and the involvement of scientists in the policy process. Science is political, and politics is scientific.

A natural scientist with the National Acid Precipitation Assessment Program insisted on the primacy of objectivity in his testimony to Congress: "I never answer policy questions. I don't tell you what to do. I am objective. Here are the facts. There must be some source of objective information." One of the most notable natural scientists working on solving the nation's air pollution problems summarizes the importance, and difficulty, of remaining objective when providing his scientific findings to policymakers:

> If we are going to become party to causes, then that is what we become, party to causes. We lose our scientific credentials when we become party to causes. If we want respect as scientific specialists [we cannot confuse] what scientists know about the facts and what they think society should do about the facts. It took me a long time

to learn this lesson. But from my congressional experience, when a congressman asked "What should we do?" I should have had the good sense to say, "You are the decision-maker and I am the scientist, and let's not confuse the two."

Other scientists are concerned about losing even the ideal of objectivity. A natural scientist from the Department of Energy makes this exact point:

> What worries me is that we have abandoned objectivity as a goal. Scientists ought to struggle for objectivity and show a disdain for advocacy. But neither the public nor the administration shares this belief of mine. You get research dollars if you choose the side they want to hear.

A natural scientist from Environment Canada explains how the scientific process works to keep scientists objective:

> The scientists in the United States have always been good. We have really had problems scientifically. Some of us, me included, got too close to the political part. But our true-blue colleagues corrected us. This is just the scientific margin of error. You want to diddle with the books, but scientists just can't get away with that. There is always someone there to correct you. Science is based on replication. That is the right way for research to be conducted.

A natural scientist with the National Center for Atmospheric Research makes the same argument, but in a slightly different way:

> We make many mistakes. The job of science is to suggest answers and to suggest far more than just one and to take our best shot and see if we are right. But most of the time we are wrong. Our work is rejected. But science is an intensely human endeavor full of mistakes. But by nature it is the best process as opposed to all the other processes. It gets us on the right track. Sooner or later it will come up with the right answer.

Two natural scientists, one working with a natural resource department in the Midwest who formerly worked with a federal environmental agency, and one working for the Environmental Protection Agency, outline the difficulties of presenting objective findings:

> The biggest problem that science has is that it becomes a value judgment. All science can tell you are the risks and benefits. We elect people to make the value judgments. But scientists are just as guilty as everyone else. They too have values. But you have to differentiate between what is the science and what is the value judgment. Science is mute on all of the great questions, anything that is humanistic or has to do with the human system. Scientists have values, but science does not.
>
> There is a body of scientists, like me, who attempt to be objective and open to alternative explanations. Part of the problem is that some scientists focus very narrowly in their own field of expertise and so see all problems as rooted in that area.

A natural scientist with the National Center for Atmospheric Research explains the power of the scientific process:

> Once a report comes out, no one ever questions its authority. The press prints headlines, and then it is just accepted, even if it is not right. Scientists should not present

arguments in a public forum. They should only present in a scientific forum. Then if it is wrong, it will be proven wrong.

A natural scientist from the University of Minnesota explains why it is important to avoid politics:

It is possible for scientists to avoid considering policy and study pollution as a fundamental science. That is what I do, and I would be insulted if someone called me an applied scientist. Now, policymakers cannot make policy without scientists, but it is possible for scientists to do science without policy and policymakers.

A social scientist from Queen's University talks about the scientific process as the key, not the scientists themselves:

Can scientists be objective? That is the wrong question. It is not objectivity, but replicability. The definition of science is not what you believe or don't believe; it is a question of replication. It would be a cruel burden to ask an individual scientist to be objective. Scientists are not objective in the least. Objectivity is irrelevant and so is passion. What counts is [whether] someone else can do it.

Finally, a Cornell University natural scientist offers a bit of a nuanced assessment of scientists and objectivity:

In all cases, subjective biases are introduced as scientists draw from their personal experience and scientific peer group to inform their choices. It is thus very difficult—and probably impossible—for scientists to present data without it having some imprint of themselves on it. This does not mean that the data is not "correct" or "true." It just means that scientists have tremendous influence over the meaning of their results.

Scientists and Advocacy. The interviews identify a broad consensus, crossing disciplines and countries, in favor of advocacy by scientists. This is true whether we are speaking of natural scientists, social scientists, Canadian scientists, or American scientists.

A common view among those interviewed is that scientists have the right to participate in policy debates as long as they make it perfectly clear to their audience that they are participating as concerned citizens and not as scientists. Typical of this view are the words of a scientist from a water resource department: "As members of a democracy, scientists have a duty to participate. It is all right for scientists to give their opinion as scientists. But they should be forthright in distinguishing the scientific facts from their own political convictions."

A scientist from a Midwestern American university provides a more detailed version of this belief:

Occasionally you get so frustrated by the lack of action that you go public to advocate. You become very frustrated with the inability of the sheer weight of the evidence to produce any action. Sometimes there comes a time in your best judgment that the ends justify the means. But this also pushes the science beyond its credibility. We are all guilty [at] one time [or] another. Scientists should advocate, with some qualifications. I do this frequently, where I say "This is what I have to say about the science" and then take off my hat as a scientist and put on my hat as a citizen. And I would even go further and say that it would be shirking one's duty not to do that, to not say what ought to be done. But doing this, you cannot claim the same expertise as a scientist.

Two other takes on this view are summarized by scientists from the University of Vermont and North Carolina State University:

> I feel very strongly that scientists should not advocate as scientists. Scientists should be objective and do objective analysis of the environment. Just do basic science, determine how nature works. If you start being an advocate, you have to take off the scientist's hat and be clear you are doing it only as a citizen. I have personal opinions, but I am very careful I am never wearing the scientific hat when I share them.
>
> Some scientists are stuck back in 1755 about their attitudes. They are technicians. They believe you can separate science and politics, that they can be objective. They do not realize the entire system is political. Scientists must be able to separate personal and professional behavior, one as citizen and one as scientist. If making a speech to the Sierra Club, I say right up front and want the press to understand that I am acting as a citizen and not as a member of my university. But when it comes to my data I can be as much [of] a damn advocate as I please, and that is my right and my responsibility to interpret my data. I am not a technician, and I have the right to go to the President and tell him the world is going to hell in a handbasket. But being an advocate is dangerous.

Some of those interviewed suggested that because scientists have special knowledge, they also have a moral responsibility to disseminate that knowledge in a public forum. A scientist from the Center for Atmospheric Research explains it this way: "If we understand our results better than any outsiders can or do and if it points to a certain policy position, then it is OK to say that. Now that might not be the same thing as advocating, but no conversation is neutral."

However, there were a good number of scientists who felt that advocacy went hand-in-hand with the loss of a scientist's credibility within the scientific community. A scientist from McMaster University sums up the concern for keeping one's credibility intact:

> My personal point of view, as one that is asked to advocate all the time, is that I am uncomfortable because it is a real risk to one's scientific reputation to advocate on any issue. There is a difference between speaking one's mind and advocating. What is really important is your scientific credibility, and you do not want to do anything to jeopardize that by having a reputation for speaking out against government or industry. I think I can be more effective with respect to an issue if I keep a low profile and keep my scientific credibility.

A scientist from the Department of Energy makes a similar point, suggesting that some scientists misuse their status as an objective observer to push their own ideological views:

> I continue to believe strongly that scientists should not advocate for policy positions. The main characteristic that distinguishes science from policy is that science is supposed to be fact-based; i.e., it is supposed to rely on findings derived by the scientific

method. In contrast, policy must consider additional "non-factual" factors, such as values and competing interests. In my judgment, scientists are no better able to weigh values and competing interests than folks in lots of other walks of life. Worse, when a scientist becomes a policy advocate, he necessarily cheapens science, as his policy advocacy cannot be purely fact-based. Rational people hearing a scientist acting as an advocate have no way of knowing where his fact-based conclusions (i.e., his science) end, versus where his own set of values and competing interests (i.e., his policy) begin.

We also found a general belief among scientists that scientists not only should advocate, but have a responsibility to do so. As a scientist tied to the Commission on Environmental Cooperation put it,

> I have always argued that scientists not only be allowed to advocate but have the responsibility to articulate their work, to describe what kinds of policy responses should result from their work. Scientists should have that right. Most do not. Scientists must be thinking about the "so what" of their work and use whatever routes available to do it, to get the word out.

Some scientists argue that while it is all right for scientists to advocate, their credentials as a scientist should not be given more merit than the opinion of any other concerned citizen. A Massachusetts Institute of Technology scientist makes this exact point:

> Science has become terribly relevant to societal needs, and it is important for scientists to mature, so that they understand what the consequences are. But I do not think scientists' choice of policies has any more legitimacy than non-scientists'. Scientists work within the scientific paradigm, but it is also known that scientists are also politically conservative as a whole. Scientists' views should not be emphasized any more than others.

Others argue that going public hurts not only the individual scientist but also the credibility of the scientific process. This point is made by a scientist from the Atmospheric Sciences Research Center:

> There is no organized structure for scientists to vent their anger. It is inappropriate for scientists to carry on debate in the media. It is usually untimely, not well received by colleagues, and provides bad information. It is a detriment to the entire process

CONCLUDING REMARKS

Our interview results suggest that scientists feel strongly about their role in the public policymaking process. Based on a review of the literature, we expected to find major differences between how natural scientists and social scientists view the science–policy linkage. The interviews did, indeed, substantiate some of those differences. In contrast, although the literature projected different views between scientists from different countries, the interviews suggest that the differences in how Canadian and American scientists perceive the science–policy linkage are slight, if they exist at all.

Advocates, Separatists, and Pragmatists

The interviews reveal three basic positions on the issues of objectivity, advocacy, and the separation of science and policy, that reflect the range of opinions offered throughout the scholarly literature: advocates, separatists, and pragmatists. Advocates believe both that advocacy is acceptable because it is possible to separate science from policymaking and that, at least through the scientific process, scientists can remain objective. Thus there are no fears that advocacy by individual scientists will contaminate the objectivity on which all scientists depend. Most natural scientists and a small number of social scientists interviewed for this study hold this view.

Separatists believe that advocacy is not acceptable because it is not possible for individual scientists to separate science and policymaking. Hence, those who advocate lose all semblance of objectivity. This view is predominant among natural scientists, who oppose advocacy because they want to retain objectivity, which they see as central to their legitimacy and their mission as scientists.

Pragmatists believe that advocacy is acceptable because science can never be separated from policymaking, so scientists should just do the very best they can to balance objectivity with influence. This view is most common among social scientists, who begin with suspicions about objectivity and conclude that science cannot be separated from policymaking. Thus, for many social scientists, advocacy makes sense because they already see themselves as an important part of the policy process (not separate from it), and believe that their task is to retain as much objectivity as they can. They share a less idealistic and more pragmatic approach, which in a way makes them more compatible with the world of the policymaker, and might make them better able to influence policy. In contrast, natural scientists who believe in objectivity are more likely to be upset about not being listened to, or about failure of scientific knowledge to affect policy.

Dialogue between Natural Scientists and Social Scientists

One of the findings that stands out from the interviews is that natural scientists remain a long way from accepting the fact that their research is (or has to be) tainted by the value constraints that characterize the world of policymaking. Despite the overwhelming findings in the literature and the almost unanimous findings from the interviews with social scientists that objectivity is at best an ideal and at worst a dangerous illusion, many natural scientists remain steadfast in their faith in the scientific process, including their ability to conduct objective research. They refuse to compromise the canons of the scientific method and continue to resist entering the policy process in any manner. The upside to this finding (at least for those who believe that objectivity is a worthy ideal) is that a good many natural scientists are fighting to keep their work strictly within the confines of the scientific process. The downside to this finding (at least for those striving to make science more policy-relevant) is that there remain a large number of natural scientists incapable of or unwilling to join science to policy in a meaningful manner.

It was clear from the interviews that social scientists' pragmatic views on objectivity and advocacy align more closely with that of policymakers and allow them to fit more easily into the policy world. Based on this finding, we suggest that a key to making science more meaningful in the policymaking process may lie not in the dialogue between scientists and policymakers, but in the dialogue between natural scientists and social scientists. The reasons for strengthening the natural science–social science connection are fairly straightforward. For natural scientists, there exist strong ties to the tenets of the scientific process that run counter to any type of policy advocacy. Yet, natural scientists also appear very frustrated because good science does not seem to be getting into the policy debate. Natural scientists find themselves in a quandary. If they advocate for specific policy outcomes, they risk losing their highly valued credibility within the scientific community. If they do not advocate, they become policy-irrelevant.

Social scientists are in a good position to alleviate this particular dilemma. They could play a mediating role, helping policymakers understand the intricacies of the scientific process and helping natural scientists to clarify their own personal biases. Social scientists could contribute by providing better explanations (hopefully leading to better understanding) of such important concepts as environment, truth, uncertainty, and so on. That is exactly where their training lies. They study the policy process, understand the ways it operates, and are in an ideal position to frame environmental science in a way that would make it more accessible to those, including policymakers, who do not have a clear grasp of the way science works. If social scientists were to be used as conduits between natural scientists and policymakers, it is possible that the science could move forward with more clarity and natural scientists could preserve their relative independence and objectivity from further erosion.

Nationalities

We started this assessment with the basic but straightforward premise that Canada and the United States are two different countries with different environmental policy frameworks and different ways of viewing science. Those differences are carefully documented above. Our expectations were that we would see those differences displayed throughout our interviews of U.S. and Canadian scientists. However, our interviews—at least regarding the four questions we asked about how science should fit into the policymaking process—showed no substantial differences between United States and Canadian respondents. It is our belief that this finding should not be seen in a negative light, but as a positive sign that, at least in a small way, the tenets of science can overcome nationalism.

It appears that scientists remain more closely bound by their scientific and professional ethics than by their nationalities. This is an important finding for several reasons. First, it provides evidence that the different national contexts of these scientists may not be the driving force determining their outlook and assessments. In essence, the lack of substantial differences between the perceptions of U.S. and Canadian scientists offers evidence of the separation of the worlds of science and politics, and shows that the institutions of science may be stronger and more independent of social and political concerns than they are generally given credit for in today's world. It also provides important evidence to support the natural scientists' contention that they can indeed do research that is relatively objective and free of the influence of personal values.

MOVING TOWARD MAKING SCIENCE MEANINGFUL

The interviews provide empirical evidence that there remain, at least among scientists, deep concerns about how science is making the link to environmental policy. Scientists do not believe that the science is getting though to policymakers—at least getting through in an unbiased, meaningful way. Scientists also continue to struggle with exactly when and how they should participate in the policymaking process. Despite the many attempts to dismiss the concept of objectivity having a place in a political world, the question of whether science and scientists possess objectivity is at the forefront of how scientists pursue their profession as they attempt to provide information about how nature works. And we are still searching for answers.

REFLECTIVE QUESTIONS

Question 8-1

Kim McDonald (*Chronicle of Higher Education,* 1999) criticizes the "convoluted wording" of a statement released by American Geophysical Union scientists regarding their stance on the earth's rising temperature. McDonald states that the scientists' statement "led to more confusion among reporters about how scientists really view climate change."

  a. Discuss why natural scientists sometimes have a difficult time translating their scientific findings into language that is understood by the public in general.
  b. If you were advising the American Geophysical Union about how better to communicate with the media and the public, what recommendations would you make?

Question 8-2

David Orrell (*Apollo's Arrow,* 2007) contends that people choose science over more lucrative careers because they want to contribute to the greater good by probing the nature of matter and helping the environment. Discuss Orrell's claim in the context of the natural scientists' goal of maintaining objectivity in their research. In your discussion, talk about how a natural scientist would defend her status as a scientist at the same time she is attempting to protect the environment.

Question 8-3

It has been suggested by Lynton Caldwell (*Policy Study Review,* 1993) that there is disinclination by natural scientists to conceptualize holistic approaches to the understanding of nature or environmental relationships. Provide an example from the physical or biological sciences that supports Caldwell's contention.

Question 8-4

Religion and science are described as independent approaches to knowledge (Richard Sloan, *Chronicle of Higher Education,* 2006). Compare and contrast the different ways that natural scientists and social scientists would attempt to link or unlink these two ways of knowing.

SUGGESTED READINGS

Kathryn Harrison and George Hoberg, *Risk, Science, and Politics: Regulating Toxic Substances in Canada and the United States* (Montreal: McGill-Queen's University Press, 1994).

James Smith, *The Idea Brokers: Think Tanks and the Rise of the New Policy Elite* (New York: Free Press, 1991).

Glen Toner, ed., *Innovation, Science, and Environment: Canadian Policies and Performance, 2008–2009* (Montreal: McGill-Queen's University Press, 2008).

Debora VanNijnatten and Robert Boardman, eds., *Canadian Environmental Policy: Context and Cases,* 2nd ed. (Don Mills, Ontario: Oxford University Press, 2002).

Norman Vig and Michael Kraft, eds., *Environmental Policy: New Directions for the Twenty-First Century,* 7th ed. (Washington, DC: CQ Press, 2010).

CHAPTER 9

Making Science Meaningful

But for new knowledge and insights to contribute to more rational and reliable public policies, scientific information must be conveyed to the public and its decision makers in language that they can understand and in the form of propositions about which decisions can be made.

Lynton Caldwell, *Environment as a Focus for Public Policy*, 1994.

THE AMERICAN PUBLIC POLICYMAKING PROCESS AND THE ENVIRONMENT

The American public policymaking process is complex, dynamic, and ideologically driven. The simple but powerful truth is that public policymaking in the United States is a purely political process consisting of a struggle over ideas and the values that underlie those ideas. There is nothing casual about how we approach policymaking in our democratic nation. Even as we move swiftly toward an increasingly globalizing world, our policy process remains rooted in the democratic ideals of participation, openness, transparency, and conflict.

The American policymaking process calls for an engaged and informed public. Citizens are consistently asked to choose sides. That is the nature of pluralism, advocacy coalitions, and our intrinsically adversarial pursuit of happiness. We want and encourage open and vigorous public debate about what values should define the direction we want to go. American policymaking is built on a foundation of adversarial conflicts; whether it be in a government split along partisan lines or in the halls of our legal system, the clarity of two sides fighting for their values is inherent in all that we do.

One of those values appears to be protecting the environment. Concern for the environment is now embedded in the core values that Americans possess. But environmental concerns do not dominate the everyday lives of most Americans. Saliency of environmental issues wanes in the shadow of concerns about economic disaster and pursuing freedom and democracy in far-off lands. We want to protect the environment, but that protection must come within the rubric of protecting jobs and protecting American lives. That is not to say that these concerns do not intersect. They do. It is to say that the fight to protect the environment is one that must be engaged on an everyday basis, or it will fall to deeper, more passionate ideals. Those who champion environmental protection must integrate their efforts with the efforts to solve the other great problems of the day. This is a way to open Kingdon's policy window without having to always wait for the next environmental crisis. If this is not done, environmentalism—though remaining of import—will always remain on the periphery of the policy cycle, and as a secondary concern to policymakers.

SCIENCE, DEMOCRACY, AND THE ENVIRONMENT

The impact of science on environmental policymaking is profound. To be more exact, solving our environmental problems, locally or globally, is not possible without the guidance of scientists. Whether acting as hidden participants, active citizens, or outright policy advocates, it is scientists who provide the parameters of our search for the solutions to our most vexing environmental problems. It is true that scientists cannot provide all of the answers, and sometimes the complexities and uncertainty ingrained in scientific analysis makes policymaking even more confusing than it need be. However, the one thing scientists can do is point us in the right direction. And this is no small thing. In the end, there is simply no way to avoid the requirement for scientists to shine the light on nature and its wonders and allow us to better judge what tarnishes them.

For policymakers and the public alike, in general terms, science crosses the spectrum from uncritical acceptance and unrelenting hope for a better world to being cited as the ultimate cause of pending global environmental destruction. What we often forget is that science does not work in isolation from the rest of society. Although the scientific method remains unique and isolated in its passion for objective analysis, it does so in a world defined by political considerations. Often obscured by ideological arguments and the desire of policymakers for certainty, science and scientists have managed to speak in terms of uncertainty and probability. This is very frustrating to those who want definitive "yes" and "no" answers. Yet, the language of uncertainty that characterizes the scientific process remains the only way scientists know how to speak about how nature works, and it serves as the very foundation that rewards scientists with considerable public prestige, public trust, and public dollars.

Thus, if we want to know about what the science tells us, we must find a way for scientists to maintain their independence from the policy world, a way for scientists to protect their scientific credibility. It is the faith we have in scientists to be above politics that gives credence to what scientists have to say. If scientists become bogged down on the policy side of environmental issues, acting as any other political interest group, the very essence of their legitimacy is in danger of disappearing, and their impact on policymaking will be marginalized. We cannot compromise the integrity built into the scientific process. It is simply not worth it. Yet if we continue on our current path, the value of science for policymaking will be lost. If scientists, to protect their integrity, simply retreat to the lab, again, policymakers and citizens are the losers. We must find a way to restore the connection between science and democracy.

SCIENCE AND ENVIRONMENTAL POLICYMAKING: SOME SUGGESTIONS

We have covered a lot of ground exploring how science connects to environmental policymaking in the United States. It is a messy process, and the questions we have asked (and explored) have never been definitively answered—more than likely because there are no answers—only more questions. We hope to have provoked the minds of our readers to come up with their own answers.

Having said that, we think it is a good idea to continue asking questions, especially of scientists, who have at times been left out—or at least somewhat marginalized—when it comes to formulating environmental policy. In the end, the question remains: What exactly is the role that scientists should play in the American environmental policymaking process?

The Need for More Proactive Scientists

If environmental questions are fundamentally questions of science—as posited throughout this book—then scientists should be playing a much larger role than generally occurs. Though science plays a critical role in the environmental policy-making process, the task of defining the meaning of scientific findings has not been carried out—for the most part—by scientists. This task has been left to other interested parties: that is, to policymakers, journalists, lobbyists, and interest groups, among others. We think this should change. The time is past when scientists can just inform the public and policymakers, and then go on with their lives.

Scientists must be more proactive. If science is going to have any chance of providing meaningful input into the policy process, scientists are the ones who will have to make stronger efforts at interacting with and talking to policymakers. Policymakers are perfectly happy to maintain their position of picking and choosing the science that fits their particular ideological beliefs. Who can blame them? Moreover, why we would we want to change the democratic system that has served us so well over the years? To ask policymakers to abide by the rules that govern science is unrealistic and unwise. Hence, it is left to the scientific community to lead the charge, to manage science in a way that fits more comfortably in the policy world. In short, scientists must do a better job of translating their scientific findings into a format that is more readily understood by both policymakers and the public. This means scientists must do a better job of educating the public and policymakers alike about the scientific process, including delving into the assumptions of science and the importance of (and reasoning behind) such concepts as probability and peer review.

Although this is no easy task, we think scientists should make the effort. Scientists should start every one of their public talks with a brief explanation of the elements that make up the scientific process, and then allow for questions.

Surprisingly, and sadly, most people do not know that the scientific process is based on severe criticism and constant checking and rechecking, trying to prove that something is not correct. Most ordinary people understand the constant criticism by scientists of other scientists' work as part of the give and take of politics and partisanship, as part of America's adversarial system. However, people simply do not know that the scientific process is built on the idea of regular and routine critiques as a means to determine where the truth lies. People do not understand that science is a dynamic, continuous, and contentious process by design; that putting things in the form of probabilities does not mean that we know nothing. It means we never know the entire, absolute truth.

Scientists must explain this to the public every chance they get because no one else will. Policymakers have no incentive to explain probabilities. As we have witnessed time after time, policymakers want answers in absolutes. They do not want probabilities. The political world is built on values, on the idea that things are right or wrong, and that absolutes do exist. That is the way of democracy. But scientists have to take the time to make sure their audience, whoever it is, knows the difference between following the scientific process and its assumptions and following the rules on the policy side. People must come to understand the part that chance plays in the scientific world, and more important, to understand that it is all right for scientists to speak in such terms. It does not show weakness, and it does not mean we cannot act. The science may muddy the waters, but that is the nature of science.

Openness, Transparency, and Protecting the Ideal of Objectivity

Getting meaningful science into the policymaking process requires that we facilitate scientists' ability to participate in the policymaking process (some would say advocate for policy positions), while at the same time protecting scientific integrity. This is one large and difficult task. However, there are ways to move in that direction. The effort to meet this challenge must focus on the idea of science as a process, and not on the idea of science as a knowledge base. We need to emphasize the qualities that make the scientific method the center of impartiality and the reason we put so much faith in scientific results. We cannot allow science to morph into politics.

What we propose is to move toward complete transparency and openness in the scientific process. When disseminating their findings, scientists should be required by their disciplines to state right up front where their personal biases may lie. Although part of revealing motives and interests involves judgment, most does not. It should be a straightforward process to lay out all the assumptions that are made and the source of all funding. It should also be uncomplicated to disclose all affiliations, including all financial and political affiliations. More important, all data used should be open for assessment. While in some cases there may be national security concerns and industrial secrets to protect, there certainly are means to set up independent reviews, while protecting what needs protecting. Calls for secrecy are too convenient for policymakers to use as cover for protecting ideological views rather than letting the science fall where it may.

Scientists should be encouraged to enter the policy process as citizens. If you believe in the scientific process, and we do, then the good science will come out in the end. That is the beauty of replication. There should be no fear of scientists carrying the day in the public forum. Our public institutions are strong enough to withstand the viewpoints of scientists. Let all scientists have their say in the public forum. Again, public debate is a hallmark of American democracy, and ultimately the final policy decisions are made, not by scientists, but by policymakers who are accountable to the people. After all, that is what democracy is supposed to be. The criticism that the public and policymakers cannot and will not understand the complexities of the science is, at best, a weak criticism. There are few people, if any, who understand the intricacies of *any* of the issues that come before us. Decisions have to be made, and they are made, without complete information and complete understanding. That is the way of public policymaking. To single out issues as too scientifically complex for public discussion is simply not a valid stance.

Scientists should simply state up front that they are advocating for a certain policy position, if that is the case. They should tell us what they believe and why they believe it to be so. If there is science that supports their view, then scientists should provide the source, fully detail all assumptions and probabilities, and explain why the science (and the policy position) makes sense to them. Scientists should disclose all their affiliations and income sources. In short, scientists should be completely open and transparent.

Integrating the Natural and Social Sciences

As argued in Chapter 8, we believe that scientists must be more articulate about their views and should refine their approach of communicating to policymakers in a way that would cause policymakers to listen in a meaningful way. Although this is unnerving for some and challenging for others, scientists must make the attempt. The easiest path to successfully linking scientists to policymakers, in our opinion, would be for closer integration of the natural and social sciences. This is not an original idea, and as one looks at the creation of interdisciplinary science and policy programs in higher education, one can see that some are already making attempts at bridging the gap between these disciplines. However, on the whole, these attempts are few and far between. Scientists are still too reticent in working, or even thinking, outside the narrow band of expertise within which they have been trained.

Social scientists and natural scientists could be linked most easily when they are first beginning their training. Colleges and universities are set up to foster such interaction, designing curriculums that require cross-discipline training. Of course, implementing this is not as simple as it may sound. Higher education possesses the same inertia and resistance to change that all large bureaucracies face. Once again, the effort to make such changes must come from the scientists themselves, and from natural scientists in particular. As a whole, social scientists are still fighting to be recognized as genuine scientists, and they are in the weaker position to bring about change; this is in no small part because such a recommendation would be viewed as self-serving. Natural scientists, despite the withering attacks on the scientific process and its claims of objectivity, still possess a high degree of respect and a formidable position of authority in the academic setting. What natural scientists say about the way the natural world works is accepted as genuine and true. For natural scientists to call for more integration of the social sciences into the natural science curriculum would go a long way toward making such training occur.

On the other hand, social scientists can contribute to closer integration with natural scientists by easing their attacks on the ideal of objectivity. It is one thing to question the specific instances of impartiality or of the reckless use of science to support unsubstantiated claims by natural scientists. It is another thing to deride the attempts at objectivity as somehow being a flaw in the scientific process and a hindrance to environmental policymaking. Social scientists should spend more time thinking about how to make the policymaking process more user-friendly for natural scientists and how to generate scientific consensus in ways that are more meaningful to policymakers. Social scientists possess special expertise and knowledge about the way the policy process works and how issues can be easily framed to fit particular ideologies. Social scientists should use this knowledge and their particular skills to generate better linkages between natural scientists and policymakers.

CONCLUDING THOUGHTS

Scientists have every right to fear for the loss of their scientific credibility as they enter into the policy world. Despite all the calls for finding a way to link scientists to the policy world in a constructive manner, the fact remains that in the American policymaking system, there does not exist a way for scientists to independently portray their science as they see it. If they participate, it has to occur within the rules already established, and those rules are defined with primacy given to political and cultural values. Moreover, once a scientist is cast as an advocate, his or her reputation for producing good science is greatly diminished within the scientific community. We need to change the rules. We need to make prominent the call for developing a way for science to enter the policymaking process that does not denigrate the scientists who produced the science. In a small way, we hope that we have contributed—along with many others—toward movement in that direction.

REFLECTIVE QUESTIONS

Question 9-1

In 1750 French economist and statesman Anne-Robert-Jaques Turgot argued that history was humanity's slow struggle to discover the scientific method (Benjamin Kline, *First Along the River,* 2007). Is Turgot's argument still valid today? Explain why or why not.

Question 9-2

What do you believe would be the most effective change that could be made to the American public policymaking process to allow for science to be properly and effectively used to make decisions regarding environmental policy in the United States?

Question 9-3

In Chapter 2, John Kingdon's model of scientists as hidden participants in the policy process is outlined. Using Kingdon's characterizations as a guide, provide a current example illustrating the value of viewing scientists in this manner.

Question 9-4

Throughout this book the authors emphasize the idea that scientists have a good deal to offer America as citizens. Illustrate the complexities of the scientist-citizen dichotomy by providing support for (1) the view that scientists should not have any more say in the development of policies than any other citizens; and (2) the view that scientists have an obligation to present their personal views of the best policy options.

SUGGESTED READINGS

Sheila Jasanoff, *Designs On Nature: Science and Democracy in Europe and the United States* (Princeton: Princeton University Press, 2005).

Roger Pielke, Jr., *The Honest Broker: Making Sense of Science in Policy and Politics* (Cambridge: Cambridge University Press, 2007).

Walter A. Rosenbaum, *Environmental Politics and Policy,* 7th ed. (Washington, DC: CQ Press, 2008).

Notes

CHAPTER 1

1. Lynton Caldwell, *Between Two Worlds: Science, the Environmental Movement, and Public Choice* (New York: Cambridge University Press, 1990), xi.
2. Sheila Jasanoff, *Designs On Nature: Science and Democracy in Europe and the United States* (Princeton: Princeton University Press, 2005), 247.
3. Jasanoff, 2005, 6.
4. Walter Rosenbaum, *Environmental Politics and Policy*, 7th ed. (Washington, DC: CQ Press, 2008), 29.
5. Alexander Keynan, "The Political Impact of Scientific Cooperation on Nature in Conflict: An Overview," in Allison deCerreno and Alexander Keynan, eds., *In Scientific Cooperation, State Conflict: The Roles of Scientists in Mitigating International Discord* (New York: The New York Academy of Sciences, 1998), 20.
6. "Making Science News," *Bioscience* 48 (1998): 843.
7. Arild Underdal, "Science and Politics: The Anatomy of an Uneasy Partnership," in Steinar Andresen et al., eds., *Science and Politics in International Environmental Regimes* (Manchester: Manchester University Press, 2000), 3.
8. Walter Baber and Robert Bartlett, *Deliberative Environmental Politics: Democracy and Ecological Rationality* (Cambridge, MA: MIT Press, 2005), 9.
9. Don Price, *The Scientific Estate* (Cambridge, MA: Harvard University Press, 1965), 172.
10. Joel Primack and Frank Von Hippel, *Advice and Dissent: Scientists in the Political Arena* (New York: Basic Books, 1974), 4.
11. Bruce Smith, *The Advisors: Scientists in the Policy Process* (Washington, DC: Brookings Institution, 1992), 207.
12. Kai N. Lee, *Compass and Gyroscope: Integrating Science and Politics for the Environment* (Washington, DC: Island Press, 1993), 5–6.
13. Roger Pielke, Jr., *The Honest Broker: Making Sense of Science in Policy and Politics* (New York: Cambridge University Press, 2007), 151.
14. Paul A. Sabatier, "The Need for Better Theories," in Paul A. Sabatier, ed., *Theories of the Policy Process*, 2nd ed. (Boulder: Westview Press, 2007), 3.
15. Sabatier, 3–4.
16. B. Guy Peters, *American Public Policy: Promise and Performance,* 7th ed. (Washington, DC: CQ Press, 2007), 4.
17. Thomas Birkland, *An Introduction to the Policy Process* (New York: M.E. Sharpe, 2001), 3.

18. Larry N. Gerston, *Public Policymaking in a Democratic Society: A Guide to Civic Engagement* (New York: M.E. Sharpe, 2008), 4.
19. B. Guy Peters and Jon Pierre, "Introduction," in B. Guy Peters and Jon Pierre, eds., *Handbook of Public Policy* (Thousand Oaks, CA: Sage Publications, 2006), 4.
20. Peter John, "Is There Life After Policy Streams, Advocacy Coalitions, and Punctuations: Using Evolutionary Theory to Explain Policy Change," *Policy Studies Journal* 31 (2003): 483.
21. Peters and Pierre, 3.
22. John, 483.
23. James Anderson, *Public Policy Making*, 5th ed. (Boston: Houghton Mifflin, 2003), 1.
24. Dean Mann, "Democratic Politics and Environmental Policy," in Sheldon Kamieniecki, Robert O'Brien, and Michael Clarke, eds., *Controversies in Environmental Policy* (Albany: State University of New York Press, 1986), 4.
25. Norman Miller, *Environmental Politics: Stakeholders, Interests, and Policymaking*, 2nd ed. (New York: Routledge, 2009), 16–17.
26. Jane Gregory and Steve Miller, *Science in Public: Communication, Culture, and Credibility* (New York, Plenum Press, 1998), 248.
27. Karen Litfin, *Ozone Discourses: Science and Politics in Global Environmental Cooperation* (New York: Columbia University Press, 1994), 29.
28. Lynton Caldwell, "A National Policy for the Environment," in Robert Bartlett and James Gladden, eds., *Environment as a Focus for Public Policy* (College Station: Texas A&M Press, 1995), 158.
29. Baber and Bartlett, 9.
30. Daniel Sarewitz and Roger Pielke, Jr., "Reconciling Supply of and Demand for Science with Science Policy," *Workshop on Carbon Science: Reconciling Supply and Demand*, 16–17 September 2004, Fort Collins, CO, 2–3.
31. M. Granger Morgan and Jon Peha, "Analysis, Governance, and the Need for Better Institutional Arrangements," in M. Granger Morgan and Jon Peha, eds., *Science and Technology Advice for Congress* (Washington, DC: Resources for the Future, 2003), 3.
32. Sheila Jasanoff, *The Fifth Branch: Science Advisers as Policymakers* (Cambridge, MA: Harvard University Press, 1994), 250.
33. Wolfgang Panofsky, "Physics and Government," *Physics Today* 52 (1999): 35.
34. Frances Lynn, "The Interplay of Science and Values in Assessing and Regulating Environmental Risks," *Science, Technology & Human Values* 11 (1986): 48.
35. Gwynne Dyer, *Climate Wars* (Toronto: Random House Canada, 2008), 144–146.
36. Dyer, 146.
37. Radford Byerly and Roger Pielke, Jr., "The Changing Ecology of United States Science," *Science* 269 (1995):1532.
38. Anne Schneider and Helen Ingram, *Policy Design for Democracy* (Lawrence: University of Kansas Press, 1997), 38.
39. Richard D. Heffner, ed., *Democracy in America* (New York: New American Library, 1956), 163–164.
40. Chris Mooney, *The Republican War on Science* (New York: Basic Books, 2005), 1.
41. Mark Rushefsky, "Elites and Environmental Policy," in James P. Lester, ed., *Environmental Politics and Policy* (Durham: Duke University Press, 1995), 283.
42. Steven Yearly, "The Environmental Challenge to Scientific Studies," in Sheila Jasanoff, Gerald E. Markle, James C. Peterson, and Trevor Pinch, eds., *Handbook of Science and Technology Studies* (Thousand Oaks, CA: Sage Publications, 1995), 462.

43. John E. Carroll et al., *The Greening of Faith: God, the Environment, and the Good Life* (Hanover: University Press of New England, 1997), 3.
44. Underdal, 3.
45. Miller, 132.
46. Litfin, 9.
47. Malcolm Scully, "Of Patronage and Exploitation," *Chronicle of Higher Education* 49 (2003): B13.
48. John Kingdon, *Agendas, Alternatives, and Public Policies*, 2nd ed. (New York: Harper Collins College Publishers, 1995), 19.
49. Daniel Sarewitz, *Frontiers of Illusion: Science, Technology, and the Politics of Progress* (Philadelphia: Temple University Press, 1996), 3.
50. Sarewitz, 71.
51. Bruce Bimber, *The Politics of Expertise in Congress: The Rise and Fall of the Office of Technology Assessment* (Albany: State University of New York Press, 1996), 1–7.
52. Lee, 163.
53. Milton Russell, "Lessons from NAPAP," *Ecological Applications* 2 (1992): 108.
54. Ellis B. Cowling, "The Performance and Legacy of NAPAP," *Ecological Applications* 2 (1992):113–114.
55. Lee, 183–184.
56. Aaron Wildavsky, *But Is it True? A Citizen's Guide to Environmental Health and Safety Issues* (Cambridge, MA: Harvard University Press, 1995), 5.
57. Rosenbaum, 119.

CHAPTER 2

1. Karen Litfin, *Ozone Discourses: Science and Politics in Global Environmental Cooperation* (New York: Columbia University Press, 1994), 106.
2. Robert Lackey, "Societal Values and the Proper Role of Restoration Ecologists," *Frontiers in Ecology and the Environment* 2 (2004): 45.
3. James Anderson, *Public Policy Making*, 5th ed. (Boston: Houghton Mifflin, 2003), 2.
4. Clarke Cochran et al., *American Public Policy*, 7th ed. (Belmont, CA: Wadsworth, 2003), 1.
5. Mark E. Rushefsky, *Public Policy in the United States: At the Dawn of the Twenty-First Century*, 4th ed. (New York: M. E. Sharpe, 2008), 3.
6. James P. Lester and Joseph Stewart, Jr., *Public Policy: An Evolutionary Approach* (Belmont, CA: Wadsworth/Thomson Learning, 2000), 4.
7. Thomas Dye, *Understanding Public Policy*, 10th ed. (Upper Saddle River, NJ: Prentice-Hall, 2002), 1.
8. Paul A. Sabatier, *Theories of the Policy Process*, 2nd ed. (Boulder: Westview Press, 2007), 3.
9. Diane Stone, "Global Public Policy," *Policy Study Journal* 36 (2008): 21.
10. Anne Schneider and Helen Ingram, *Policy Design for Democracy* (Lawrence: University of Kansas Press, 1997), 3.
11. E. E. Schattschneider, *The Semisovereign People: A Realist's View of Democracy in America* (Hinsdale, Illinois: Dryden Press, 1960), 127–128.
12. Georg Sorensen, *Democracy and Democratization: Processes and Prospects in a Changing World* (Boulder: Westview Press, 1998), 3.
13. See Freedom House: http://www.freedomhouse.org and POLITY IV: http://www.systemicpeace.org/polity/polity4.htm.

14. Echoes of this concept of democracy are found in Federalist X, by James Madison: "Complaints are everywhere heard . . . that measures are too often decided, not according to the rules of justice and the rights of the minor party, but by the superior force of an interested and overbearing majority. . . . If a faction consists of less than a majority, relief is supplied by the republican principle, which enables the majority to defeat its sinister views by regular vote. . . . To secure the public good and private rights against the danger of such a [majority] faction, and at the same time to preserve the spirit and the form of popular government, is then the great object to which our inquiries are directed."

15. Kai N. Lee, *Compass and Gyroscope: Integrating Science and Politics for the Environment* (Washington, DC: Island Press, 1993), 34.

16. Larry N. Gerston, *Public Policymaking in a Democratic Society: A Guide to Civic Engagement* (New York: M. E. Sharpe, 2008), 4.

17. Robert D. Putnam, "Bowling Alone: America's Declining Social Capital," *Journal of Democracy* 6 (1995): 65–78.

18. Leonard Cole, *Element of Risk: The Politics of Radon* (New York: Oxford University Press, 1993), 3; Andrew Dobson and Derek Bell, "Introduction," in Andrew Dobson and Derek Bell, eds., *Environmental Citizenship* (Cambridge, MA: MIT Press, 2006), 6.

19. David Collingridge and Colin Reeve, *Science Speaks to Power: The Role of Experts in Policy Making* (New York: St. Martin's Press, 1986), 158.

20. Transparency International, http://www.transparency.org/news_room/faq/corruption_faq#faqcorr2 (14 August 2009).

21. Daniel Fiorina, *The New Environmental Regulation* (Cambridge, MA: MIT Press, 2006), 191–192.

22. Christopher Bosso, *Environment, Inc.: From Grassroots to Beltway* (Lawrence: University of Kansas Press, 2005), 153.

23. Lynton Caldwell, *Between Two Worlds: Science, the Environmental Movement, and Public Choice* (New York: Cambridge University Press, 1990), x.

24. Gerston, 3–14.

25. Robert Duffy, *The Green Agenda in American Politics: New Strategies for the Twenty-First Century* (Lawrence: University of Kansas Press, 2003), 41.

26. Rushefsky, 2008, 22–34.

27. Roger Clark et al., *Integrating Science and Policy in Natural Resource Management: Lessons and Opportunities from North America*, U.S. Department of Agriculture, Forest Service, Pacific Northwest Research Station, General Technical Report, PNW-GTR-441, September, 1998, 2–3.

28. United States Intelligence Community. http://www.intelligence.gov/1-members .shtml (14 August 2009).

29. Walter Rosenbaum, *Environmental Politics and Policy*, 7th ed. (Washington, DC: CQ Press, 2008), 30.

30. James Smith, *The Idea Brokers: Think Tanks and the Rise of the New Policy Elite* (New York: Free Press, 1991), xxi.

31. Glen Krutz, and Paul Jorgensen, "Winnowing in Environmental Policy: Jurisdictional Challenges and Opportunities," *Review of Policy Research* 25 (2008): 222.

32. Judith Layzer, *The Environmental Case: Translating Values into Policy*, 2nd ed. (Washington, DC: CQ Press, 2006), 491.

33. Rushefsky, 2008, 31.

34. Rushefsky, 2008, 32.

35. Roger Pielke, Jr., *The Honest Broker: Making Sense of Science in Policy and Politics* (New York: Cambridge University Press, 2007), 11.
36. Bruce Williams and Albert Matheny, *Democracy, Dialogue, and Environmental Disputes: The Contested Languages of Social Regulation* (New Haven, CT: Yale University Press, 1995), 42–46.
37. Charles E. Lindblom, *Politics and Markets* (New York: Basic Books, 1977), 356.
38. Williams and Matheny, 42.
39. Adam Finkel and Dominic Golding, *Worst Things First? The Debate over Risk-Based National Environmental Priorities* (Washington, DC: Resources for the Future, 1994), 27.
40. Andrew Bacevich, *The Limits of Power: The End of American Exceptionalism* (New York: Henry Holt & Company, 2008), 102–103; Dorothy Nelkin, "Science Controversies: The Dynamics of Public Disputes in the United States," in Sheila Jasanoff et al., eds., *Handbook of Science and Technology Studies* (Thousand Oaks, CA: Sage Publications, 1995), 445–447.
41. Sheila Jasanoff, *The Fifth Branch: Science Advisers as Policymakers* (Cambridge, MA: Harvard University Press, 1994), 9; Schneider and Ingram, 38.
42. Eric Herzik and John Dobra, "What's Science Got to Do with It? The Use of Public Opinion in Developing Nuclear Waste Policy," *Proceeding of the 5th Annual International Conference on High Level Radioactive Waste Management* (American Nuclear Society, 1994), 119.
43. Brian Silver, *The Ascent of Science* (New York: Solomon Press, 1998), xv.
44. Schneider and Ingram, 6–7.
45. Megan Jones, David Guston, and Lewis Branscomb, *Informed Legislatures: Coping with Science in a Democracy* (Cambridge, MA: Harvard University Press, 1996), 1.
46. Stone, Diane, 32.
47. Robert Wood, "Scientists and Politics: The Rise of an Apolitical Elite," in Robert Gilpin and Christopher Wright, eds., *Scientists and National Policy-Making* (New York: Columbia University Press, 1964), 44.
48. Daniel Kleinman, *Politics on the Endless Frontier: Postwar Research Policy in the United States* (Durham, NC: Duke University Press, 1995), 2.
49. See Richard Hofferbert, *The Study of Public Policy* (Indianapolis: Bobbs-Merrill, 1974).
50. See Larry Kiser and Elinor Ostrom, "The Three Worlds of Action," in Elinor Ostrom, ed., *Strategies of Political Inquiry* (Beverly Hills, CA: Sage Publications, 1982), 179–222.
51. See Charles Bonser, Eugene McGregor, and Clinton Oster, *American Public Policy Problems: An Introductory Guide*, 2nd ed. (Upper Saddle River, NJ: Prentice Hall, 2000); Lester and Stewart; Rushefsky, 2008.
52. See B. Guy Peters and Jon Pierre, "Introduction," in B. Guy Peters and Jon Pierre, eds., *Handbook of Public Policy* (Thousand Oaks, CA: Sage Publications, 2006), 1–9.
53. See David Robertson and Dennis Judd, *The Development of American Public Policy: The Structure of Policy Restraint* (Glenview, IL: Scott, Foresman and Company, 1989).
54. Paul A. Sabatier, *Theories of the Policy Process*, 2nd ed. (Boulder: Westview Press, 2007), 5–10.
55. Peters and Pierre, 1.
56. See Sabatier, 8–10. Sabatier offers a more comprehensive listing of frameworks in addition to what we have listed. Also, see Peter John, "Is There Life after Policy Streams, Advocacy Coalitions, and Punctuations: Using Evolutionary Theory to

Explain Policy Change," *Policy Studies Journal* 31 (2003): 481–498; and Louis Weschler, "Taming the Common Pool," *Journal of Public Administration Research and Theory: J-Part* 1 (1991): 488–492.

57. Weschler, 489.
58. See John Kingdon, *Agendas, Alternatives, and Public Policies*, 2nd ed. (New York: Harper Collins College Publishers, 1995).
59. See Paul Sabatier and Hank Jenkins-Smith, *Policy Change and Learning* (Boulder, CO: Westview Press, 1993); and Paul Sabatier and Christopher Weible, "The Advocacy Coalition Framework: Innovations and Clarifications," in Paul Sabatier, ed., *Theories of the Policy Process*, 2nd ed. (Boulder, CO: Westview Press, 2007), 191.
60. See Frank Baumgartner and Bryan Jones, *Agendas and Instability in American Politics* (Chicago. IL: University of Chicago Press, 1993); and James True, Bryan Jones, and Frank Baumgartner, "Punctuated Equilibrium Theory: Explaining Stability and Change in Public Policymaking," in Paul Sabatier, ed., *Theories of the Policy Process*, 2nd ed. (Boulder, CO: Westview Press, 2007), 155–187.
61. See Elinor Ostrom, *Governing the Commons: The Evolution of Institutions for Collective Action* (New York: Cambridge University Press, 1990); and Elinor Ostrom, "Institutional Rational Choice: An Assessment of the Institutional Analysis and Development Framework," in Paul Sabatier, ed., *Theories of the Policy Process* (Boulder, CO: Westview Press, 1999), 35–71.
62. Ostrom, 1990, 182.
63. Weschler, 488–492.
64. Deborah Stone, *Policy Paradox: The Art of Political Decision Making*, rev. ed. (New York: W. W. Norton & Co., 2002), 376.
65. Stone, Deborah, 376.
66. Sheila Jasanoff, *Designs on Nature: Science and Democracy in Europe and the United States* (Princeton: Princeton University Press, 2005), 23; Rushefsky, 2008, 4–6.
67. Roger Pielke, Jr., "Asking the Right Questions: Atmospheric Sciences Research and Societal Needs," *Bulletin of the American Meteorological Society* 78 (1997): 258.
68. Karen Greif and Jon Merz, *Current Controversies in the Biological Sciences: Case Studies of Policy Challenges from New Technologies* (Cambridge, MA: MIT Press, 2007), 2.
69. David Guston, *Between Politics and Science: Assuring the Integrity and Productivity of Research* (New York: Cambridge University Press, 2000), 2.
70. Richard Sclove, "Better Approaches to Science Policy," *Science* 279 (1998): 1283.
71. Thomas Beierle and Jerry Cayford, "Dispute Resolution as a Method of Public Participation," in Rosemary O'Leary and Lisa Bingham, eds., *The Promise and Performance of Environmental Conflict Resolution* (Washington, DC: Resources for the Future, 2003), 53.
72. Sarah Pralle, *Branching Out, Digging In: Environmental Advocacy and Agenda Setting* (Washington, DC: Georgetown University Press, 2007), 220.
73. Jasanoff, 1994, 17.
74. Sanford Lakoff, "The Disconnect Between Scientists and the Public," *Chronicle of Higher Education* 51 (2005): B18.
75. Jasanoff, 2005, 5–6.
76. Sabatier, 3.
77. Kingdon's hidden cluster of participants includes academics, researchers, career bureaucrats, congressional staffers, and administrative appointees.
78. Kingdon, 200.
79. Kingdon, 201.

80. Eugene Rosa, Riley Dunlap, and Michael Kraft, "Prospects for Public Acceptance of a High-Level Nuclear Waste Repository in the United States: Summary and Implications," in Riley Dunlap, Michael Kraft, and Eugene Rosa, eds., *Public Reactions to Nuclear Waste: Citizens' Views of Repository Siting* (Durham, NC: Duke University Press, 1993), 291.

81. Walter Baber and Robert Bartlett, *Deliberative Environmental Politics: Democracy and Ecological Rationality* (Cambridge, MA: MIT Press, 2005), 5–11.

82. Mark Bowen, *Censoring Science: Inside the Political Attack on Dr. James Hansen and the Truth of Global Warming* (New York: Dutton, 2008), 265–304.

83. Baber and Bartlett, 11.

84. Nelkin, 446.

85. Rushefsky, 2008, 3.

86. Evan Goldstein, "The New Paternalism," *Chronicle of Higher Education* 59 (2008): B8.

87. Greif and Merz, 3.

88. Edward O. Wilson, *Consilience: The Unity of Knowledge* (New York: Alfred A. Knopf, 1998), 182.

89. Litfin, 31.

90. Alexander Farrell, Jill Jager, and Stacy VanDeveer, "Understanding Design Choices," in Alexander Farrell and Jill Jager, eds., *Assessments of Regional and Global Environmental Risks: Designing Processes for the Effective Use of Science in Decisionmaking* (Washington, DC: Resources for the Future, 2006), 1.

91. Tora Skodvin and Arild Underdal, "Exploring the Dynamics of the Science–Politics Interaction," in Steiner Andresen et al., eds., *Science and Politics in International Environmental Regimes* (Manchester: Manchester University Press, 2000), 30.

92. George E. Brown, "Environmental Science under Siege in the U.S. Congress," *Environment* 39 (1997): 19.

93. Sarewitz, 78.

94. Steve Rayner, "Prediction and Other Approaches to Climate Change Policy," in Daniel Sarewitz, Roger Pielke, Jr., and Radford Byerly, Jr., eds., *Prediction: Science, Decision-Making, and the Future of Nature* (Washington, DC: Island Press, 2000), 270–271.

95. Wade Robison, *Decisions in Doubt: The Environment and Public Policy* (Hanover, NH: University Press of New England, 1994), 40.

96. Sheila Jasanoff and Marybeth Long Martello, "Conclusion: Knowledge and Governance," in Sheila Jasanoff and Marybeth Long Martello, eds., *Earthly Politics: Local and Global in Environmental Governance* (Cambridge, MA: MIT Press, 2004), 336.

97. George E. Brown, Jr. "Guest Comment: The Objectivity Crisis," *American Journal of Physics* 60 (1992): 780.

98. Mark Rushefsky, "The Misuse of Science in Governmental Decisionmaking," *Science, Technology, and Human Values* 9 (1984): 47.

99. Skodvin and Underdal, 30.

100. Robison, 7; Rosenbaum, 59.

101. Paul Sabatier, "The Need for Better Theories," in Paul Sabatier, ed., *Theories of the Policy Process*, 2nd ed. (Boulder: Westview Press, 2007), 4.

102. Rushefsky, 1984, 47.

CHAPTER 3

1. See Benjamin Kline, *First Along the River: A Brief History of the U.S. Environmental Movement,* 3rd ed. (New York: Rowman & Littlefield Publishers, Inc., 2007).

2. For a concise summary of the history of the environmental movement, see also Zachary Smith, *The Environmental Paradox*, 5th ed. (Upper Saddle River, NJ: Pearson/Prentice Hall, 2009), 16–20.

3. Kline, 82.

4. Kline, 99.

5. For a listing of mainstream environmental organizations and their revenues, as well as a discussion of the environmental movement in the twenty-first century, see Deborah Guber and Christopher Bosso, "Past the Tipping Point? Public Discourse and the Role of the Environmental Movement in a Post-Bush Era," in Norman Vig and Michael Kraft, eds., *Environmental Policy: New Directions for the Twenty-First Century*, 7th ed. (Washington, DC: CQ Press, 2010), 51–74.

6. Kline, 163.

7. Norman Vig and Michael Kraft, eds., *Environmental Policy: New Directions for the Twenty-First Century*, 7th ed. (Washington, DC: CQ Press, 2010), xi.

8. Kline, 173.

9. Lynton Caldwell, *Between Two Worlds: Science, the Environmental Movement, and Public Choice* (New York: Cambridge University Press, 1990), 101.

10. Willett Kempton, James Boster, and Jennifer Hartley, *Environmental Values in American Culture* (Cambridge, MA: MIT Press, 1995), 13.

11. Walter A. Rosenbaum, *Environmental Politics and Policy*, 7th ed. (Washington, DC: CQ Press, 2008), 52.

12. W. Douglas Costain and James Lester, "The Evolution of Environmentalism," in James Lester, ed., *Environmental Politics & Policy: Theories and Evidence*, 2nd ed. (Durham, NC: Duke University Press, 1995), 34.

13. Robert Duffy, *The Green Agenda in American Politics: New Strategies for the Twenty-first Century* (Lawrence: University of Kansas Press, 2003), 6.

14. Walter Baber and Robert Bartlett, *Deliberative Environmental Politics: Democracy and Ecological Rationality* (Cambridge, MA: MIT Press, 2005), 215.

15. Christopher Bosso, *Environment, Inc.: From Grassroots to Beltway* (Lawrence: University of Kansas Press, 2005), 157.

16. Paul Ehrlich and Anne Ehrlich, *Betrayal of Science and Reason: How Anti-Environmental Rhetoric Threatens Our Future* (Washington, DC: Island Press, 1996), 12.

17. Gregg Easterbrook, "Good News from Planet Earth," *USA Weekend*, 14–16 April 1995, 4.

18. Christopher Bosso and Deborah Gruber, "Maintaining Presence: Environmental Advocacy and the Permanent Campaign," in Norman Vig and Michael Kraft, *Environmental Policy: New Directions for the Twenty-First Century*, 6th ed. (Washington, DC: CQ Press, 2006), 80–84.

19. Gallup Poll, "Increased Number Think Global Warming Is 'Exaggerated,'" 11 March 2009, http://www.gallup.com/poll/116590/Increased-Number-Think-Global-Warming -Exaggerated.aspx (14 August 2009).

20. Christopher Bosso and Deborah Gruber, "The Boundaries and Contours of American Environmental Activism," in Norman Vig and Michael Kraft, *Environmental Policy: New Directions for the Twenty-First Century*, 5th ed. (Washington, DC: CQ Press, 2003), 94.

21. Duffy, 6.

22. Duffy, 9.

23. Duffy, 4.

24. Smith, 297.

25. Paul Harris, "Bringing the In-Between Back In: Foreign Policy in Global Environmental Politics," *Politics & Policy* 36 (2008): 914.

26. Rosenbaum, 6.

27. James Speth, "Environmental Failure: A Case for a New Green Politics," *Environment360*, 21 October 2008, http://e360.yale.edu/content/feature.msp?id =2075 (29 August 2009), 1.

28. Evan Ringquist and Tatiana Kostadinova, "Assessing the Effectiveness of International Environmental Agreements: The Case of the 1985 Helsinki Protocol," *American Journal of Political Science* 49 (2005): 88.

29. Kai N. Lee, *Compass and Gyroscope: Integrating Science and Politics for the Environment* (Washington, DC: Island Press, 1993), 49.

30. Duffy, 5.

31. Gwynne Dyer, *Climate Wars* (Toronto: Random House Canada, 2008), 142.

32. Duffy, 10.

33. CNN Election Center 2008, Presidential Exit Polls, 4 November 2008, http://www.cnn.com/ELECTION/2008/results/polls/#val=USP00p6 (21 August 2009).

34. Bosso, 1; Frank Davis, Albert Wurth, and John Lazarus, "The Green Vote in Presidential Elections: Past Performance and Future Promise," *Social Science Journal* 45 (2008): 540.

35. Jeffrey Kash, "Enemies to Allies: The Role of Policy-Design Adaptation in Facilitating a Farmers-Environmentalist Alliance," *Policy Studies Journal* 36 (2008): 39–40.

36. Morton Keller, *America's Three Regimes: A New Political History* (New York: Oxford University Press, 2007), 250.

37. Lester Milbrath, *Environmentalists: Vanguard for a New Society* (Albany: State University Press of New York, 1984), 21.

38. Rosenbaum, 52; Vig and Kraft, xi–xiii.

39. Neil Harrison and Gary Bryner, *Science and Politics in the International Environment* (New York: Rowman and Littlefield, 2004), 1–3; Rosenbaum, 333.

40. Arthur Mol, *Globalization and Environmental Reform: The Ecological Modernization of the Global Economy* (Cambridge, MA: MIT Press, 2001), ix.

41. Robert Paehlke, *Democracy's Dilemma: Economic, Social Equity, and the Global Economy* (Cambridge, MA: MIT Press, 2003), 8.

42. Jennifer Clapp, "Responses to Environmental Threats in an Age of Globalization," in Robert Paelke and Douglas Torgereson, eds., *Managing Leviathan: Environmental Politics and the Administrative State*, 2nd ed. (Peterborough, Ontario: Broadview Press, 2005), 271.

43. Stephen D. Krasner, "Structural Causes and Regime Consequences: Regimes as Intervening Variables," in Stephen D. Krasner, ed., *International Regimes* (Ithaca, NY: Cornell University Press, 1982), 2.

44. Lamont C. Hempel, "Climate Policy on the Installment Plan," in Norman Vig and Michael Kraft, eds., *Environmental Policy*, 6th ed. (Washington, DC: CQ Press, 2006), 298.

45. Gary Bryner, "Global Interdependence," in Robert Durant, Daniel Fiorino, and Rosemary O'Leary, eds., *Environmental Governance Reconsidered: Challenges, Choices, and Opportunities* (Cambridge, MA: MIT Press, 2004), 69.

46. *The Environmental Professional* 16 (1994): 118.

47. Robert Durant, Daniel Fiorino, and Rosemary O'Leary, "Conclusion," in Robert Durant, Daniel Fiorino, and Rosemary O'Leary, eds., *Environmental Governance*

Reconsidered: Challenges, Choices, and Opportunities (Cambridge, MA: MIT Press, 2004), 515.

48. Rosenbaum, 1–24; Vig and Kraft, 2010, 1–23.
49. Glen Sussman, Byron Daynes, and Jonathon West, *American Politics and the Environment* (New York: Longman Publishers, 2002), 313.
50. Frank Wijen, Kees Zoeteman, and Jan Pieters, *A Handbook of Globalization and Environmental Policy: National Government Interventions in a Global Arena* (Cheltenham, UK: Edward Elgar, 2005), 2.
51. Ken Conca and Geoffrey Dabelko, "Three Decades of Global Environmental Politics," in Ken Conca and Geoffrey Dabelko, eds., *Green Planet Blues* (Boulder, CO: Westview Press, 2004), 1.
52. Joseph DiMento, *The Global Environment and International Law* (Austin: University of Texas Press, 2003), 13.
53. John Sigmon, "Saving the Environment (from Ourselves): An Educator's Perspective," *Human Dimension's Quarterly* 1 (1996): 11.
54. Richard Benedick, *Ozone Diplomacy: New Directions in Safeguarding the Planet* (Cambridge, MA: Harvard University Press, 1998), xi.
55. David Fahrenthold, "Ready for Challenges," *Washington Post National Weekly* 26 (2008): 34.
56. Malcolm Scully, "Protecting the Endangered Species Act," *Chronicle of Higher Education* 49 (2003): B16.
57. Donald Kettl, "Environmental Policy: The Next Generation," *The LaFollette Policy Report* 9 (1999): 16.
58. Rosenbaum, 7.
59. Denise Scherberle, *Federalism and Environmental Policy: Trust and the Politics of Implementation*, 2nd ed. (Washington, DC: Georgetown University Press, 2004), 2.
60. Ronnie Lipschutz, *Global Environmental Politics: Power, Perspectives, and Practice* (Washington, DC: CQ Press, 2004), xi.
61. Evan Ringquist, *Environmental Protection at the State Level: Politics and Progress in Controlling Pollution* (Armonk, NY: M.E. Sharpe, 1993), 8.
62. Dean Mann, "Democratic Politics and Environmental Policy," in Sheldon Kamieniecki, Robert O'Brien, and Michael Clarke, eds., *Controversies in Environmental Policy* (Albany: State University of New York Press, 1986), 4.
63. Kline, 84–100; Christoph Knill, "Environmental Policy," in B. Guy Peters and Jon Pierre, eds., *Handbook of Public Policy* (Thousand Oaks, CA: Sage Publications, 2006), 249–259.
64. Harris, 930.
65. Caldwell, 1990, 4.
66. Baber and Bartlett, 208; Lynton Caldwell, *Between Two Worlds: Science, the Environmental Movement, and Public Choice* (New York: Cambridge University Press, 1990), 4; Duffy, 41.
67. Paehlke, 3.
68. Lynton Caldwell, "Environmental Policy as a Political Problem," *Policy Studies Review* 12 (1993): 111.
69. Knill, 259.
70. Baber and Bartlett, 209.
71. Rosenbaum, 41.
72. Judith Layzer, *The Environmental Case: Translating Values Into Policy*, 2nd ed. (Washington, DC: CQ Press, 2006), 279.

73. Vig and Kraft, 2010, 9–17.
74. Caldwell, 1990, 87.
75. Evan Ringquist, "Environmental Protection Regulation," in Kenneth Meier, E. Thomas Garman, and Lael Keiser, eds., *Regulation and Consumer Protection: Politics, Bureaucracy and Economics*, 3rd ed. (Houston, TX: Dame Publications, 1998), 143–180.
76. Evan Goldstein, "The New Paternalism," *Chronicle of Higher Education* 54 (2008): B9.
77. Goldstein, B9.
78. Elizabeth McNie, "Reconciling Supply and Demand of Scientific Information: A Review of the Literature," *Workshop on Carbon Cycle Science: Reconciling Supply and Demand*, 16–17 September 2004, Fort Collins, CO, 27.
79. Sheila Jasanoff and Marybeth Long Martello, "Conclusion: Knowledge and Governance," in Sheila Jasanoff and Marybeth Long Martello, eds., *Earthly Politics: Local and Global in Environmental Governance* (Cambridge, MA: MIT Press, 2004), 335.
80. Caldwell, 1993, 112.
81. Jasanoff and Martello, 336; Mark Rushefsky, "Elites and Environmental Policy," in James P. Lester, ed., *Environmental Politics and Policy* (Durham: Duke University Press, 1995), 283.
82. Daniel Sarewitz and Roger Pielke, Jr., "Reconciling Supply of and Demand for Science with Science Policy," *Workshop on Carbon Science: Reconciling Supply and Demand*, 16–17 September 2004, Fort Collins, CO, 10.
83. Smith, 1.
84. Layzer, 6.
85. Rosenbaum, 366.
86. Rosenbaum, 57.
87. James Rosenau, "Environmental Challenges in a Global Context," in Sheldon Kamieniecki, ed., *Environmental Politics in the International Arena: Movements, Parties, Organizations, and Policy* (Albany: State University of New York Press, 1993), 258.
88. John Carroll, Paul Brockelman, and Mary Westfall, eds., *The Greening of Faith: God, the Environment, and the Good Life* (Hanover, NH: University Press of New England, 1997), 3.
89. Karen Litfin, *Ozone Discourses: Science and Politics in Global Environmental Cooperation* (New York: Columbia University Press, 1994), 13; Richard Pouyat, "Science and Environmental Policy: Making Them Compatible," *Bioscience* 49 (1999): 282.
90. Dale Jamieson, "Prediction in Society," in Daniel Sarewitz, Roger Pielke, Jr., and Radford Byerly, Jr., eds., *Prediction: Science, Decision-Making, and the Future of Nature* (Washington, DC: Island Press, 2000), 322–323.
91. George E. Brown, Jr., "Guest Comment: The Objectivity Crisis," *American Journal of Physics* 60 (1992): 779.
92. Daniel Sarewitz, *Frontiers of Illusion: Science, Technology, and the Politics of Progress* (Philadelphia: Temple University Press, 1996), 4.
93. Brown, 779–780.
94. Richard Somerville, "The Ethics of Climate Change," *Environment360*, 4 June 2008, http://www.e360.yale.edu (8 June 2008), 1.
95. William Leiss, *Under Technology's Thumb* (Montreal: McGill-Queen's University Press, 1990), 148.
96. Sarewitz, 109.

CHAPTER 4

1. Karen Greif and Jon Merz, *Current Controversies in the Biological Sciences: Case Studies of Policy Challenges from New Technologies* (Cambridge, MA: MIT Press, 2007), 1.

2. Daniel Sarewitz and Roger Pielke, Jr., "Reconciling Supply of and Demand for Science with Science Policy," *Workshop on Carbon Science: Reconciling Supply and Demand*, 16–17 September 2004, Fort Collins, CO, 10; Jac Van Beek and Frances Isaacs, "Convergence and Scientific Management," in Glen Toner, ed., *Innovation, Science, and Environment: Canadian Policies and Performance, 2008–2009* (Montreal: McGill-Queen's University Press, 2008), 211.

3. Nicholas Ashford, "Value Judgments and Risk Assessment," in C. Mark Smith, David Christiana, and Karl Kelsey, eds., *Chemical Risk Assessment and Occupational Health* (Westport, CT: Auburn House, 1994), 199; Jurgen Schmandt, "Regulation and Science," *Science, Technology, and Human Values* 9 (1984): 26.

4. Jane Gregory and Steve Miller, *Science in Public: Communication, Culture, and Credibility* (New York: Plenum Trade, 1998), 248; Edward O. Wilson, *Consilience: The Unity of Knowledge* (New York: Alfred A. Knopf, 1998), 190.

5. Jeffrey Brainard, "The Waning Influence of Scientists on National Policy," *Chronicle of Higher Education* 48 (2001): A19; Kenneth Hoover and Todd Donovan, *The Elements of Social Science Thinking*, 9th ed. (Boston: Thomson-Wadsworth, 2008), 2.

6. Brian Silver, *The Ascent of Science* (New York: Solomon Press, 1998), xii.

7. Don Price, *The Scientific Estate* (Cambridge, MA: Harvard University Press, 1965), 120.

8. Bruce Williams and Albert Matheny, *Democracy, Dialogue, and Environmental Disputes: The Contested Languages of Social Regulation* (New Haven, CT: Yale University Press, 1995), 11.

9. Mark Bowen, *Censoring Science: Inside the Political Attack on Dr. James Hansen and the Truth of Global Warming* (New York: Dutton, 2008), 231–232.

10. Francis Collins, *The Language of God* (New York: Free Press, 2006), 6.

11. William Leiss, *Under Technology's Thumb* (Montreal: McGill-Queen's University Press, 1990), 6.

12. Deborah Stone, *Policy Paradox: The Art of Political Decision Making*, rev. ed. (New York: W. W. Norton & Co., 2002), 203.

13. Karen Litfin, *Ozone Discourses: Science and Politics in Global Environmental Cooperation* (New York: Columbia University Press, 1994), 35; Dorothy Nelkin, "Science Controversies: The Dynamics of Public Disputes in the United States," in Sheila Jasanoff et al., eds., *Handbook of Science and Technology Studies* (Thousand Oaks, CA: Sage Publications, 1995), 452.

14. Michael Shermer, *The Borderlands of Science: Where Sense Meets Nonsense* (New York: Oxford University Press, 2001), 43; Sheldon Steinbach, "How Frivolous Litigation Threatens Good Science," *Chronicle of Higher Education* 45 (1998): A56.

15. Paul Sabatier, "The Need for Better Theories," in Paul Sabatier, ed., *Theories of the Policy Process*, 2nd ed. (Boulder: Westview Press, 2007), 5.

16. Litfin, 24.

17. Hoover and Donovan, 3–4.

18. Alan C. Isaak, *Scope and Methods of Political Science*, 4th ed. (Homewood, Illinois: Dorsey Press, 1985), 28–31.

19. Isaak, 31.

20. Sabatier, 5.

21. Sabatier, 5.

22. Silver, xiii.
23. Silver, 25.
24. Eugene Buck, M. Lynne Corn, and Pamela Baldwin, "The Endangered Species Act and 'Sound Science,'" *CRS Report for Congress* (Washington, DC: CRS, 2007), 7.
25. Buck, Corn, and Baldwin, 8.
26. Buck, Corn, and Baldwin, 10.
27. Dominique Foray and Ali Kazancigil, "Science, Economics, and Democracy: Selected Issues." Prepared for the World Conference on Science, UNESCO-ICSU, Budapest, Hungary, 26 June–1 July, 1999, 12.
28. H. Sterling Burnett, "Openness Protects Science and the Decisions That Follow," *Idaho Statesman*, 1 August 1999, 7B.
29. Burnett, 7B.
30. Bill Joy, "Why the Future Doesn't Need Us," *Wired* 8 (2000): 254.
31. United States General Accounting Office, *Climate Change Research*, (Washington, D.C., GAO-07-1172, 2007), 2.
32. Ashford, 201.
33. Daniel Greenberg, "Self-Restraint by Scientists Can Avert Federal Intrusion," *Chronicle of Higher Education* 49 (2002): B20.
34. Arild Underdal, "Science and Politics: The Anatomy of an Uneasy Partnership," in Steinar Andresen et al., eds., *Science and Politics in International Environmental Regimes* (Manchester: Manchester University Press, 2000), 10.
35. Richard Somerville, "The Ethics of Climate Change," *Environment360*, 4 June 2008, http://www.e360.yale.edu (8 June 2008), 1.
36. David Guston, *Between Politics and Science: Assuring the Integrity and Productivity of Research* (New York: Cambridge University Press, 2000), 23.
37. Roger Masters, *Beyond Relativism: Science and Human Values* (Hanover, NH: University of New England Press, 1993), 17–19.
38. William Bixby, "Newton's Principia," in Jerry Marion, ed., *A Universe of Physics: A Book of Readings* (New York: John Wiley and Sons, 1970), 48–52; A.J. Hahn, *Basic Calculus: From Archimedes to Newton to Its Role in Science* (New York: Springer-Verlag, 1998), 515–516.
39. Roger Masters, *Beyond Relativism: Science and Human Values* (Hanover, NH: University of New England Press, 1993), 12–26.
40. David Ricci, *The Tragedy of Political Science: Politics, Scholarship, and Democracy* (New Haven, CT: Yale University Press, 1984), 191–194; Silver, 22.
41. Norman Miller, *Environmental Politics: Stakeholders, Interests, and Policymaking*, 2nd ed. (New York: Routledge, 2009), 132; See also Walter Baber and Robert Bartlett, *Deliberative Environmental Politics: Democracy and Ecological Rationality* (Cambridge, MA: MIT Press, 2005), 9; John Myers and Joshua Reichert, "Perspectives on Nature's Services," in Gretchen Daily, ed., *Nature's Services: Societal Dependence on Natural Ecosystems* (Washington, DC: Island Press, 1997), xix; and Walter A. Rosenbaum, *Environmental Politics and Policy*, 7th ed. (Washington, DC: CQ Press, 2008), 333.
42. Eugene Skolnikoff, "The Role of Science in Policy: The Climate Change Debate in the United States," *Environment* 41 (1999): 17; Glen Toner, "Contesting the Green: Canadian Environmental Policy at the Turn of the Century," in Uday Desai, ed., *Environmental Politics and Policy in Industrialized Countries* (Cambridge, MA: MIT Press, 2002), 74.
43. Marvin Soroos, *The Endangered Atmosphere: Preserving a Global Commons* (Columbia: University of South Carolina Press, 1997), 14–15.

44. Robert Gilpin, "Introduction: Natural Scientists in Policy Making," in Robert Gilpin and Christopher Wright, eds., *Scientists and National Policy-Making* (New York: Columbia University Press, 1964), 12; Rosenbaum, 341; Bruce Smith, *The Advisors: Scientists in the Policy Process* (Washington, DC: Brookings Institution, 1992), 202.

45. Steven Mufson, "A Scientist Will Tackle Climate Change," *Washington Post National Weekly* 26 (2008): 35.

46. Zachary Smith, *The Environmental Policy Paradox* (Upper Saddle River, NJ: Pearson-Prentice Hall, 2009), 12.

47. Silver, xiv.

48. Sheila Jasanoff, *The Fifth Branch: Science Advisers as Policymakers* (Cambridge, MA: Harvard University Press, 1994), 7; Daniel Sarewitz, Roger Pielke, Jr., and Radford Byerly, Jr., "Introduction: Death, Taxes, and Environmental Policy," in Daniel Sarewitz, Roger Pielke, Jr., and Radford Byerly, Jr., eds., *Prediction: Science, Decision-Making, and the Future of Nature* (Washington, DC: Island Press, 2000), 4.

49. John Graham, Laura Green, and Marc Roberts, *In Search of Safety: Chemicals and Cancer Risk* (New York: Plenum Press, 1988), viii.

50. Roger Pielke, Jr., "Scientific Information and Global Change Policymaking," *Climate Change* 28 (1994): 318.

51. Brian Martin and Evelleen Richards, "Scientific Knowledge, Controversy, and Public Decision Making," in Sheila Jasanoff et al., eds., *Handbook of Science and Technology Studies* (Thousand Oaks, CA: Sage Publications, 1995), 507.

52. Rosenbaum, 17.

53. Baber and Bartlett, 8.

54. Roger Clark et al., *Integrating Science and Policy in Natural Resource Management: Lessons and Opportunities from North America*, U.S. Department of Agriculture, Forest Service, Pacific Northwest Research Station, General Technical Report, PNW-GTR-441, September, 1998, 16; Sheila Jasanoff and Marybeth Long Martello, "Conclusion: Knowledge and Governance," in Sheila Jasanoff and Marybeth Long Martello, eds., *Earthly Politics: Local and Global in Environmental Governance* (Cambridge, MA: MIT Press, 2004), 337.

55. Marvin Soroos, "Arctic Haze and Transboundary Air Pollution: Conditions Governing Success and Failure," in Oran Young and Gail Osherenko, eds., *Polar Politics: Creating International Environmental Regimes* (Ithaca, NY: Cornell University Press, 1993), 216.

56. David Collingridge and Colin Reeve, *Science Speaks to Power: The Role of Experts in Policy Making* (New York: St. Martin's Press, 1986), 5; Jasanoff, 1994, 8; Robert Wood, "Scientists and Politics: The Rise of an Apolitical Elite," in Robert Gilpin and Christopher Wright, eds., *Scientists and National Policy-Making* (New York: Columbia University Press, 1964), 45.

57. Pielke, 1994, 316.

58. William Leiss, "Governance and the Environment," in Thomas Courchene, ed., *Policy Framework for a Knowledge Economy* (Kingston, Ontario: John Deutch Institute for the Study of Economic Policy, 1996), 125–126.

59. Good science is defined by Leiss as being based on a thorough understanding of the leading edge of published scientific research findings.

60. Leiss, 125–126.

61. Stone, 379.

62. Litfin, 198.

63. Clark et al., 16.

64. George E. Brown, "Environmental Science under Siege in the U.S. Congress," *Environment* 39 (1997): 20.
65. Leonard Cassuto, "A Humorist's Sojourn among Scientists," *Chronicle of Higher Education* 49 (2003): B5.
66. Underdal, 10.
67. Miller, 132.
68. Chris Mooney, "Beware 'Sound Science,'" *Washington Post National Weekly Edition* 21 (2004): 23.
69. Underdal, 6.
70. Radford Byerly and Roger Pielke, Jr., "The Changing Ecology of United States Science," *Science* 269 (1995): 1532.
71. Smith, Zachary, 16.
72. C. P. Snow, *Science and Government* (Cambridge, MA: Harvard University Press, 1961), 76.
73. Pielke, 1994, 317.
74. Rosenbaum, 31.
75. Helen Ingram et al., "Scientists and Agenda Setting: Advocacy and Global Warming." Prepared for the Western Political Science Association Annual Meeting, Newport Beach, CA, 23 March 1990, 2–4; Litfin, 9–10.
76. Jasanoff and Martello, 337; Judith Layzer, *The Environmental Case: Translating Values into Policy*, 2nd ed. (Washington, DC: CQ Press, 2006), 289; Nelkin, 1995, 452.
77. Skolnikoff, 19.
78. Lynton Caldwell, "Binational Responsibilities for a Shared Environment," in Charles Doran and John Sigler, eds., *Canada and the United States: Enduring Friendship, Persistent Stress* (Englewood Cliffs, NJ: Prentice Hall, 1985), 222–223.
79. Graham, Green, and Roberts, 189.
80. Roger Pielke, Jr., *The Honest Broker: Making Sense of Science in Policy and Politics* (New York: Cambridge University Press, 2007), 87.
81. Dorothy Nelkin, *Nuclear Power and Its Critics: The Cayuga Lake Controversy* (Ithaca, NY: Cornell University Press, 1971), 43.
82. Norman Meyers, "Truth or Consequences?" *Earthwatch* March (2000): 8.
83. Richard Pouyat, "Science and Environmental Policy—Making Them Compatible," *Bioscience* 49 (1999): 281–282.
84. Pielke, 2007, 142.
85. Susan Cozzens and Edward Woodhouse, "Science, Government, and the Politics of Knowledge," in Sheila Jasanoff et al., eds., *Handbook of Science and Technology Studies* (Thousand Oaks, CA: Sage Publications, 1995), 533.
86. Underdal, 3–4.
87. Nina Burkardt, Emily Ruell, and Douglass Clark, "An Exploration of Bureau of Reclamation Approaches for Managing Conflict over Diverging Science," U.S. Department of Interior, Denver, CO, 2008, 5–6; Rosenbaum, 57.
88. Patrick Hamlett, *Understanding Technological Politics: A Decision-Making Approach* (Englewood Cliffs, NJ: Prentice Hall, 1992), 134.
89. Silver, 250.
90. Litfin, 81.
91. Alexander Farrell, Jill Jager, and Stacy VanDeveer, "Understanding Design Choices," in Alexander Farrell and Jill Jager, eds., *Assessments of Regional and Global Environmental Risks: Designing Processes for the Effective Use of Science in Decision-making* (Washington, DC: Resources for the Future, 2006), 2.

92. Jasanoff, 1994, 8.

93. Smith, Zachary, 13.

94. Sanford Lakoff, "The Disconnect between Scientists and the Public, *Chronicle of Higher Education* 51 (2005): B18; Peter Montague, "The Uses of Scientific Uncertainty," *Rachel's Environment and Health Weekly* 657 (1999): 2.

95. Skolnikoff, 19.

96. Daniel Sarewitz, *Frontiers of Illusion: Science, Technology, and the Politics of Progress* (Philadelphia: Temple University Press, 1996), 92.

97. Tora Skodvin and Arild Underdal, "Exploring the Dynamics of the Science–Politics Interaction," in Steiner Andresen et al., eds., *Science and Politics in International Environmental Regimes* (Manchester: Manchester University Press, 2000), 31.

98. Ryan Meyer, "Intractable Debate: Why Congressional Hearings on Climate Fail to Advance Policy," *Perspectives in Public Affairs* 3 (2006): 87.

99. Silver, 24.

100. Robert Lackey, "Normative Science," *Fisheries* 29 (2004): 38.

101. Sheila Jasanoff, *Designs on Nature: Science and Democracy in Europe and the United States* (Princeton: Princeton University Press, 2005), 16.

102. Walter Isaacson, *Einstein: His Life and Universe* (New York: Simon and Schuster, 2007), 6.

103. Dennis Soden, "At the Nexus: Science Policy," in Dennis Sodden, ed., *At the Nexus: Science Policy* (New York: Nova Science Publishers, 1996), 4.

104. Aaron Wildavsky, *But Is It True? A Citizen's Guide to Environmental Health and Safety Issues* (Cambridge, MA: Harvard University Press, 1995), 10.

105. Bruce Bimber, *The Politics of Expertise in Congress: The Rise and Fall of the Office of Technology Assessment* (Albany: State University of New York Press, 1996), 97; Graham, Green, and Roberts, 218.

106. Jasanoff, 1994, 7–8.

107. Lynton Caldwell, "Environmental Policy as a Political Problem," *Policy Studies Review* 12 (1993): 107–110.

108. Guy Benveniste, *The Politics of Expertise* (San Francisco: Boyd and Fraser Publishing Company, 1977), 5.

109. Brent Steel, Richard Clinton, and Nicholas Lovrich, *Environmental Politics and Policy: A Comparative Approach* (Boston: McGraw Hill, 2003), 55.

110. Graham, Green, and Roberts, 198.

111. Cozzens and Woodhouse, 542; Underdal, 5.

112. Wade Robison, *Decisions in Doubt: The Environment and Public Policy* (Hanover, NH: University Press of New England, 1994), 80.

113. Shermer, 177.

114. Gregory and Miller, 250.

115. Roger Masters, *Beyond Relativism: Science and Human Values* (Hanover, NH: University of New England Press, 1993), viii.

116. Williams and Matheny, 46.

117. Hamlett, 62–63; Sarewitz, 11; Daniel Sarewitz and Roger Pielke, Jr., "Prediction in Science and Policy," in Daniel Sarewitz, Roger Pielke, Jr., and Radford Byerly, Jr., eds., *Prediction: Science, Decision-Making, and the Future of Nature* (Washington, DC: Island Press, 2000), 11.

118. Bimber, 2.

119. Arthur Lupia, "Evaluating Political Science Research: Information for Buyers and Sellers," *PS: Political Science and Politics* 33 (2000): 7–13.

120. Underdal, 5.
121. Andrew Ross, "Introduction," in Andrew Ross, ed., *Science Wars* (Durham, NC: Duke University Press, 1996), 13.
122. Pielke, 2007, 32.
123. Alexander Keynan, "The Political Impact of Scientific Cooperation on Nature in Conflict: An Overview," in Allison deCerreno and Alexander Keynan, eds., *In Scientific Cooperation, State Conflict: The Roles of Scientists in Mitigating International Discord* (New York: The New York Academy of Sciences, 1998), 23.
124. Philip Kitcher, *Science, Truth, and Democracy* (New York: Oxford University Press, 2001), 195.
125. Gregory and Miller, 250.
126. Silver, xiii.
127. Silver, xiv.

CHAPTER 5

1. Kai N. Lee, *Compass and Gyroscope: Integrating Science and Politics for the Environment* (Washington, DC: Island Press, 1993), 17.
2. William Leiss, "Governance and the Environment," in Thomas Courchene, ed., *Policy Frameworks for a Knowledge Economy* (Kingston, Ontario: John Deutsch Institute for the Study of Economic Policy, 1996), 125–127.
3. Leiss, 124.
4. Judith Layzer, *The Environmental Case: Translating Values into Policy*, 2nd ed. (Washington, DC: CQ Press, 2006), 1–2.
5. Arild Underdal, "Science and Politics: The Anatomy of an Uneasy Partnership," in Steinar Andrescn et al., eds., *Science and Politics in International Environmental Regimes* (Manchester: Manchester University Press, 2000), 7.
6. Richard Benedick, *Ozone Diplomacy: New Directions in Safeguarding the Planet* (Cambridge, MA: Harvard University Press, 1998), 9.
7. Richard Monastersky, "Climate Science on Trial," *Chronicle of Higher Education* 53 (2006): A15.
8. Dale Jamieson, "Prediction in Society," in Daniel Sarewitz, Roger Pielke, Jr., and Radford Byerly, Jr., eds., *Prediction: Science, Decision-Making, and the Future of Nature* (Washington, DC: Island Press, 2000), 322.
9. *Environmental Professional* 16 (1994): 115–117.
10. Stephen Meyer, "The Role of Scientists in the 'New Politics,'" *Chronicle of Higher Education* 41 (1995): B1.
11. Walter A. Rosenbaum, *Environmental Politics and Policy*, 7th ed. (Washington, DC: CQ Press, 2008), 59.
12. Zachary Smith, *The Environmental Policy Paradox* (Upper Saddle River, NJ: Pearson-Prentice Hall, 2009), 15.
13. Lee, 15.
14. Karen Litfin, *Ozone Discourses: Science and Politics in Global Environmental Cooperation* (New York: Columbia University Press, 1994), 30.
15. Marybeth Long Martello and Sheila Jasanoff, "Globalization and Environmental Governance," in Sheila Jasanoff and Marybeth Long Martello, eds., *Earthly Politics: Local and Global in Environmental Governance* (Cambridge, MA: MIT Press, 2004), 3.
16. Eugene Rosa, Riley Dunlap, and Michael Kraft, "Prospects for Public Acceptance of a High-Level Nuclear Waste Repository in the United States: Summary and

Implications," in Eugene Rosa, Riley Dunlap, Michael Kraft, eds., *Public Reactions to Nuclear Waste: Citizens' Views of Repository Siting* (Durham, NC: Duke University Press, 1993), 291. Also see Sheila Jasanoff and Marybeth Long Martello, "Conclusion: Knowledge and Governance," in Sheila Jasanoff and Marybeth Long Martello, eds., *Earthly Politics: Local and Global in Environmental Governance* (Cambridge, MA: MIT Press, 2004), 337.

17. Roger Clark et al., *Integrating Science and Policy in Natural Resource Management: Lessons and Opportunities from North America*, U.S. Department of Agriculture, Forest Service, Pacific Northwest Research Station, General Technical Report, PNW-GTR-441, September, 1998, 1.

18. Sheila Jasanoff, *Designs on Nature: Science and Democracy in Europe and the United States* (Princeton: Princeton University Press, 2005), 288.

19. Benedick, 9.

20. Tora Skodvin and Arild Underdal, "Exploring the Dynamics of the Science–Politics Interaction," in Steiner Andresen et al. eds., *Science and Politics in International Environmental Regimes* (Manchester: Manchester University Press, 2000), 22.

21. Sheila Jasanoff, *The Fifth Branch: Science Advisors as Policymakers* (Cambridge, MA: Harvard University Press, 1994), 230.

22. Litfin, 184.

23. John Graham, Laura Green, and Marc Roberts, *In Search of Safety: Chemicals and Cancer Risk* (New York: Plenum Press, 1988), 218.

24. Roger Pielke, Jr., *The Honest Broker: Making Sense of Science in Policy and Politics* (New York: Cambridge University Press, 2007), 10.

25. Stephen Bocking, *Ecologists and Environmental Politics: A History of Contemporary Ecology* (New Haven, CT: Yale University Press, 1997), 8–9; Jasanoff, 2005, 4.

26. Pielke, 9–10.

27. Jasanoff, 1994, 250.

28. Tim Clark, "Developing Policy-Oriented Curricula for Conservation Biology: Professional and Leadership Education in the Public Interest," *Conservation Biology* 15 (2001): 36.

29. Helen Ingram et al., "Scientists and Agenda Setting: Advocacy and Global Warming." Presented at the annual meeting of the Western Political Science Association, Newport Beach, CA, 23 March 1990, 11.

30. Litfin, 4.

31. Ingram et al., 11.

32. Stephen Schneider, "Is the 'Citizen–Scientist' an Oxymoron?" in David Kleinman, ed., *Science, Technology, and Democracy* (Albany: State University of New York, 2000), 105.

33. Don Price, "The Scientific Establishment," in Robert Gilpin and Christopher Wright, eds., *Scientists and National Policy-Making* (New York: Columbia University Press, 1964), 28.

34. Daniel Sarewitz, *Frontiers of Illusion: Science, Technology, and the Politics of Progress* (Philadelphia: Temple University Press, 1996), 11.

35. Jasanoff, 2005, 5–6.

36. Don Price, *The Scientific Estate* (Cambridge, MA: Harvard University Press, 1965), 191.

37. Pielke, 5.

38. Jamieson, 322.

39. David Guston, *Between Politics and Science: Assuring the Integrity and Productivity of Research* (New York: Cambridge University Press, 2000), xv.

40. Jasanoff, 2005, 288.
41. Pielke, 150.
42. Price, 1964, 28–29.
43. George E. Brown, "Environmental Science under Siege in the U.S. Congress," *Environment* 39 (1997): 20.
44. Skodvin and Underdal, 22.
45. Alexander Keynan, "The Political Impact of Scientific Cooperation on Nature in Conflict: An Overview," in Allison deCerreno and Alexander Keynan, eds., *In Scientific Cooperation, State Conflict: The Roles of Scientists in Mitigating International Discord* (New York: The New York Academy of Sciences, 1998), 22; Albert Wohlstetter, "Strategy and the Natural Scientists," in Robert Gilpin and Christopher Wright, eds., *Scientists and National Policymaking* (New York: Columbia University Press, 1964), 174.
46. Graham, Green, Roberts, 189.
47. Litfin, 187.
48. John W. Zillman, "Atmospheric Science and Public Policy," *Science* 276 (1997): 1084.
49. David Collingridge and Colin Reeve, *Science Speaks to Power: The Role of Experts in Policy Making* (New York: St. Martin's Press, 1986), 158.
50. Jasanoff, 1994, 16.
51. Brown, 1997, 20–21.
52. Brown, 1997, 20–21.
53. Norman Miller, *Environmental Politics: Stakeholders, Interests, and Policymaking*, 2nd ed. (New York: Routledge, 2009), 132.
54. Sam Earman, "The Intersection of Science and the Law: Who Has the Right-of-Way?" in Dennis Sodden, ed., *At the Nexus: Science Policy* (New York: Nova Science Publishers, 1996), 13.
55. Alexander Farrell, Jill Jager, and Stacy VanDeveer, "Understanding Design Choices," in Alexander Farrell and Jill Jager, eds., *Assessments of Regional and Global Environmental Risks: Designing Processes for the Effective Use of Science in Decisionmaking* (Washington, DC: Resources for the Future, 2006), 13.
56. Richard Dowd, "The Role of Science in EPA Decisionmaking," *American Chemical Society* 15 (1981): 1138.
57. Elizabeth McNie, "Reconciling Supply and Demand of Scientific Information: A Review of the Literature," *Workshop on Carbon Cycle Science: Reconciling Supply and Demand*, 16–17 September 2004, Fort Collins, CO, 27.
58. Bruce Williams and Albert Matheny, *Democracy, Dialogue, and Environmental Disputes: The Contested Languages of Social Regulation* (New Haven, CT: Yale University Press, 1995), 53.
59. Skodvin and Underdal, 31.
60. Rosenbaum, 118–119.
61. Smith, 14.
62. Smith, 13.
63. Eugene Buck, M. Lynne Corn, and Pamela Baldwin, "The Endangered Species Act and 'Sound Science,'" *CRS Report for Congress* (Washington, DC: CRS, 2007), 10.
64. Jasanoff, 2005, 247.
65. Williams and Matheny, 56–57.
66. Leiss, 126.
67. Rosenbaum, 119.
68. Litfin, 184–188.

69. Litfin, 188. Epistemic environmental communities are generally defined as knowledge-based, heavily dependent on such cognitive factors as scientific knowledge, philosophical ideas, and public opinion.
70. Litfin, 104.
71. Underdal, 6.
72. Pielke, 89.
73. Ryan Meyer, "Intractable Debate: Why Congressional Hearings on Climate Fail to Advance Policy," *Perspectives in Public Affairs* 3 (2006): 85.
74. Alexander Zakaria, "Science and the State," in Allison deCerreno and Alexander Keynan, eds., *In Scientific Cooperation, State Conflict: The Roles of Scientists in Mitigating International Discord* (New York: The New York Academy of Sciences, 1998), 260–261.
75. Richard Somerville, "The Ethics of Climate Change," *environment360*, 4 June 2008, http://www.e360.yale.edu (8 June 2008).
76. Clark, 33.
77. Litfin, 29.
78. Skodvin and Underdal, 32.
79. Bruno Latour, *Science in Action: How to Follow Scientists and Engineers through Society* (Cambridge, MA: Harvard University Press, 1987), 15.
80. Litfin, 8.
81. Guston, xv.
82. McNie, 23.
83. Guston, xv.
84. McNie, 23.
85. McNie, 22.
86. Guy Benveniste, *The Politics of Expertise* (San Francisco: Boyd and Fraser Publishing Company, 1977), 28; Jean-Jacques Solomon, "Scientists' Social Responsibility," in Allison deCerreno and Alexander Keynan, eds., *In Scientific Cooperation, State Conflict: The Roles of Scientists in Mitigating International Discord* (New York: The New York Academy of Sciences, 1998), 260; Robert Wood, "Scientists and Politics: The Rise of an Apolitical Elite," in Robert Gilpin and Christopher Wright, eds., *Scientists and National Policy-Making* (New York: Columbia University Press, 1964), 71.
87. George E. Brown, "Guest Comment: The Objectivity Crisis," *American Journal of Physics* 60 (1992): 779.
88. Jeffrey Brainard, "The Waning Influence of Scientists on National Policy," *Chronicle of Higher Education* 48 (2001): A19; Miller, 132–134.
89. Roger Masters, *Beyond Relativism: Science and Human Values* (Hanover, NH: University of New England Press, 1993), 24.
90. Robert Lackey, "Normative Science," *Fisheries* 29 (2004): 39.
91. Guston, xv.
92. McNie, 23.
93. Clark et al., 17.
94. Sarewitz, 171–172.
95. Dorothy Nelkin, "Science Controversies: The Dynamics of Public Disputes in the United States," in Sheila Jasanoff et al., eds., *Handbook of Science and Technology Studies* (Thousand Oaks, CA: Sage Publications, 1995), 453.
96. Deborah Stone, *Policy Paradox: The Art of Political Decision Making, Revised Edition* (New York: W. W. Norton & Co., 2002), 8.

97. Pielke, 4–5.
98. Litfin, 29.
99. Benedick, 9.
100. Layzer, 283.
101. Monastersky, A10.
102. Nelkin, 1995, 447.
103. Eric Ginsburg, and Ellis Cowling, "Future Directions in Air-Quality Science, Policy, and Education," *Environment International* 29 (2003): 133; Leiss, 127.
104. Richard Sloan, "The Critical Distinction between Science and Religion," *Chronicle of Higher Education* 53 (2006): B13.
105. Sarewitz, 94–95.
106. Brainard, A22.
107. Wade Robison, *Decisions in Doubt: The Environment and Public Policy* (Hanover, NH: University Press of New England, 1994), 81.
108. Litfin, 5.
109. Pielke, 139–140.
110. Jasanoff, 1994, 250.
111. Pielke, 137.
112. Sarewitz, 77.
113. Clark et al., 9.
114. McNie, 20.
115. Underdal, 3–4.
116. Thomas Prugh, Robert Costanza, and Herman Daly, *The Local Politics of Global Sustainability* (Washington, DC: Island Press, 2000), 94–95.
117. Price, 1965, 275.
118. Daniel Sarewitz and Roger Pielke, Jr., "Reconciling Supply of and Demand for Science with Science Policy," *Workshop on Carbon Science: Reconciling Supply and Demand*, 16–17 September 2004, Fort Collins, CO, 9.
119. Sarewitz, 94–95.
120. Sarewitz, 94–95.
121. Sarewitz, 94–95.
122. Sarewitz and Pielke, 12.
123. Graham, Green, Roberts, viii.
124. Victor Weisskopf, "The Privilege of Being a Physicist," in Jerry Marion, ed., *A Universe of Physics: A Book of Readings* (New York: John Wiley and Sons, 1970), 8.
125. Dorothy Nelkin, *Nuclear Power and Its Critics: The Cayuga Lake Controversy* (Ithaca, NY: Cornell University Press, 1971), 106–108.
126. Rosenbaum, 58.
127. Pielke, 9–10.
128. Nelkin, 1971, 106–108.
129. Meyer, Stephen, B2.
130. Robert Proctor, *Value-Free Science? Purity and Power in Modern Knowledge* (Cambridge, MA: Harvard University Press, 1991), 270.
131. Meyer, Ryan, 94–95.
132. Kathryn Harrison and George Hoberg, *Risk, Science, and Politics: Regulating Toxic Substances in Canada and the United States* (Montreal: McGill-Queen's University Press, 1994), 6.
133. Harrison and Hoberg, 8.
134. Lackey, 38.

135. Eugene Skolnikoff, "The Role of Science in Policy: The Climate Change Debate in the United States," *Environment* 41 (1999): 44.
136. Wood, 42.
137. David Orrell, *Apollo's Arrow: The Science of Prediction and the Future of Everything* (Toronto: Harper Collins, 2007), 107.
138. Guston, 27.
139. Pielke, 151.
140. Pielke, 88.
141. Karen Greif and Jon Merz, *Current Controversies in the Biological Sciences: Case Studies of Policy Challenges from New Technologies* (Cambridge, MA: MIT Press, 2007), 9.
142. Graham, Green, Roberts, 189.
143. Orrell, 107.
144. Jasanoff, 1994, 7.
145. Latour, 159.
146. Ingram et al., 5.
147. Brainard, A20.
148. Miller, 132–134.
149. Schneider, 112.
150. Paul Erlich and Ann Erlich, *Betrayal of Science and Reason: How Anti-Environmental Rhetoric Threatens Our Future* (Washington, DC: Island Press, 2001), 22.
151. Norman Meyers, "Truth or Consequences? *Earthwatch* March (2000): 8.
152. Andrew Ross, "Introduction," in Andrew Ross, ed., *Science Wars* (Durham: Duke University Press, 1996), 4.
153. Dorothy Nelkin, "The Science Wars," in Andrew Ross, ed., *Science Wars* (Durham: Duke University Press, 1996), 114.
154. Bill Joy, "Why the Future Doesn't Need Us," *Wired* 8 (2000): 246.
155. Malcolm Scully, "Of Patronage and Exploitation," *Chronicle of Higher Education* 49 (2003): B13.
156. Kenneth Wilkening, "Science/Politics as Yin/Yang: The Role of Scientists and Scientific Knowledge in Regime formation on the Acid Deposition Issue in East Asia. Presented at the annual meeting of the International Studies Association, Toronto, Canada, 1997, 12.
157. Gretchen Daily, *Nature's Services: Societal Dependence on Natural Ecosystems* (Washington, DC: Island Press, 1997), xv.
158. Jasanoff, 1994, 7.
159. Jane Gregory and Steve Miller, *Science in Public: Communication, Culture, and Credibility* (New York: Plenum Press, 1998), 1.

CHAPTER 6

1. Steve Rayner, "Prediction and Other Approaches to Global Climate Change Policy," in Daniel Sarewitz, Roger Pielke, Jr., and Radford Byerly, Jr., eds., *Prediction: Science, Decision-Making, and the Future of Nature* (Washington, DC: Island Press, 2000), 292.
2. Brian Martin and Evelleen Richards, "Scientific Knowledge, Controversy, and Public Decision Making," in Sheila Jasanoff et al., eds., *Handbook of Science and Technology Studies* (Thousand Oaks, CA: Sage Publications, 1995), 507.
3. Janet Denhardt and Robert Denhardt, *The New Public Service: Serving, Not Steering* (New York: M. E. Sharpe, 2007), 9; Marvin Soroos, *The Endangered Atmosphere: Preserving a Global Commons* (Columbia: University of South Carolina Press, 1997), 17.

4. David Guston, *Between Politics and Science: Assuring the Integrity and Productivity of Research* (New York: Cambridge University Press, 2000), 15; U.S. General Accounting Office, *Scientific Integrity: EPA's Efforts to Enhance the Credibility and Transparency of Its Scientific Processes* (Washington, DC: GAO-09-773T, 2009), 2–7.
5. Mark Tercek, "Driven by Science," *Nature Conservancy Magazine* 58 (2008): 2.
6. Karen Litfin, *Ozone Discourses: Science and Politics in Global Environmental Cooperation* (New York: Columbia University Press, 1994), 33.
7. Brian Silver, *The Ascent of Science* (New York: Solomon Press, 1998), 236.
8. Sheryl Stolberg, "Obama Puts His Own Spin on Mix of Science with Politics," *The New York Times*, 10 March 2009, A18.
9. Litfin, 24; Dorothy Nelkin, "Science Controversies: The Dynamics of Public Disputes in the United States," in Sheila Jasanoff et al., eds., *Handbook of Science and Technology Studies* (Thousand Oaks, CA: Sage Publications, 1995), 452.
10. Patrick Hamlett, *Understanding Technological Politics: A Decision-Making Approach* (Englewood Cliffs, NJ: Prentice Hall, 1992), 62–63.
11. Gordon Durnil, *The Making of a Conservative Environmentalist* (South Bend: Indiana University Press, 1995), 129.
12. Arthur Kantrowitz, "Controlling Technology Democratically," *American Scientist* 63 (1975): 507.
13. Sheila Jasanoff, *Designs on Nature: Science and Democracy in Europe and the United States* (Princeton: Princeton University Press, 2005), 231.
14. Jennifer Allen, "Institutions, Culture, and the Role of Scientific Information in Wetland Policy Development: A Comparative Study of the United States and Canada." Paper prepared for the biennial meeting of the Association for Canadian Studies in the United States, Minneapolis, MN, 19–23 November 1997, 4.
15. Helen Ingram et al., "Scientists and Agenda Setting: Advocacy and Global Warming." Presented at the annual meeting of the Western Political Science Association, Newport Beach, CA, 23 March 1990, 6.
16. Roger Masters, *Beyond Relativism: Science and Human Values* (Hanover, NH: University of New England Press, 1993), 4.
17. Robert Wood, "Scientists and Politics: The Rise of an Apolitical Elite," in Robert Gilpin and Christopher Wright, eds., *Scientists and National Policy-Making* (New York: Columbia University Press, 1964), 43.
18. Ingram et al., 9.
19. Don Price, *The Scientific Estate* (Cambridge, MA: Harvard University Press, 1965), 118.
20. Tim Clark, "Developing Policy-Oriented Curricula for Conservation Biology: Professional and Leadership Education in the Public Interest," *Conservation Biology* 15 (2001): 33.
21. Daniel Sarewitz, *Frontiers of Illusion: Science, Technology, and the Politics of Progress* (Philadelphia: Temple University Press, 1996), 33.
22. Mark Bowen, *Censoring Science: Inside the Political Attack on Dr. James Hansen and the Truth of Global Warming* (New York: Dutton, 2008), 53.
23. Philip Kitcher, *Science, Truth, and Democracy* (New York: Oxford University Press, 2001), 3.
24. Litfin, 16.
25. Kerry Emanuel, *What We Know about Climate Change* (Cambridge, MA: MIT Press, 2007), 67.
26. Arnold Meltsner, *Policy Analysts in the Bureaucracy* (Berkeley: University of California Press, 1976), 52.

27. Phyllis Coontz, "Ethics in Systematic Research," in Gerald Miller and Marcia Whicker, eds., *Handbook of Research Methods in Public Administration* (New York: Marcel Dekker, 1999), 18.
28. Bruce Bimber, *The Politics of Expertise in Congress: The Rise and Fall of the Office of Technology Assessment* (Albany: State University of New York Press, 1996), 12.
29. Bimber, 14.
30. Guston, 2000, xv; Bradford Wilson, "Politicizing Academic Freedom, Vulgarizing Scholarly Discourse," *Chronicle of Higher Education* 44 (1997): A52.
31. Ryan Meyer, "Intractable Debate: Why Congressional Hearings on Climate Fail to Advance Policy," *Perspectives in Public Affairs* 3 (2006): 86.
32. Alan Miller, "The Role of Analytical Science in Natural Resource Decision Making," *Environmental Management* 17 (1993): 570.
33. Robert Proctor, *Value-Free Science? Purity and Power in Modern Knowledge* (Cambridge, MA: Harvard University Press, 1991), 269.
34. Jasanoff, 2005, 288.
35. Hope Yen, "Obama Names 4 Top Members of Science Team," *Idaho Statesman*, 21 December, 2008, 16 Main.
36. Litfin, 15.
37. Sheila Jasanoff and Marybeth Long Martello, "Conclusion: Knowledge and Governance," in Sheila Jasanoff and Marybeth Long Martello, eds., *Earthly Politics: Local and Global in Environmental Governance* (Cambridge, MA: MIT Press, 2004), 338.
38. Proctor, 267.
39. Deborah Stone, *Policy Paradox: The Art of Political Decision Making*, rev. ed. (New York: W. W. Norton & Co., 2002), 309.
40. Nicholas Ashford, "Disclosure of Interest: A Time for Clarity," *American Journal of Industrial Medicine* 28 (1995): 611; Meyer, 86; Andrew Ross, "Introduction," in Andrew Ross, ed., *Science Wars* (Durham: Duke University Press, 1996), 10.
41. Sheila Jasanoff, *The Fifth Branch: Science Advisors as Policymakers* (Cambridge, MA: Harvard University Press, 1994), 16–17.
42. Bruce Williams and Albert Matheny, *Democracy, Dialogue, and Environmental Disputes: The Contested Languages of Social Regulation* (New Haven, CT: Yale University Press, 1995), 39.
43. Kitcher, 31.
44. Ross, 4.
45. Williams and Matheny, 40.
46. Michael Shermer, *The Borderlands of Science: Where Sense Meets Nonsense* (New York: Oxford University Press, 2001), 189.
47. Stanley Aronowitz, "The Politics of the Science Wars," in Andrew Ross, ed., *Science Wars* (Durham: Duke University Press, 1996), 205.
48. Jasanoff, 1994, 250.
49. Steve Fuller, "Does Science Put an End to History, or History to Science," in Andrew Ross, ed., *Science Wars* (Durham: Duke University Press, 1996), 45.
50. Wade Robison, *Decisions in Doubt: The Environment and Public Policy* (Hanover, NH: University Press of New England, 1994), 2.
51. Eugene Buck, M. Lynne Corn, and Pamela Baldwin, "The Endangered Species Act and 'Sound Science,'" *CRS Report for Congress* (Washington, DC: CRS, 2007), 11.
52. Walter A. Rosenbaum, *Environmental Politics and Policy*, 7th ed. (Washington, DC: CQ Press, 2008), 125.
53. Kitcher, 61.

54. K. C. Cole, "Is There Such a Thing as Scientific Objectivity," *Discover* 6 (1985): 99.

55. Nicholas Ashford, "Value Judgments and Risk Assessment," in C. Mark Smith, David Christiani, and Karl Kelsey, eds., *Chemical Risk Assessment and Occupational Health* (Westport, CT: Auburn House, 1994), 198–199.

56. Rosenbaum, 125.

57. Stephen Bocking, *Ecologists and Environmental Politics: A History of Contemporary Ecology* (New Haven, CT: Yale University Press, 1997), xi; Proctor, 271; Stone, 310.

58. Sarewitz, 48.

59. Susan Cozzens and Edward Woodhouse, "Science, Government, and the Politics of Knowledge," in Sheila Jasanoff et al., eds., *Handbook of Science and Technology Studies* (Thousand Oaks, CA: Sage Publications, 1995), 553; Jasanoff, 1994, 12; Jasanoff, 2005, 251; Jasanoff and Martello, 338; Litfin, 8; Masters, 146–147.

60. J. Baird Callicott, "Science, Value, and Ethics: A Hierarchical Theory," in Ben Minteer and Bob Taylor, eds., *Democracy and the Claims of Nature: Critical Perspectives for a New Century* (Lanham, MD: Rowman and Littlefield, 2002), 92; Kitcher, 7.

61. Nelkin, 1995, 445.

62. Richard Pouyat, "Science and Environmental Policy—Making Them Compatible," *Bioscience* 49 (1999): 282; Silver, 109.

63. Sarewitz, 114.

64. Litfin, 33.

65. David Guston, "Boundary Organizations in Environmental Policy and Science: An Introduction," *Science, Technology, and Human Values* 26 (2001): 399; Dorothy Nelkin, *Nuclear Power and Its Critics: The Cayuga Lake Controversy* (Ithaca, NY: Cornell University Press, 1971), 100; Rosenbaum, 124; Masters, 146.

66. Shermer, 308.

67. Cozzens and Woodhouse, 534.

68. Daniel Metlay, "From Tin Roof to Torn Wet Blanket: Predicting and Observing Ground Water Movement at a Proposed Nuclear Waste Site," in Daniel Sarewitz, Roger Pielke, Jr., and Radford Byerly, Jr., eds., *Prediction: Science, Decision-Making, and the Future of Nature* (Washington, DC: Island Press, 2000), 216.

69. Dorothy Nelkin, "The Science Wars," in Andrew Ross, ed., *Science Wars* (Durham: Duke University Press, 1996), 114.

70. Jean-Jacques Solomon, "Scientists' Social Responsibility," in Allison deCerreno and Alexander Keynan, eds., *In Scientific Cooperation, State Conflict: The Roles of Scientists in Mitigating International Discord* (New York: The New York Academy of Sciences, 1998), 260.

71. Bocking, 145–146.

72. Bocking, 183.

73. Bocking, 5–6.

74. Bimber, 14.

75. Sarewitz, 93.

76. Durnil, 128.

77. Stone, 313.

78. Jasanoff and Martello, 337.

79. Kitcher, 31.

80. Roger Pielke, Jr., *The Honest Broker: Making Sense of Science in Policy and Politics* (New York: Cambridge University Press, 2007), 147.

81. Bimber, xi.

82. Sarewitz, 14.

83. Clark, 32.
84. Masters, 27.
85. Arild Underdal, "Science and Politics: The Anatomy of an Uneasy Partnership," in Steinar Andresen et al., eds., *Science and Politics in International Environmental Regimes* (Manchester: Manchester University Press, 2000), 5–6.
86. James Smith, *The Idea Brokers: Think Tanks and the Rise of the New Policy Elite* (New York: Free Press, 1991), xviii.
87. John Graham, Laura Green, and Marc Roberts, *In Search of Safety: Chemicals and Cancer Risk* (New York: Plenum Press, 1988), viii.
88. Ronald Brunner, "Alternatives to Production," in Daniel Sarewitz, Roger Pielke, Jr., and Radford Byerly, Jr., eds., *Prediction: Science, Decision-Making, and the Future of Nature* (Washington, DC: Island Press, 2000), 308.
89. Ashford, 1994, 198.
90. Kitcher, 180.
91. Shermer, 20.
92. Miller, 570.
93. Paul Ehrlich and Anne Ehrlich, *Betrayal of Science and Reason: How Anti-Environmental Rhetoric Threatens Our Future* (Washington, DC: Island Press, 1996), 35.
94. Aaron Wildavsky, *But Is It True? A Citizen's Guide to Environmental Health and Safety Issues* (Cambridge, MA: Harvard University Press, 1995), 9.
95. Alan Leshner, "Science and Public Engagement," *Chronicle of Higher Education* 53 (2006): B20.
96. Silver, 104.
97. Emanuel, 17.
98. Kitcher, 102.
99. Emanuel, 55.
100. David Orrell, *Apollo's Arrow: The Science of Prediction and the Future of Everything* (Toronto: Harper Collins, 2007), 59.
101. Albert Wohlstetter, "Strategy and the Natural Scientists," in Robert Gilpin and Christopher Wright, eds., *Scientists and National Policy-Making* (New York: Columbia University Press, 1964), 174.
102. Nelkin, 1971, 102.
103. Proctor, x.
104. Kitcher, 29.
105. Zachary Smith, *The Environmental Policy Paradox* (Upper Saddle River, NJ: Pearson-Prentice Hall, 2009), 14.
106. Robert Lackey, "Normative Science," *Fisheries* 29 (2004): 38.
107. Edward O. Wilson, *Consilience: The Unity of Knowledge* (New York: Alfred A. Knopf, 1998), 60–61.
108. Silver, 106.
109. Silver, 106.
110. Guston, 2000, 163.

CHAPTER 7

1. Mark Tercek, "Driven by Science," *Nature Conservancy Magazine* 58 (2008): 2.
2. Mark Bowen, *Censoring Science: Inside the Political Attack on Dr. James Hansen and the Truth of Global Warming* (New York: Dutton, 2008), 229.

3. Patrick Hamlett, *Understanding Technological Politics: A Decision-Making Approach* (Englewood Cliffs, NJ: Prentice Hall, 1992), 63.

4. Lynton K. Caldwell, "Binational Responsibilities for a Shared Environment," in Charles F. Doran and John H. Sigler, eds., *Canada and the United States: Enduring Friendship, Persistent Stress* (Englewood Cliffs, NJ: Prentice Hall, 1985), 222; Helen Ingram et al., "Scientists and Agenda Setting: Advocacy and Global Warming." Presented at the annual meeting of the Western Political Science Association, Newport Beach, CA, 23 March 1990, 24–25; Karen T. Litfin, *Ozone Discourses: Science and Politics in Global Environmental Cooperation* (New York: Columbia University Press, 1994), 9; Steve Lyttle, "Gore Gets a Cold Shoulder," *Sydney Morning Herald*, 14 October 2007, 1; Marvin Soroos, *The Endangered Atmosphere: Preserving a Global Commons* (Columbia: South Carolina Press, 1997), 14.

5. Bruce Smith, *The Advisors: Scientists in the Policy Process* (Washington, DC: Brookings Institution, 1992), 3.

6. David Collingridge and Colin Reeve, *Science Speaks to Power: The Role of Experts in Policy Making* (New York: St. Martin's Press, 1986), 17; Judith Layzer, *The Environmental Case: Translating Values into Policy*, 2nd ed. (Washington, DC: CQ Press, 2006), 2.

7. Stephen Schneider, "Is the 'Citizen–Scientist' an Oxymoron?" in Daniel Kleinman, ed., *Science, Technology, and Democracy* (Albany: State University of New York, 2000), 113.

8. Roger Pielke, Jr., *The Honest Broker: Making Sense of Science in Policy and Politics* (New York: Cambridge University Press, 2007), 121.

9. K. C. Cole and Robert Hotz, "Rapid Spread of Information Distorts Scientific Discoveries," *Idaho Statesman*, 1 January 1999, 4A.

10. Ingram et al., 24.

11. Stephen Bocking, *Ecologists and Environmental Politics: A History of Contemporary Ecology* (New Haven, CT: Yale University Press, 1997), ix.

12. Collingridge and Reeve, 16.

13. Bruce Bimber, *The Politics of Expertise in Congress: The Rise and Fall of the Office of Technology Assessment* (Albany: State University of New York, 1996), 3; Robert Gilpin, "Introduction: Natural Scientists in Policy Making," in Robert Gilpin and Christopher Wright, eds., *Scientists and National Policy-Making* (New York: Columbia University Press, 1964), 1.

14. Bowen, 65.

15. Bimber, 4–5; Bruno Latour, *Science in Action: How to Follow Scientists and Engineers through Society* (Cambridge, MA: Harvard University Press, 1987), 30.

16. Hamlett, 6.

17. Don Price, *The Scientific Estate* (Cambridge, MA: Harvard University Press, 1965), 276.

18. Matthew Nisbet and Chris Mooney, "Blinded with Science," *Washington Post National Weekly Edition* 24 (2007): 27.

19. Robert Lackey, "Normative Science," *Fisheries* 29 (2004): 39.

20. Pielke, 2007, 95.

21. Ingram et al., 2–5.

22. Hamlett, 16.

23. Jane Lubchenco, "Entering the Century of the Environment: A New Social Contract for Science," *Science, Technology, & Human Values* 279 (1998): 491–497; John P. Myers and Joshua S. Reichert, "Perspectives on Nature's Services," in Gretchen C. Daily, ed., *Nature's Services: Societal Dependence on Nature's Ecosystems* (Washington, DC:

Island Press, 1997), xix; Carl Safina, "To Save the Earth, Scientists Should Join Policy Debates," *Chronicle of Higher Education* 45 (1998): A80.

24. Thomas Prugh, Robert Costanza, and Herman Daly, *The Local Politics of Global Sustainability* (Washington, DC: Island Press, 2000), 92.

25. Andrew Revkin, "Climate Expert Says NASA Tried to Silence Him," *New York Times*, 29 January 2006, 2.

26. Jeffrey Brainard, "The Waning Influence of Scientists on National Policy," *Chronicle of Higher Education* 48 (2001): A21.

27. Seth Dunn, "Scientific Society Speaks Out on Climate," *Worldwatch* 12 (1999): 10.

28. Stephen Meyer, "The Role of Scientists in the 'New Politics,'" *Chronicle of Higher Education* 41 (1995): B1.

29. Brainard, A21; Fareed Zakaria, "Science and the State," in Allison deCerreno and Alexander Keynan, eds., *In Scientific Cooperation, State Conflict: The Roles of Scientists in Mitigating International Discord* (New York: The New York Academy of Sciences, 1998), 261.

30. Joel Primack and Frank Von Hippel, *Advice and Dissent: Scientists in the Political Arena* (New York: Basic Books, 1974), 5.

31. Kai N. Lee, *Compass and Gyroscope: Integrating Science and Politics for the Environment* (Washington, DC: Island Press, 1993), 167.

32. Ingram et al., 8–9.

33. William Leiss, "Governance and the Environment," in Thomas Courchene, ed., *Policy Framework for a Knowledge Economy* (Kingston, Ontario: John Deutch Institute for the Study of Economic Policy, 1996), 126–127.

34. Pielke, 2007, 117.

35. Gordon Durnil, *The Making of a Conservative Environmentalist* (South Bend: Indiana University Press, 1995), 131.

36. Paul Ehrlich and Anne Ehrlich, *Betrayal of Science and Reason: How Anti-Environmental Rhetoric Threatens Our Future* (Washington, DC: Island Press, 1996), 204.

37. Bimber, 22; Eric Ginsburg and Ellis Cowling, "Future Directions in Air-Quality Science, Policy, and Education," *Environment International* 29 (2003): 133.

38. Bocking, 192.

39. Pielke, 2007, 135.

40. Daniel Sarewitz, *Frontiers of Illusion: Science, Technology, and the Politics of Progress* (Philadelphia: Temple University Press, 1996), 73.

41. Sheila Jasanoff, *The Fifth Branch: Science Advisors as Policymakers* (Cambridge, MA: Harvard University Press, 1994), vi.

42. Phyllis Coontz, "Ethics in Systematic Research," in Gerald Miller and Marcia Whicker, eds., *Handbook of Research Methods in Public Administration* (New York: Marcel Dekker, 1999), 17.

43. Lackey, 39; Pielke, 2007, 82–83.

44. Collingridge and Reeve, 17.

45. Collingridge and Reeve, x.

46. Sarewitz, 76.

47. Hamlett, 6.

48. Zachary Smith, *The Environmental Policy Paradox* (Upper Saddle River, NJ: Pearson-Prentice Hall, 2009), 14.

49. George E. Brown, "Environmental Science under Siege in the U.S. Congress," *Environment* 39 (1997): 18–19.

50. Pielke, 2007, 63.

51. Ingram et al., 2.
52. Alan Leshner, "Science and Public Engagement," *Chronicle of Higher Education* 53 (2006): B20.
53. Bowen, 215–216.
54. Durnil, 131; Also, see Seth Dunn, "Clearing the Haze," *Worldwatch* 11 (1998): 35–36.
55. Tim Callahan, "Trees and Volcanoes Cause Smog (More Myths from the Wise Use Movement)," *The Humorist* January/February (1996): 34.
56. Collingridge and Reeve, 16.
57. Ray Pierre, "The Debate Is Just Beginning—On the Cretaceous!" *Real Climate: Climate Science from Climate Scientists*, 23 January 2008, http://www.realclimate.org/index.php?p=526 (1 February 2008), 1.
58. Pierre, 1.
59. Brown, 15.
60. Lyttle, 1; David Orrell, *Apollo's Arrow: The Science of Prediction and the Future of Everything* (Toronto: HarperCollins, 2007), 333; Malcom Scully, "Of Patronage and Exploitation," *Chronicle of Higher Education* 49 (2003): B13.
61. Megan Jones, David Guston, and Lewis Branscomb, *Informed Legislatures: Coping with Science in a Democracy* (Lanham, MD: University Press of America, 1996), 3.
62. Lee, 167.
63. Roger Clark et al., *Integrating Science and Policy in Natural Resource Management: Lessons and Opportunities from North America*, U.S. Department of Agriculture, Forest Service, Pacific Northwest Research Station, General Technical Report, PNW-GTR-441, September 1998, 13.
64. Clark Chapman, "The Asteroid/Comet Impact Hazard: Homo Sapiens as Dinosaur," in Daniel Sarewitz, Roger Pielke, Jr., and Radford Byerly, Jr., eds., *Prediction: Science, Decision-Making, and the Future of Nature* (Washington, DC: Island Press, 2000), 122.
65. Bowen, 71; Zakaria, 261.
66. Jane Gregory and Steve Miller, *Science in Public: Communication, Culture, and Credibility* (New York: Plenum Press, 1998), 249.
67. Alexander Keynan, "Cross-Cutting Issues and Lessons Learned," in Allison deCerreno and Alexander Keynan, eds., *In Scientific Cooperation, State Conflict: The Roles of Scientists in Mitigating International Discord* (New York: The New York Academy of Sciences, 1998), 278.
68. Brown, 29.
69. Lackey, 39.
70. Roger Pielke, Jr., and Michael Glantz, "Serving Science and Society: Lessons from Large-Scale Atmospheric Science Programs," *Bulletin of the American Meteorological Society* 76 (1995): 2446.
71. Radford Byerly and Roger Pielke, Jr., "The Changing Ecology of United States Science," *Science* 269 (1995): 1531; Nisbet and Mooney, 27; Eugene Skolnikoff, "The Role of Science in Policy: The Climate Change Debate in the United States," *Environment* 41 (1999): 45.
72. Kerry Emanuel, *What We Know about Climate Change* (Cambridge, MA: MIT Press, 2007), 72–73; Gregory and Miller, 249; Pielke and Glantz, 2446.
73. Gretchen Daily, "Introduction: What Are Ecosystem Services," in *Nature's Services: Societal Dependence on Natural Ecosystems* (Washington, DC: Island Press, 1997), 2; *The Environmental Professional*, "Linkages Are Weak between Science and Environmental Decisionmaking," 16 (1994): 111; Smith, Zachary, 14.

74. Nisbet and Mooney, 27.
75. Dale Jamieson, "Prediction in Society," in Daniel Sarewitz, Roger Pielke, Jr., and Radford Byerly, Jr., eds., *Prediction: Science, Decision-Making, and the Future of Nature* (Washington, DC: Island Press, 2000), 324; Ryan Meyer, "Intractable Debate: Why Congressional Hearings on Climate Fail to Advance Policy," *Perspectives in Public Affairs* 3 (2006): 88.
76. James Smith, *The Idea Brokers: Think Tanks and the Rise of the New Policy Elite* (New York: Free Press, 1991), xx.
77. Lynton Caldwell, *Environment as a Focus for Public Policy* (College Station: Texas A&M University Press, 1995), 294; Elizabeth McNie, "Reconciling Supply and Demand of Scientific Information: A Review of the Literature," *Workshop on Carbon Cycle Science: Reconciling Supply and Demand*, 16–17 September 2004, Fort Collins, CO, 24; Roger Pielke, Jr., "Usable Information for Policy: An Appraisal of the U.S. Global Change Research Program," *Policy Sciences* 28 (1995): 66; Randy Showstack, "Community-Based Research Proposal as Model to Make Science More Accessible," *EOS* 79 (1998): 370; Soroos, 1997, 284.
78. Bowen, 230; Jane Lubchenco, "Restoring Science to U.S. Climate Policy," *environment360*, 9 July 2009, http://www.e360.yale.edu/content/feature.msp?id=2169 (10 July 2009), 1.
79. Glen Sussman, Byron Daynes, and Jonathon West, *American Politics and the Environment* (New York: Longman Publishers, 2002), 11.
80. Gregory and Miller, 1.
81. Kenneth Prewitt, "The Public and Science Policy," *Science, Technology, and Human Values* 7 (1982): 5–6.
82. Richard Feynman, "The Value of Science," in Jerry Marion, ed., *A Universe of Physics: A Book of Readings* (New York: John Wiley and Sons, 1970), 4; Roger Pielke, Jr., Daniel Sarewitz, and Radford Byerly, Jr., "Decisionmaking and the Future of Nature: Understanding and Using Predictions," in Daniel Sarewitz, Roger Pielke, Jr., and Radford Byerly, Jr., eds., *Prediction: Science, Decision-Making, and the Future of Nature* (Washington, DC: Island Press, 2000), 384.
83. Richard Pouyat, "Science and Environmental Policy—Making Them Compatible," *Bioscience* 49 (1999): 285.
84. Leshner, B20.
85. Pielke and Glantz, 2450.
86. Eugene Rosa, Riley Dunlap, and Michael Kraft, "Prospects for Public Acceptance of a High-Level Nuclear Waste Repository in the United States: Summary and Implications," in Eugene Rosa, Riley Dunlap, Michael Kraft, eds., *Public Reactions to Nuclear Waste: Citizens' Views of Repository Siting* (Durham, NC: Duke University Press, 1993), 312.
87. Ehrlich and Ehrlich, 200.
88. *Bioscience* 48 (1998): 894; Nisbet and Mooney, 27.
89. Meyer, Stephen, B2.
90. Daniel Sarewitz and Roger Pielke, Jr., "Reconciling Supply of and Demand for Science with Science Policy," *Workshop on Carbon Science: Reconciling Supply and Demand*, 16–17 September 2004, Fort Collins, CO, 19.
91. *Bioscience*, 893.
92. Myers and Reichert, xix.
93. Layzer, 283; Leshner, B20.
94. Roger Masters, *Beyond Relativism: Science and Human Values* (Hanover, NH: University of New England Press, 1993), 3–4.

95. Robert Paehlke, "Cycles of Closure in Environmental Politics and Policy," in Ben Minteer and Bob Taylor, eds., *Democracy and the Claims of Nature: Critical Perspectives for a New Century* (Lanham, MD: Rowman and Littlefield, 2002), 296; Sarewitz, 75; Bruce Williams and Albert Matheny, *Democracy, Dialogue, and Environmental Disputes: The Contested Language of Social Regulation* (New Haven: Yale University Press, 1995), 42.
96. Brown, 20; Ginsburg, and Cowling, 134.
97. Brainard, A22; Chapman, 130–131.
98. Primack and Von Hippel, ix.
99. Dorothy Nelkin, "The Science Wars," in Andrew Ross, ed., *Science Wars* (Durham: Duke University Press, 1996), 122.
100. Ehrlich and Ehrlich, 204.
101. Lee, 184.
102. Matthew Paterson, *Understanding Global Environmental Politics: Domination, Accumulation, Resistance* (New York: Palgrave, 2001), 12.
103. Peter Haas, "Stratospheric Ozone: Regime Formation in Stages," in Oran Young and Gail Osherenko, eds., *Polar Politics: Creating International Environmental Regimes* (Ithaca, NY: Cornell University Press, 1993), 152; Gail Osherenko and Oran Young, "The Formation of International Regimes: Hypotheses and Cases," in Oran Young and Gail Osherenko, eds., *Polar Politics: Creating International Environmental Regimes* (Ithaca, NY: Cornell University Press, 1993), 19.
104. Henrik Selin and Stacy VanDeveer, "Political Science and Prediction: What's Next for U.S. Climate Change Policy?" *Review of Policy Research* 24 (2007): 1.
105. Collingridge and Reeve, ix; Sarewitz, 77; Williams and Matheny, 41.
106. Sarewitz, 76.
107. Marvin Soroos, "Science and International Climate Change Policy," in Neil Harrison and Gary Bryner, eds. *Science and Politics in the International Environment* (Boulder, CO: Rowman & Littlefield, 2004), 83–107.
108. Emanuel, 74.
109. Marc Morano, "U.S. Senate Report: Over 400 Prominent Scientists Disputed Man-Made Global Warming Claims in 2007," *The Inhoff EPW Press Blog*, 20 December 2007, 1.
110. S. Fred Singer and Dennis Avery, *Unstoppable Global Warming: Every 1,500 Years* (Boulder, CO: Rowman and Littlefield, 2007), 6.
111. Soroos, 1997, 145.
112. Skolnikoff, 45.
113. Jasanoff, 234; Litfin, 4.
114. Tora Skodvin and Arild Underdal, "Exploring the Dynamics of the Science–Politics Interaction," in Steiner Andresen et al., eds., *Science and Politics in International Environmental Regimes* (Manchester: Manchester University Press, 2000), 30–31.
115. Walter A. Rosenbaum, *Environmental Politics and Policy*, 7th ed. (Washington, DC: CQ Press, 2008), 40.
116. Bowen, 188.
117. Ingram et al., 9.
118. Ehrlich and Ehrlich, 190; Howard Neufeld, "The Nemisis Effect," *Worldwatch* 12 (1999): 6.
119. Orrell, 330.
120. Emanuel, 59.

121. Bowen, 205; Cole and Hotz, 4A; Bruce Lewenstein, "Science and the Media," in Sheila Jasanoff et al., eds., *Handbook of Science and Technology Studies* (Thousand Oaks, CA: Sage Publications, 1995), 348.
122. Brown, 15; Ingram et al., 8.
123. Chapman, 122.
124. Lewenstein, 347.
125. Pielke, 2007, 63.
126. Merrill Goozer, "Credibility of Scientists: Industry versus Public Interest," *Environmental Health Perspectives* 114 (2006): A147.
127. Craig Barrow and James Conrad, "Assessing the Reliability and Credibility of Industry Science and Scientists," *Environmental Health Perspectives* 114 (2006): 153.
128. Barrow and Conrad, 153–155.
129. Jennifer Sass, "Credibility of Scientists: Conflict of Interest and Bias," *Environmental Health Perspectives* 114 (2006): A147–148.
130. Chris Mooney, "Beware 'Sound Science,'" *Washington Post National Weekly Edition* 21 (2004): 23.
131. H. Joseph Hebert, "Does Ethanol Help Climate Fight?" *Idaho Statesman*, 4 May 2009, A7–8.
132. Matthew Nisbet and Chris Mooney, "Blinded with Science," *Washington Post National Weekly Edition* 24 (2007): 27.
133. Jane Lubchenco, "Restoring Science to U.S. Climate Policy," *Environment360*, 9 July 2009, http://www.e360.yale.edu/content/feature.msp?id=2169 (10 July 2009), 1.
134. Philip Kitcher, *Science, Truth, and Democracy* (New York: Oxford University Press, 2001), 197.

CHAPTER 8

1. Edward O. Wilson, *Consilience: The Unity of Knowledge* (New York: Alfred A. Knopf, 1998), 49.
2. Sheila Jasanoff and Marybeth Long Martello, "Conclusion: Knowledge and Governance," in Sheila Jasanoff and Marybeth Long Martello, eds., *Earthly Politics: Local and Global in Environmental Governance* (Cambridge, MA: MIT Press, 2004), 340.
3. Sheila Jasanoff, *Designs On Nature: Science and Democracy in Europe and the United States* (Princeton, NJ: Princeton University Press, 2005), 290.
4. Daniel Sarewitz, *Frontiers of Illusion: Science, Technology, and the Politics of Progress* (Philadelphia: Temple University Press, 1996), 35.
5. Karen T. Litfin, *Ozone Discourses: Science and Politics in Global Environmental Cooperation* (New York: Columbia University Press, 1994), 25.
6. Jean-Guy Vaillancourt, "Environment," in Robert Paehlke, ed., *Conservation and Environmentalism* (New York: Garland Publishing, Inc., 1995), 218.
7. Alexander Keynan, "The Political Impact of Scientific Cooperation on Nations in Conflict: An Overview," in Allison deCerreno and Alexander Keynan, eds., *In Scientific Cooperation, State Conflict: The Roles of Scientists in Mitigating International Discord* (New York: The New York Academy of Sciences, 1998), xii.
8. Litfin, 36.
9. Litfin, 40.
10. Michael Shermer, *The Borderlands of Science: Where Sense Meets Nonsense* (New York: Oxford University Press, 2001), 319.

11. Eugene Skolnikoff, "Science and Technology: The Sources of Change," in Nazli Choucri, ed., *Global Accord: Environmental Challenges and International Responses* (Cambridge, MA: MIT Press, 1995), 260.

12. Courtney Brown, "Politics and the Environment," *American Political Science Review* 88 (1994): 292.

13. Nicholas Ashford, "Disclosure of Interest: A Time for Clarity," *American Journal of Industrial Medicine* 28 (1995): 612; Bruce Bimber, *The Politics of Expertise in Congress: The Rise and Fall of the Office of Technology Assessment* (Albany: State University of New York, 1996), 7–12; Stephen Bocking, *Ecologists and Environmental Politics* (New Haven: Yale University Press, 1997), 5–6; David Collingridge and Colin Reeve, *Science Speaks to Power: The Role of Experts in Policy Making* (New York: St. Martin's Press, 1986), 28; John Graham, Laura Green, and Marc Roberts, *In Search of Safety: Chemicals and Cancer Risk* (New York: Plenum Press, 1988), 187; Kathryn Harrison and George Hoberg, *Risk, Science, and Politics: Regulating Toxic Substances in Canada and the United States* (Montreal: McGill-Queen's University Press, 1994), 33; Helen Ingram et al., "Scientists and Agenda Setting: Advocacy and Global Warming," presented at the annual meeting of the Western Political Science Association, Newport Beach, CA, 23 March 1990, 17; Keynan, 8; Frances M. Lynn, "The Interplay of Science and Values in Assessing and Regulating Environmental Risks," *Science, Technology, & Human Values* 11 (1986): 48; Dorothy Nelkin, "The Science Wars," in Andrew Ross, ed., *Science Wars* (Durham: Duke University Press, 1996), 118; Don Price, *The Scientific Estate* (Cambridge, MA: Harvard University Press, 1965), 26; Shermer, 17.

14. Ed Ayres, "Specialization and Tunnel Vision," *Worldwatch* 12 (1999): 4; Gordon Durnil, *The Making of a Conservative Environmentalist* (South Bend: Indiana University Press, 1995), 131–132; Kai N. Lee, *Compass and Gyroscope: Integrating Science and Politics for the Environment* (Washington, DC: Island Press, 1993), 164.

15. Deborah Stone, *Policy Paradox: The Art of Political Decision Making*, Revised Edition (New York: W.W. Norton & Co., 2002), 189.

16. Paul Stern, Oran Young, and Daniel Druckman, *Global Environmental Change: Understanding the Human Dimensions* (Washington, DC: National Academy Press, 1992), 25; Sarewitz, 4–5.

17. Roger Masters, *Beyond Relativism: Science and Human Values* (Hanover, NH: University of New England Press, 1993), vii; David Schlosberg and Thomas Sisk, "The Environmental Science/Policy Interface: Crossing Disciplinary Boundaries with a Team Teaching Approach," *PS: Political Science and Politics* 33 (2000): 75.

18. Roger Clark et al., *Integrating Science and Policy in Natural Resource Management: Lessons and Opportunities from North America*, U.S. Department of Agriculture, Forest Service, Pacific Northwest Research Station, General Technical Report, PNW-GTR-441, September 1998, 17; David Orrell, *Apollo's Arrow: The Science of Prediction and the Future of Everything* (Toronto: Harper Collins, 2007), 283.

19. Kurt Campbell et al., *The Age of Consequences: The Foreign Policy and National Security Implications of Global Climate Change* (Washington, DC: Center for a New American Security, 2007), 13; Wilson, Edward, 125.

20. Litfin, 41.

21. Roy Macridis and Mark Hulliung, *Contemporary Political Ideologies: Movement and Regimes*, 6th ed. (New York: Harper Collins, 1996), 3.

22. Sarewitz, 29.

23. Wilson, Edward, 191.

24. *Environmental Professional* 16 (1994): 118; William Hagan, Jr., "Culture Wars," *Science* 256 (1994): 853; Roger Pielke, Jr., "Asking the Right Questions: Atmospheric Sciences Research and Social Needs," *Bulletin of the American Meteorological Society* 78 (1997): 255–264; Sarewitz, 26; Richard Sclove, "Better Approaches to Science Policy," *Science* 279 (1998): 1283; Smith, James, 14; Stern, Young, and Druckman, 25.

25. Hagan, 853.

26. Jasanoff and Martello, 337.

27. William Bowen and Chieh-Chen Bowen, "Typologies, Indexing, Content Analysis, Meta-Analysis, and Scaling as Measurement Techniques," in Gerald Miller and Marcia Whicker, eds., *Handbook of Research Methods in Public Administration* (New York: Marcel Dekker, 1999), 53.

28. Wilson, Edward, 184.

29. Smith, James, xii.

30. Arthur Lupia, "Evaluating Political Science Research: Information for Buyers and Sellers," *PS: Political Science and Politics* 33 (2000): 9.

31. Lynton Caldwell, *Environment as a Focus for Public Policy* (College Station: Texas A&M University Press, 1995), 315.

32. Eville Gorham, "Human Impacts on Ecosystems and Landscapes," in J. I. Nassauer, ed., *Placing Nature: Culture and Landscape Ecology* (Washington, DC: Island Press, 1997), 30–31.

33. Wilson, Edward, 183.

34. Wilson, Edward, 126.

35. Wilson, Edward, 11.

36. Wilson, Edward, 13.

37. Wilson, Edward, 191.

38. Jean-Jacques Solomon, "Scientists' Social Responsibility," in Allison deCerreno and Alexander Keynan, eds., *In Scientific Cooperation, State Conflict: The Roles of Scientists in Mitigating International Discord* (New York: The New York Academy of Sciences, 1998), 260.

39. Masters, vii.

40. Dominique Foray and Ali Kazancigil, "Science, Economics, and Democracy: Selected Issues," Prepared for the World Conference on Science, UNESCO-ICSU, Budapest, Hungary, 26 June–1 July 1999, 8; Jane Gregory and Steve Miller, *Science in Public: Communication, Culture, and Credibility* (New York: Plenum Press, 1998), 248–250; Pielke, 262; Richard Sclove, "For U.S. Science Policy, It's Time for a Reality Check," *Chronicle of Higher Education* 45 (1998): B4.

41. Jasanoff and Martello, 340.

42. Patrick Hamlett, *Understanding Technological Politics: A Decision-Making Approach* (Englewood Cliffs, NJ: Prentice Hall, 1992), 62; Victor Weisskopf, "The Privilege of Being a Physicist," in Jerry Marion, ed., *A Universe of Physics: A Book of Readings* (New York: John Wiley and Sons, 1970), 5–10; Wilson, Edward, 39.

43. Jeffrey Brainard, "U.S. Agencies Look to Interdisciplinary Science," *Chronicle of Higher Education* 48 (2001): A20; Paul Ehrlich and Anne Ehrlich, *Betrayal of Science and Reason: How Anti-Environmental Rhetoric Threatens Our Future* (Washington, DC: Island Press, 1996), 205; Jac Van Beek and Frances Isaacs, "Convergence and Science Management," in Glen Toner, ed., *Innovation, Science, and Environment: Canadian Policies and Performance, 2008–2009* (Montreal: McGill-Queen's University Press, 2008), 209.

44. Claude Philips, "Political Scientists Need to Pay Attention to Developments in Biology," *PS: Political Science and Politics* 32 (1999): 536.
45. Norman Hillmer, "A Border People," *Canada World View* 24 (2005): 4; Doug Struck, "Canada's Confidence," *Washington Post National Weekly Edition* 23 (2006): 18.
46. Don Munton, "Dependence and Interdependence in Trans-boundary Environmental Relations," *International Journal* 36 (1980–1981): 142–143.
47. Alice Chamberlin and Leonard Legault, "International Joint Commission Looks to the 21st Century," *Focus* 22 (1997): 5; Roger Gibbins, *Canada as a Borderlands Society* (Orono, ME: The Canadian Society, 1989), 2–11; David Leyton-Brown and Christopher Sands, "Introduction," *American Review of Canadian Studies* 27 (1997): 164–165; Allen M. Springer, "From Trail Smelter to Devil's Lake: The Need for Effective Federal Involvement in Canadian-American Environmental Disputes," *American Review of Canadian Studies* 37 (2007): 77.
48. Michael Adams, *Fire and Ice: The United States, Canada, and the Myth of Converging Values* (Toronto: Penguin Canada, 2003), 143; David Kumar and James Altschuld, "Science, Technology, and Society," *American Behavioral Scientist* 47 (2004): 1360.
49. Paul Martin, "Foreword from the Prime Minister," *Canada's International Policy Statement*, Ottawa, 2005, 1; Brian Russell, "Canada–United States Relations: Why Can't We Be Friends?" *Globe and Mail*, 20 December 2005, 1; Debora VanNijnatten, "Canadian-American Environmental Relations: Interoperability and Politics," *American Review of Canadian Studies* 34 (2004): 650.
50. George Hoberg, "Canadian-American Environmental Relations: A Strategic Framework," in Debora VanNijnatten and Robert Boardman, eds., *Canadian Environmental Policy: Context and Cases*, 2nd ed. (Don Mills, Ontario: Oxford University Press, 2002), 173–180.
51. Barry Rabe and William Lowry, "Comparative Analysis of Canadian and American Environmental Policy," *Policy Studies Journal* 27 (1999): 264.
52. Jennifer Allen, "Institutions, Culture, and the Role of Scientific Information in Wetland Policy Development: A Comparative Study of the United States and Canada," Paper prepared for the biennial meeting of the Association for Canadian Studies in the United States, Minneapolis, MN, 19–23 November 1997, 9–11.
53. Richard Benedick, *Ozone Diplomacy: New Directions in Safeguarding the Planet* (Cambridge, MA: Harvard University Press, 1998), 316; Robert Boardman, "Milk-and-Potatoes Environmentalism: Canada and the Turbulent World," in Debora VanNijnatten and Robert Boardman, eds., *Canadian Environmental Policy: Context and Cases*, 2nd ed. (Don Mills, Ontario: Oxford University Press, 2002), 195; Sheldon Kamieniecki and Michael Kraft, "Foreword," in Uday Desai, ed., *Environmental Politics and Policies in Industrialized Countries* (Cambridge, MA: MIT Press, 2002), ix; Elizabeth Desombre, "Understanding United States Unilateralism: Domestic Sources of U.S. International Environmental Policy," in Regina Axelrod, David Downie, and Norman Vig, eds., *The Global Environment: Institutions, Laws, and Policy* (Washington, DC: CQ Press, 2005), 182–183; Litfin, 107; Robert Paehlke, "Environmentalism in One Country: Canadian Environmental Policy in an Era of Globalization," *Policy Studies Journal* 28 (2000): 161; Marvin Soroos, *The Endangered Atmosphere: Preserving a Global Commons* (Columbia: University of South Carolina Press, 1997), 160; Glen Toner, "The Harper Minority Government and ISE: Second Year–Second Thoughts," in Glen Toner, ed., *Innovation, Science, and Environment: Canadian Policies and Performance, 2008–2009* (Montreal: McGill-Queen's University Press, 2008), 3.

54. Christopher Bosso and Deborah Gruber, "Maintaining Presence: Environmental Advocacy and the Permanent Campaign," in Norman Vig and Michael Kraft, eds., *Environmental Policy: New Directions for the Twenty-First Century*, 6th ed. (Washington, DC: CQ Press, 2006), 95; Centre for Research and Information on Canada, "Portraits of Canada 2004," Ottawa, Ontario, 2005, 2; Neil Harrison, "Political Responses to Changing Uncertainty," in Neil Harrison and Gary Bryner, eds., *Science and Politics in the International Environment* (Boulder, CO: Rowman and Littlefield, 2004) 120; Walter A. Rosenbaum, *Environmental Politics and Policy*, 7th ed. (Washington, DC: CQ Press, 2008), 39.

55. Rosenbaum, 359; Debora VanNijnatten and Robert Boardman, "Introduction," in Debora VanNijnatten and Robert Boardman, eds., *Canadian Environmental Policy: Context and Cases*, 2nd ed. (Don Mills, Ontario: Oxford University Press, 2002), x–xii.

56. Bocking, 195; Debora VanNijnatten, "Participation and Environmental Policy in Canada and the United States: Trend Over Time," *Policy Studies Journal* 27 (1999): 270.

57. Jeremy Wilson, "'Internationalization' and the Conservation of Canada's Boreal Ecosystems," *Canadian-American Public Policy* 56 (2003): 6.

58. Brent S. Steel et al., "The Role of Scientists in the Natural Resource Policy Process: A Comparison of Canadian and American Publics," Prepared for the 42nd Annual Western Social Sciences Association Conference, San Diego, CA, 26–29 April 2000, 14.

59. Douglas Ross, "Canada, A Land of Deep Ambivalence: Understanding the Divergent Response to United States Primacy after 9/11," *Canadian-American Public Policy* 68 (2006): 4–5.

60. Donald Barry, "Chrétien, Bush, and the War in Iraq," *American Review of Canadian Studies* 35 (2005): 216.

61. Jon Alston, Theresa Morris, and Arnold Vedlitz, "Comparing Canadian and American Values: New Evidence from National Surveys," *American Review of Canadian Studies* 26 (1996): 311; Seymour Lipset, "North American Cultures," *Borderlands Monograph Series #3* (1990): 2.

62. John Carroll, *Acid Rain: An Issue in Canadian-American Relations* (Washington, DC: National Planning Association, 1982), 2–3; Don Munton and Geoffrey Castle, "Air, Water, and Political Fire: Building a North American Environmental Regime," in A. Claire Cutler and Mark Zacher, eds., *Canadian Foreign Policy and International Economic Regimes* (Vancouver: University of British Columbia Press, 1992), 313.

63. Leslie Alm and Ross Burkhart, "Canada and the United States: Approaches to Global Environmental Policymaking," *International Journal of Canadian Studies* 31 (2005): 261–279; Earl Fry, "State of Canada/U.S. Relations," Seminar on United States–Canadian Relations at the United States Air Force Academy, Colorado Springs, CO), 1988.

64. Debora VanNijnatten, "Analyzing the Canada–U.S. Relationship: A Multi-Faceted Approach," *American Review of Canadian Studies* 33 (2003): 95.

65. Harrison and Hoberg, 8–13.

66. Bruce Smith, *The Advisors: Scientists in the Policy Process* (Washington, DC: Brookings Institution, 1992), 8.

67. Bocking, 195–201; Jasanoff, 18.

68. Allen, 30–31.

69. Allen, 11–16.

70. Clark et al., 3.

71. Clark et al., 12.
72. Bocking, 163–167.
73. Allen, 33.
74. Rosenbaum, 342.
75. Peter Calamai, "$100 Million from Ottawa Will Link Canadian Scientists to World's Best," *Toronto Star*, 14 March 2008, 1.
76. William Leiss, "Governance and the Environment," in Thomas Courchene, ed., *Policy Framework for a Knowledge Economy* (Kingston, Ontario: John Deutch Institute for the Study of Economic Policy, 1996), 126–129.

Index

About the Authors

LESLIE R. ALM

Professor Alm teaches for both the Department of Public Policy & Administration and the Department of Political Science at Boise State University. He has served as the chair of both departments and as the director of the Masters of Public Administration Program. Dr. Alm has served on the executive council of the Borderlands Studies Association and is currently serving on the executive council of the Western Social Science Association. His book, *Crossing Borders, Crossing Boundaries: The Role of Scientists in the U.S. Acid Rain Debate*, was published by Praeger in 2000. He has published book chapters in *Environmental Politics and Public Policy in the West, Handbook of Research Methods in Public Administration,* and *Global Environmental Policy and Administration,* as well as articles in *Policy Studies Journal, Journal of Environmental Systems, The American Review of Canadian Studies, Canadian-American Public Policy, Journal of Environmental Systems,* and *Science, Technology, and Human Values.*

ROSS E. BURKHART

Dr. Burkhart is an associate professor and chair of the Department of Political Science at Boise State University. Dr. Burkhart's research interests are in analyzing cross-national democratization patterns and United States–Canada environmental relations. His research has been published in several journals and books, including the *American Political Science Review, European Journal of Political Research, International Journal of Canadian Studies, Journal of Politics, Social Science Quarterly,* and *Studies in Comparative International Development.*

MARC V. SIMON

Dr. Simon is an associate professor in the Department of Political Science at Bowling Green State University. He is also coordinator of Peace and Conflict Studies at BGSU. After serving for eight years as department chair, in 2008 he received a Fulbright award to teach environmental policy and international relations at the Diplomatic Academy in Vienna, Austria. His research examines war and revolution, environmental policy, and techniques of conflict resolution. He has published articles in *International Studies Quarterly, the Journal of Conflict Resolution, Journal of Environmental Education, Journal of Borderlands Studies, Journal of Peace Research* and *Environment and Planning.*